VICTORIAN PANORAMA

Christopher Wood is an established expert on Victorian art, and his *Dictionary of Victorian Painters* is a standard work. He has also written a number of other books including *Tissot, Paradise Lost: Paintings of English Life and Landscape 1860–1914* and *Pre-Raphaelites*. He was for a number of years in charge of Victorian sales at Christie's. He now runs his own picture gallery in London.

HENRY COURTNEY SELOUS (1811–1890) *The Inauguration of the Great Exhibition, 1st May, 1851* (detail)
Victoria and Albert Museum

VICTORIAN PANORAMA

Paintings of Victorian Life

CHRISTOPHER WOOD

FABER AND FABER LIMITED · LONDON

For Sarah

First published in 1976
by Faber and Faber Limited
3 Queen Square London WC1N 3AU
This paperback edition first published in 1990

Printed in Great Britain by
BAS Printers Limited, Over Wallop, Hampshire

A CIP record for this book
is available from the British Library
ISBN 0-571-14375-X

ACKNOWLEDGEMENTS

The illustrations in this book are all reproduced by kind permission of their owners, and I can only thank them collectively, whether they be private individuals, trustees, curators of museums, auctioneers or dealers. Many of them have been tremendously kind and helpful in supplying information as well as photographs. My biggest debt, once again, is to my assistant Margaret Richardson, who also helped me with my *Dictionary of Victorian Painters*. Her painstaking research has been of enormous help, and produced much new and interesting information. I discussed aspects of this book with many people, in particular with Richard and Leonée Ormond, for whose helpful advice and suggestions I record my gratitude. I also wrote some of the book in friends' houses, and I would like to thank them for putting up with me –especially Monny Curzon in France, and Jamie and Bea Zobell in Spain. Thanks also to the Christie's girls who typed (in their spare time, of course!) my manuscript so efficiently – Vivien Harrison and Alison Campbell. Finally, I must pay those ritual, but nonetheless sincere, thanks to my wife Sarah, for her patience during that often tiresome and difficult period when a husband becomes an author.

CHRISTOPHER WOOD,
1976

CONTENTS

INTRODUCTION

Victorian Painting and 'Modern Life'

I think I can confidently assert that this book includes all the best 'modern-life' paintings produced in the Victorian period. I have deliberately avoided included drawings, water-colours and illustrations, as these need a separate survey of their own. Many artists used illustration to explore modern-life subjects they would not have dared to tackle in paint; this is especially true of Millais, Sandys, Fred Walker, Fildes, Holl and Herkomer – and numerous other illustrators of the sixties. There may of course be more paintings awaiting rediscovery, but I doubt if they will fall outside the themes I have outlined in these chapters which embody all the preoccupations of the modern-life painter.

They also form a remarkable iconography of the preoccupations of Victorian society, its aspirations and failures, its hopes and fears, its likes and dislikes, its prejudices and paradoxes. Some of the pictures may not be great art, but they are often very good social history. They are fascinating records of a period, documents of how a society saw itself. In addition, they represent a perhaps unique struggle by academic art to come to terms with a new, industrialized society, with 'modern life' as we now understand it. For this reason it was a brief experiment. Fashion changed, modern life was left to the photographer and the illustrator, and painting went its own separate way.

Narrative Painting

When looking at Victorian pictures of 'modern life', it is essential to know something of the tradition of narrative painting of which they form a part. Many painters of modern life were also painters of literary and historical subjects – Frith, Egley, Eyre Crowe, for example – and they used the same methods in both genres.

Sir David Wilkie (1785–1841) is often quoted as the originator of modern-life subjects, but this is only partly true. His humorous scenes of Scottish village life, painted in the rich old-masterish tones of Teniers and Ostade, look back to the picturesque eighteenth-century tradition of Morland and Wheatley. Wilkie was, as Hazlitt described him, 'a serious, prosaic, literal narrator of facts', but his true Victorian descendants are artists like William Collins, Thomas Webster and F. D. Hardy, and other such painters of rustic and domestic genre.

9

The real ancestor of modern-life painting was Hogarth; followed by the historical and literary painters of the 1830s and 1840s, such as E. M. Ward and C. R. Leslie. Their endless scenes from *The Vicar of Wakefield* and *Le Bourgeois Gentilhomme*, anecdotal, sentimental, humorous – frequently exhibited with immensely long captions of explanation – first taught the Victorian public to equate painting with literature; taught them that a picture was something to be read, a novel in a rectangle. The artist became story-teller, novelist, as well as painter. A picture had to tell a story by means of objects, clues, costumes, facial expressions, literary quotations; the spectator was invited to create a past and a future, as it were, outside the frame. These were the methods which the historical painters brought with them when they approached modern-life subjects.

Richard Redgrave 1804–1888

The true pioneer of modern-life pictures, particularly of social themes, was Redgrave, whose importance in this respect has never been sufficiently recognized. A sensitive man, he was appalled by the social evils of the age, and records in his memoirs that they worried him even as a child. The traumatic event of his life seems to have been the death of his sister, who was sent away to be a governess, pined, and died in 1829. She must have been the inspiration for his most famous picture *The Poor Teacher* (**133**), and may also account for his obsession with the theme of suffering womanhood. At first he painted the usual historical subjects, from Chaucer, *Pilgrim's Progress* and, inevitably, *The Vicar of Wakefield*, but, in the words of his son, he 'longed to fight for the oppressed and help the weak, and could do it only with his brush'. His first attempt was *The Reduced Gentleman's Daughter* of 1840, showing a girl applying for a place. It was based on an article in *The Rambler*, and still set in eighteenth-century dress. For his next picture, *The Poor Teacher*, of 1843, he returned to the same theme but this time took the important step of using modern dress. The success of the picture was so great that he followed it up with *The Seamstress* (**127**), *Fashion's Slaves* (**128**) and *The Outcast* (**141**). Later, his official duties much curtailed his output of paintings. In the 1850s and 1860s he painted mainly landscapes with figures, while staying at his summer house at Leith Hill, Abinger, though he still occasionally returned to social themes, as with the beautiful *Emigrant's Last Sight of Home* (**236**). Perhaps his only direct imitator was Emily Mary Osborn, with her penchant for heart-rending scenes of ladies in distress (**112**). However, his influence in encouraging social subjects and the use of modern dress was very important.

Redgrave's social-message pictures echo a distinct movement in the literature of the 1840s. Mrs. Gaskell's *Mary Barton* and Kingsley's *Yeast* were both published in 1848. Redgrave's *Seamstress* of 1844 was inspired by Thomas Hood's poem *Song of the Shirt*; the spirit of G. F. Watts' *Found Drowned* (**142**) corresponds exactly to another Hood poem, *The Bridge of Sighs*. By the 1840s and 1850s everyone was beginning to think more seriously about social problems.

The Pre-Raphaelites

It is an often-repeated fallacy that the Pre-Raphaelites were the first to make modern-life subjects acceptable. As always, it was their influence which was important, if not their actual achievements. J. L. Tupper in the first 1849 issue of *The Germ*, the short-lived Pre-Raphaelite periodical, proclaimed the battle cry for modern subjects, as against 'High Art': 'why teach us to hate a Nero or an Appius, and not an underselling oppressor of workmen and betrayer of woman and children? Why to love a Ladie in Bower, and not a wife's fireside?' Rossetti tried his hand at modern life with *Found* (**144**), but the picture was still unfinished at his death. He soon returned to Ladies in Bowers and Burne-Jones persisted in painting angels. The work of Millais and of Arthur Hughes is in general either too poetic or too historical to be considered as modern-life painting, except for *The Rescue* (**5**) and *The Long Engagement* (**78**). Only Holman Hunt and Ford Madox Brown really struck out into the treacherous waters of modern life. Hunt brought his own brand of moral and biblical symbolism to *The Awakening Conscience* (**143**), the first Victorian picture to grapple with the thorny problem of prostitution, and to *The Hireling Shepherd*, an elaborate fable of flirtation. Ford Madox Brown's *Work* (**116**) and *The Last of England* (**232**) are two masterpieces of modern-life painting, combining the narrative methods of Frith, the moral symbolism of Hunt, and Brown's own forceful realism. Other Pre-Raphaelite ventures into modern life were sporadic, such as Martineau's *Last Day in the Old Home* (**41**) and Bell Scott's *Iron and Coal* (**117**).

William Powell Frith 1819–1909

It was Frith who really created the vogue for modern-life subjects in the 1850s and 1860s, and produced its most memorable masterpieces – *Ramsgate Sands* (**200**), *Derby Day* (**186**) and *The Railway Station* (**220**), three great panoramas of Victorian life. In his *Autobiography* he claims that he was 'always strongly drawn to painting modern life', and was tired of historical subjects when he first decided to paint *Ramsgate Sands* in 1851. The picture was a tremendous success, and was bought by Queen Victoria. Encouraged by this, he went on to even greater success with *Derby Day* and *The Railway Station*, although he still continued to paint historical subjects as well, right up to the end of his career. His modern-life pictures were enormously popular with the public (*Derby Day* was the first picture to have a rail put up to protect it at the Royal Academy since Wilkie's *Chelsea Pensioners* of 1822), but they were disliked by the critics and most of his fellow-artists. In reading reviews of the period, many of which I will be quoting, this prejudice against modern-life subjects comes up again and again. It seems that all Victorian critics thought of their own age as hopelessly ugly and unpicturesque; and they were brought up on the academic precepts laid down in Reynold's *Discourses*, that great art must only deal with sublime generalities; to descend into the realm of particularity was a step downward. But Frith knew he could afford to ignore the critics. Also, his modern-life pictures brought him large sums of money. He had a mercenary side to his nature, and records most of the prices obtained for his pictures, just as Trollope listed receipts from all his novels in his *Autobiography*. Frith sold *The Railway Station* to Flatou for £4,500; Gambart offered him £10,000 for the three *Times of Day* (**153–5**); huge sums of money by the standards of the day. The financial rewards of modern-life painting attracted other artists – it is perhaps significant that both George Elgar Hicks and William Maw Egley kept meticulous account books, listing prices for every picture, sketch and drawing sold. It also explains why so many historical painters felt bound to attempt one or two modern-life subjects; for example, Alfred Elmore (**35**), John Ritchie (**187–8**), Alfred Rankley (**99**), Abraham Solomon (**225–7**), and A. L. Egg (**224**).

Frith's big panoramas are remarkable feats of organization: 'I cannot say I have ever found difficulty in composing great numbers of figures into a more or less harmonious whole,' he wrote. He used the painstaking, academic methods of the historical painter, posing models for every figure, making sketches for every group, using photography to help with backgrounds, and also sometimes with figures. As a result, his big pictures have a curiously static, immobile appearance, as if all the figures were suddenly frozen into an immense tableau. They are better examined in detail. Frith also used the historical painters' method of weaving endless narrative sub-plots into the story; almost all the figures in *Derby Day* are in some way involved or related to each other. But, taken as a whole, these panoramas are fascinating sources of information about Victorian life, and one can only regret that Frith did not paint more of them.

Frith and Hogarth

Frith, a great admirer of Hogarth, wrote of him that 'In colour, form, composition and execution, Hogarth's works are a "continual feast" to every true artist,' and lamented his fall from fashion in the nineteenth century. Frith consciously tried to emulate Hogarth in his modern-life panoramas, but more particularly in his three moralistic series, *The Times of Day* (**153–5**), *The Road to Ruin* (**36–40**) and *The Race for Wealth* (**26–30**). Of course, Frith's pictures are vastly different in spirit from those of Hogarth. The bitter satires of Hogarth are turned into sentimental homilies. Frith himself realized this, and wrote of *The Road to Ruin* that it was 'a kind of Gambler's Progress, avoiding the satirical vein of Hogarth, for which I knew myself to be unfitted.' He also commented on his picture of a lady smoking a cigarette (**1**) which was strongly criticized for impropriety, 'I think Hogarth would have made a picture of such an incident, with the addition, perhaps, of matter unpresentable to the present age. It might have adorned our National Gallery, whilst I was mercilessly attacked for painting such a subject at all. I knew very well that if I or any other painter dared to introduce certain incidents (such as bristle over Hogarth's works) into our pictures, they would have no chance of shocking the public that admires the Hogarths on the walls in Trafalgar Square, for the Council of the Royal Academy would prevent any such catastrophe.'

1 WILLIAM POWELL FRITH, R.A. (1819–1909) *At Homburg 1869* Private collection, signed and dated 1870, 23 × 19¼ in. (59·7 × 48·9cm.)
Frith exhibited this picture at the R.A. in 1870, and according to his *Autobiography*, 'I was mercilessly attacked for painting such a subject at all.' A picture of a lady smoking, and in public, was thought highly improper. Painters of modern-life subjects had to be careful not to offend Victorian morality

1A CHARLES WEST COPE, R.A. (1811–1890) *A Life Well Spent* Private collection, signed and dated (with monogram) 1862, 23¾ × 19¾in. (60·3 × 50·2cm.)

Pictures like these encapsulate the Victorian cult of home as a domestic fortress. The room is comfortably and cosily furnished; the children neat, dutiful and quiet; the mother lovingly watchful, and busy with her needle. In the Victorian scheme of things, a woman's place could only be the home

Modern Dress

One of the great obstacles to modern-life painting was the supposed ugliness of Victorian dress, an attitude which we may now find difficult to understand. Frith constantly refers to it, and compares a bank-holiday crowd on Hampstead Heath – 'dirty, or primly snug' – with the peasants of Teniers or Jan Steen, 'gay, with bright colours and dresses that call aloud to be painted'. Most people would now think the reverse. The greatest problem was thought to be trousers, then a recent invention. Millais thought it almost impossible to make a modern portrait look dignified: 'Just imagine Van Dyck's "Charles I" in a pair of check trousers!' Another difficulty was hats, particularly the stove-pipe topper worn at all times by the mid-Victorian gentleman. Painting large numbers of them in one picture was a tricky problem, and Ansdell overcame it well in his huge portrait-group of *The Royal Agricultural Society* (**163**).

No one in England would have agreed with Baudelaire's statement: 'how great and poetic we are in our patent-leather boots.' Baudelaire intended to write a long article on English painting, but only got as far as the tantalizingly brief comments he made about the pictures at the Exposition Universelle in 1855. One longs to know what he might have had to say about Frith. For all his dislike of modern dress, Frith realized that his pictures would record for posterity the costume of the period; this was his intention in painting *English Archers* (**198**) and *The Private View* (**215**). But for most artists modern dress was too much to stomach, and the Pre-Raphaelites' worship of medieval dress and ornament was a reaction against it.

The Search for Subjects

Another problem which gave Frith trouble was 'the terrible difficulty of finding a satis-factory subject'. He hit on the surprising expedient of advertizing in the press for sug-gestions, offering a reward if the subject was used. Among the subjects suggested were a Review in Hyde Park, Whiteley's Store, the Eton and Harrow Match, the Trial of the Tichborne Claimant, and the Boat Race, but for some reason Frith turned all these down. It seems that modern-life painters had to choose their subjects as carefully as the modern film producer chooses the subject for a popular film. Another problem was that once one artist had painted a certain subject, it seemed to discourage any other artist from using it again. Frith's principal imitator, George Elgar Hicks, requisitioned *Billingsgate* (**151**), *The Post Office* (**180** and **jacket**) and *The Bank of England* (**31**), thus preventing Frith from tackling these tempting subjects.

The vogue for modern subjects was at its height during the 1850s and 1860s. There-after it declined, except for a brief outburst of social realism in the 1870s, and later examples, such as G. W. Joy's *Bayswater Omnibus* of 1895 (**231**), tend to be isolated and rare. Of Frith's many imitators and followers, most jumped on the bandwagon while the going was good, and thereafter returned to their normal work. Only Hicks, Eyre

2
GEORGE ELGAR HICKS (1824–1914)
Woman's Mission – Companion of Manhood
Tate Gallery, London, signed and dated 1863,
30 × 25¼in. (76·2 × 64·1cm.)
Many features of the Victorian narrative picture
of modern life are combined here – the emotional
moment, the letter conveying news, the ideal of
consoling womanhood, the cosy domesticity,
the detail. The picture was one of a series of
three on the theme of Woman's Mission; the
others were *Guide of Childhood* and *Comfort of
Old Age*

Crowe and Arthur Boyd Houghton showed any real, lasting interest. After *The Private View* of 1883 (**215**), even Frith gave up, and turned back once more to the well-trodden paths of Boswell, Pepys and Shakespeare.

The Victorian Interior

The interior has an important part to play in Victorian narrative painting. Many of the pictures in this book are set in cluttered middle-class sitting rooms, and they tell us an enormous amount about Victorian interior decoration. But in narrative pictures, interiors are more than just decoration. Objects have a purpose; they provide clues to the story, and take on the character of their owner. This animation of objects corresponds exactly to Dickens' many descriptions of interiors; for example, Arthur Clennam in *Little Dorrit* returns to his invalid mother's gloomy old house, and in one of the bedrooms finds 'a maimed table, a crippled wardrobe, a lean set of fire-irons like the skeleton of a set deceased . . . and a bedstead with four bare atomies of posts, each terminating in a spike, as if for the dismal accommodation of lodgers who might prefer to impale themselves.' In the same way Holman Hunt uses objects to build up the elaborate moral symbolism of *The Awakening Conscience* (**143**). The garish middle-class interiors of Barwell's *Adopting a Child* (**3**) or Egley's *Military Aspirations* (**65**), like Mrs. Thornton's drawing room in

3
FREDERICK BACON BARWELL (fl. 1855–1897)
Adopting a Child Photo: M. Newman Ltd.,
signed and dated 1857, 40 × 31in. (101·6 × 78·7cm.)
Another emotional moment, as a woman brings her
child to the house of a middle-aged couple who
are going to adopt it. Ruskin in his *Academy
Notes* praised the picture, although deploring
'the unmanageable phenomena of modern life,
in dress and bookcases'. He also urged the
spectator 'not to miss the indication of the
reason for the adoption, in the portrait of their
own lost child, which hangs behind the parents;
and to which the girl shrinking from them to her
mother's side, evidently bears a close resemblance' –
a typical example of the use of objects as clues to
expand the narrative

Mrs. Gaskell's novel *North and South* have 'a painfully spotted, spangled, speckled look'
and tell us much about the characters and situations of their owners. Letters, books,
pictures, statues, clocks, keys, newspapers, pets – all are brought into service of art, to
provide clues and help expand the narrative. In outdoor scenes, posters were a popular
method of emphasizing the message, for example in Brown's *Work* (116), Egg's *Past and
Present* (145–7) and Solomon's *Second Class – The Parting* (227).

The Victorian interior is also an expression of the Victorian cult of Home. Home
was a haven of rest and protection, a padded and cushioned fortress, protecting its inmates from the world outside. The same *horror vacui* which infected the Victorian interior
spills over into Victorian paintings. And just as ornamentation and over-decoration
tended to obscure the practical use of objects, as with so many of the exhibits at the
Great Exhibition, so detail in Victorian narrative paintings tends to get out of hand, to
become a riot of stifling, condensed, sometimes confusing information. Ruskin criticized
a picture by G. B. O'Neill on this score, 'There is too much in it to be natural. It is a
map of a market-day, instead of a picture of one.' (*Academy Notes*, 1856)

Detail

Much has been written about the Victorian passion for detail, which affected not only painting but all the arts, architecture and literature especially. For painters, detail was an article of faith, a sign that they had worked hard and conscientiously. Ruskin loved detail because of 'the sense of human labour and care spent on it', and always carried a magnifying glass with him to exhibitions. Detail is also an expression of the rational, scientific spirit of the Victorians. Facts had to be collected, labelled, documented, codified; Ruskin's *Modern Painters* for example is an encyclopaedic attempt to record all the minutiae of nature.

The lengths to which Victorian painters went to make their pictures authentic and exact in detail is legendary. Hunt went to the Holy Land to paint *The Scapegoat*, and brought back a goat and some Dead Sea mud to use in his studio; Millais put Elisabeth Siddal fully clothed in a bath to pose for *Ophelia*; Frith, as we have seen, took infinite pains with his models and settings; Luke Fildes constructed an entire fisherman's cottage in his studio in which to paint *The Doctor* (**102**); both Egley and G. W. Joy went to the trouble of borrowing omnibuses to paint *Omnibus Life* (**228**) and *The Bayswater Omnibus* (**231**). This incredibly earnest, conscientious approach was part of the Victorian belief

4 ATTRIBUTED TO W. C. MERCIER *Charles Reade in his Study* National Portrait Gallery, London, $43\frac{1}{4} \times 55\frac{1}{4}$in. (109·9 × 140·4cm.)
The clutter of the Victorian interior plays an important part in narrative pictures. Objects not only help to tell a story, by providing clues, but reflect the personality of their owner

5
SIR JOHN EVERETT MILLAIS, Bt., P.R.A.
(1829–1896) *The Rescue* National Gallery of
Victoria, Melbourne, signed and dated 1855,
46 × 34¼ in. (116 × 87·1cm.)
For his only deliberately 'modern-life' picture,
Millais chose a typically dramatic moment – a
fireman carries two children out of a burning
house to their waiting mother. Millais was
inspired to paint the subject by a fire he
witnessed one night in London; his intention
was 'to honour a set of men quietly doing noble
work – firemen.' The picture was painted in
F. B. Barwell's studio, and C. A. Collins helped
to paint the fire-hose. With typical thoroughness,
Millais posed models for the figures, made many
drawings, and a full-size cartoon. He also put a
lighted brand on the floor of his studio, which
filled it with smoke, and put coloured glass over
the windows to get the right effects of light.
The picture was at first skied at the R.A. but
Millais made a fuss, and had it re-hung. In
general it was well received, especially by Ruskin,
who wrote, 'the only *great* picture exhibited this
year; but this is *very* great.'

that art should contribute to knowledge. Art should have a serious moral purpose, to teach, to 'turn the minds of men to good reflections' (Millais).

Realism

For all their devotion to accuracy and detail, it would be wrong to think of Victorian modern-life pictures as totally realistic. Painters were hampered by two important limitations – their own attitudes, and the attitudes of the Victorian public, many of whom believed, like Dickens' Mrs. General in *Little Dorrit*, that 'nothing disagreeable should ever be looked at.' Facts had to be tailored to fit current taste, and there is therefore an unwillingness to face up to unpleasant facts, such as poverty, death, deserted children, seduction. Themes such as these had to be handled with care, which usually meant a liberal coating of sentiment or humour to sugar the pill. Everyone knows, for example, that nasty things went on in Victorian schools, but we find little trace of this in the many pictures of school life by Thomas Webster and others. Painters studied a subject in detail, 'as if devotion to realism in small matters licensed evasion in larger ones', as Peter Conrad observed in *A Victorian Treasure-House*. Some facts are omitted altogether – although motherhood is the theme of many pictures (**56–8**), I have never seen a pregnant woman in any Victorian picture. Morality was also a powerful influence, as we have already

6 JOHN HENRY HENSHALL (1856–1928) *The Public Bar* Photo: M. Newman Ltd., signed, 24½ × 43¾in. (62·2 × 111·1cm.) Realistic, honest pictures of ordinary Victorian life, like this one, are surprisingly rare. Most Victorians thought their own age hopelessly vulgar and unpicturesque. Modern-life painting was considered an inferior branch of art, and critics almost invariably attacked modern-life pictures on the grounds that such prosaic, literal facts were not suitable material for art, and had better be left to the photographer

seen with Frith's picture of a lady smoking (**1**). The most striking example is the two versions of Solomon's *First Class – The Meeting* (**225–6**). As Thackeray complained, in the preface to Pendennis, 'Since the author of Tom Jones was buried, no writer of fiction among us has been permitted to depict, to his utmost power, a man – we must drape him, and give him a certain conventional simper.' Modern life too had to be draped, given a certain conventional simper.

But this is not to say that all modern-life painting was pure evasion. Some subjects are more realistically handled than others, and many painters earnestly tried to face up to social issues. Genuine poverty and distress, for example, are to be found in the pictures of Holl, Herkomer and Fildes, whose brief outburst of social realism in the 1870s and 1880s offended the critics and shocked the public. For all its limitations, Victorian modern-life painting presents us with a uniquely comprehensive picture of the age. Few periods in history have been so well and so attractively documented in painting. Even if it is life seen through the painters' eyes, at least the painters' attitudes are a reflection of those of their time. In these pictures we see not just how the painters looked at life, but how the Victorians themselves looked at it.

1

VICTORIA REGINA

'Her virtues are not those of a great woman, like Elizabeth or
Catherine II or Maria Theresa, but are the virtues and powers of
an ordinary woman; things that any person, however humble, can
appreciate and imitate.'

Diary of Arthur Joseph Munby (1901)

A book about Victorian narrative painting should begin with Queen Victoria. Perhaps
no British monarch has become so identified with the age in which he or she lived. 'Her
prejudices and her convictions were so exactly those dominant in her age that she seemed
to embody its very nature within herself' (Kingsley Martin, *The Triumph of Lord Palmerston*,
1963). And like the age to which she has given her name, she was a complex and paradoxical
character. As a girl she was always laughing; in later life she was not amused. She raised
a large family, but disliked babies. She was strict with her children, though she adored
pets. She was strong-willed, yet dependent on a succession of father-figures. History
has labelled her a prude, but her letters and journals reveal a passionate nature. She
could be both broadminded and intolerant, generous and mean, kind and spiteful,
honest and devious, cosy and terrifying; the domesticated bourgeois or the proud autocrat.
It was her destiny to preside over the fortunes of England during perhaps the greatest
period in her history and by her long reign of sixty-three years to give a sense of continuity to a period of tremendous change, very little of which she understood, or even
sympathized with. In spite of her many failings, Victoria had two great virtues – human
sympathy and downright common sense – and it was these that made her, in the end,
a great Queen.

Most pictures of Victoria are, of course, portraits. Through these we can follow all
the phases of her career and also trace the changing image of the Victorian woman.
In the 1830s, Sir George Hayter, John Partridge, Robert Thorburn, Edmund Thomas
Parris and many others portrayed her as a little early-Victorian doll – plump, round-
eyed and ringleted. They cast her in the 'keepsake' mould, the ideal of early Victorian
womanhood, submissive and entirely ornamental. This image of the young Queen
persists in her Coronation portraits. Both Hayter and A. E. Chalon almost submerged
the tiny Victoria in ermine and regalia, converting the keepsake beauty into a sultana
under an oriental canopy; a Victorian odalisque. For the picture of her Coronation cere-

7 HENRY TANWORTH WELLS, R.A. (1828–1903)
Victoria Regina Tate Gallery, London, signed and dated
1880, 96½ × 75½in. (238·8 × 191·8cm.)
Victoria had already been on the throne over forty years
by the time this picture was painted, and the result is a
romantic re-creation of the event in vaguely Regency
style. The kneeling figures of Lord Conyngham and the
Archbishop of Canterbury, in his ill-fitting wig, could
have walked straight out of a Marcus Stone 'quality
street' picture, and the young Queen out of a Victorian
romantic novel. The picture could equally well have
been given an innocuous title like 'The Rivals', and no-
one would have been any the wiser

mony (8) C. R. Leslie chose the romantic moment when the Virgin Queen kneels humbly
at the altar to take the sacrament after the crowning, fulfilling her famous promise 'I
will be good.'

The Victorians admired a woman who sat well on a horse. To ride well was one of
the few accomplishments which a Victorian lady could show off in public, whether it
was the Queen herself, or the courtesans in Rotten Row. Victoria was a dashing rider,
and loved to lead huge cavalcades out into Windsor Park. These outings were recorded
by Sir Francis Grant, R. B. Davis and Landseer. Victoria was especially proud of being
able to review the Life Guards on horseback, instead of in the safety of an open carriage,
a scene recorded by Landseer in one of his most superb sketches (9). Earlier the same
year, 1837, the youthful Queen refused point blank to take a review in Hyde Park in a
carriage, and her threat of 'no horse, no review' leaked out to the press:

> 'I will have a horse, I'm determined on that,
>   If there is to be a review,
> No horse, no review, my Lord Melbourne, that's flat,
>   In spite of Mama and of you.'
>   (Mr. J. S. Haldane's Papers, Miss Haldane, 1837)

9 (*right*) SIR EDWIN LANDSEER, R.A. (1802–1873) *Queen Victoria reviewing the Life Guards with the Duke of
Wellington, 28th Sept. 1837* Private collection, London, 22 × 34½in. (55·9 × 87·6cm.)
'The whole went off beautifully', wrote Queen Victoria, 'and I felt for the first time like a man, as if I could fight
myself at the head of my Troops.' Landseer's brilliant sketch has captured the dashing spirit of the occasion, and of
the youthful Queen

8 CHARLES ROBERT LESLIE, R.A. (1794–1859) *The Coronation of Queen Victoria, 28th June 1838*
(detail) Reproduced by gracious permission of Her Majesty the Queen, 38 × 73½in. (97 × 186·8cm.)

The young Queen, divesting herself of the Crown and Regalia, kneels at the altar to receive the sacrament from the Archbishop. A ray of sunlight suddenly lit up her head, and the Duchess of Kent, sitting in the middle of the front row, burst into tears. Lord Melbourne stands holding the Sword of State, which he found 'excessively heavy', and next to him is the Duke of Wellington. The lady standing behind the Queen is the Mistress of the Robes, the Duchess of Sutherland, with six of the train bearers. Although it took place in Westminster Abbey, Leslie has painted the scene as if it were a private family affair. The Queen did not commission the picture, but agreed to buy it when she heard that Leslie had begun it; the price was 600 guineas

10 SIR EDWIN LANDSEER, R.A. (1802–1873) *Queen Victoria and Prince Albert at Windsor with the Princess Royal* (detail) Reproduced by gracious permission of Her Majesty the Queen, 44½ × 56½in. (113 × 143·5cm.) Landseer has portrayed the happy young couple as romantic Walter Scott figures, in a baronial interior littered with game, fawned on by pets instead of courtiers. Victoria thought Albert particularly handsome in his long leather boots, but the English court thought he looked like an Italian tenor. Albert's attitude to shooting was also rather un-English, his idea being to kill the largest possible number of birds in the shortest possible time

Victoria inherited a discredited and unpopular crown, tolerated but not respected. As a young Queen she was not herself popular. Her crush on the Whig leader, Lord Melbourne, and the scandal of the Lady Flora Hastings affair, led to hisses at Ascot and mutters of 'Mrs. Melbourne'. Her marriage in 1840 to an obscure German princeling, Prince Albert of Saxe-Coburg, did little to improve matters at first, and there was a nasty public row over the size of his allowance. But under the serious influence of Albert, and with the steady arrival of royal babies at yearly intervals, the monarchy seized the three impregnable positions – morality, industry and domesticity – behind which it was safe. The portraits by Landseer and Winterhalter of the 1840s and 1850s reflect the changing image of the young Queen, now the maturer figure of wife and mother. Winterhalter, who arrived in England in 1842, brought a Continental elegance and chic to the English royal family, but it is Landseer who has left us with the most faithful and enduring record of

Victoria, Albert, their children and their pets (**10**). His pictures show us a mid-Victorian family, romantic rather than royal; and they reflect that gradual identification of the monarchy with the people which was a feature of the Victorian age.

The Great Exhibition of 1851 was the first event of the reign to bring the monarchy and the people closer. This is reflected in the official picture of the Inauguration Ceremony by H. C. Selous (**11**). Unlike the early events of Victoria's reign, her Coronation, her Marriage, the Christening of her children, which were painted by Hayter and C. R. Leslie as small, private, almost family occasions, the Great Exhibition was a public event, in which both monarchy and people could take justifiable pride. Of course, Queen Victoria saw it as a day of triumph for Albert – 'I do feel proud of what my beloved Albert's great mind has conceived.' The opening day, 1st May, 1851, was bright and sunny and Victoria and her family drove to the ceremony in an open carriage. As she moved down the central

11 HENRY COURTNEY SELOUS (1811–1890) *The Inauguration of the Great Exhibition, 1st May, 1851*
(detail) Victoria and Albert Museum, signed and dated 1851–2, 66¾ × 95¼ in. (169·5 × 237cm.)
Victoria and Albert, who stand on the dais with their two eldest children, Vicky and Bertie, were deeply moved by their tumultuous reception. Selous has included the celebrated Chinaman on the right, who suddenly appeared from the crowd, and prostrated himself before the throne. Assuming that he must be an envoy from the Emperor of China, the Lord Chamberlain placed him in the procession between the Duke of Wellington and the Archbishop of Canterbury. The next day it was discovered that he was a Chinese sailor whose junk, moored on the Thames, was open to the public at a shilling a head

12 PROSPER LAFAYE (1806–1883) *Queen Victoria and Prince Albert in the Indian Pavilion of the Great Exhibition 1851* (detail) Victoria and Albert Museum, 29¾ × 44¼in. (77·5 × 112·5cm.)
After the opening on 1st May, Victoria went back to the Exhibition several times a week until it closed in October. She went through all sections systematically, and is here shown visiting the Indian pavilion, where she admired the large Indian pearls, jewels, and a stuffed elephant. Lafaye was a Parisian painter of historical subjects, and landscapes, who only seems to have made this one brief excursion into English life

aisle of Paxton's Crystal Palace to the dais, she was deeply moved by the tumultuous cheering of the crowds, and the deafening music of the organs. Afterwards she cut out a report in *The Times* which compared it to the Day of Judgement and wrote, 'it was the happiest, proudest day in my life.' She went back to the Exhibition with her children almost every day, going through each section systematically. She was particularly interested by the Indian pavilion, which she is shown visiting in the picture by Lafaye (**12**), mixing quite happily with the crowds. Winterhalter was afterwards commissioned to paint a portrait of Victoria and Albert with Prince Arthur, whose first birthday was on 1st May. In the foreground, the aged Duke of Wellington, who was to die the following year, presents his godson the Prince with a casket; and in the background rises the Crystal Palace, symbol of the peace, prosperity and progress of the mid-Victorian epoch.

Of the other pictures of Victoria and Albert, the curious Thomas Jones Barker (13) reminds us of those public duties that are now the only activity left to an English constitutional monarch – taking parades, launching ships, laying foundation stones, opening Parliament, pinning on medals. Ever since the Crimean War, the Queen had had a soft spot for soldiers, which much endeared her to her subjects. She enjoyed distributing medals, visiting military hospitals, and talking to the soldiers (14). After the death of Albert and the Duchess of Kent in 1861, Victoria was plunged into an orgy of mourning and widowhood and her public appearances ceased. She went far beyond the usual limits of Victorian mourning, elevating it to a kind of suttee. When Landseer painted her at Osborne in 1865 (15), four years after Albert's death, she was still in deep mourning. For nearly ten years this dark shadow hung over the Royal Family. No one ever saw

13 THOMAS JONES BARKER (1815–1882) *Queen Victoria presenting a Bible in the Audience Chamber at Windsor* (detail) National Portrait Gallery, London, signed with monogram and dated 1861, 45 × 66in. (114·4 × 167·6cm.) Prince Albert stands on the left, with Lord John Russell and Palmerston talking on the right, not apparently much interested in the scene. The dusky potentate reaches out gingerly for the Bible, as if afraid it might bite him. This curious picture expresses clearly the belief held by many Victorians that the Bible was the foundation of England's greatness, and that her mission was to spread Christianity throughout the world. These simplistic but humane views were held by Victoria herself, who thought England's duty in building an Empire was 'to protect the poor natives, and advance civilisation'

16 ANDREW CARRICK GOW, R.A. (1848–1920) *St. Paul's Cathedral, the Queen's Diamond Jubilee, 22nd June 1897* (detail) Guildhall Gallery, London, 56 × 96in. (142· × 238·8cm.)
The Diamond Jubilee was a grand imperial spectacular, and a unique expression of loyalty to the aged Queen, whose reign was by then the longest in English history. Victoria wrote afterwards in her diary, 'No one ever, I believe, has met with such an ovation as was given to me . . . the crowds were quite indescribable, and their enthusiasm truly marvellous and deeply touching.' A cinematograph was made of the scene outside St. Paul's, but the result was almost indecipherable, and Gow's picture remains much the best record of the occasion

the Queen; her popularity began to wane; there was even Republican talk in the 1860s. In the end Disraeli and Gladstone coaxed her back into the limelight. The Empire needed a first lady; Britannia wanted an Empress. So during the last thirty years of her reign, the small stumpy figure of the 'grandmother of Europe' became a national symbol. Pictures of this period are mainly straightforward records of historical events, reaching a climax at the Diamond Jubilee of 1897 (16), when the little old lady in a bonnet became the focus of an Empire's loyalty.

14 (*left, above*) JERRY BARRETT (1814–1906) *Victoria and Albert visiting the Crimean wounded at Chatham Hospital in 1855* Private collection, Wales, 55 × 83in. (139·7 × 210·8cm.)
Victoria visited Chatham Hospital in 1855, and was disgusted by the crowded rooms 'not built for the purpose', and felt great pity for the wounded and disabled men. She also distributed medals personally, and instituted the Victoria Cross in 1857. Barrett's picture was exhibited in 1856 with enormous success at 162 Piccadilly, and thousands of engravings of it were sold. The *Art Journal* wrote approvingly, 'happily, in all things the example of the Queen of England influences for good every class and order of her subjects'

15 (*left, below*) SIR EDWIN LANDSEER, R.A. (1802–1873) *Osborne 1865* (detail) Reproduced by gracious permission of her Majesty the Queen, 57 × 82in. (144·7 × 208·3cm.)
The faithful John Brown holds the horse's head, and the equally faithful dog, Prince, sits up to beg. On the left are two of the Royal Princesses, Helena and Alice, and in the background, Osborne, best-loved of all Victoria's residences, where she died in 1901, having faithfully preserved Albert's rooms for forty years. King Edward VII so hated the house he gave it to the nation, and it became a convalescent home for officers. The Private Apartments, preserved exactly as Victoria and Albert left them, were opened to the public in 1954

17 JACQUES JOSEPH TISSOT (1836–1902) *Too Early* Guildhall, London, 28 × 40in. (71·1 × 101·6cm.)

Tissot arrived in London in 1871, and *Too Early* was one of his first successes at the R.A. in 1873. Mrs Louise Jopling wrote of it in *Twenty Years of My Life* as 'a new departure in art, this witty representation of modern life'. Tissot's three large society scenes *Too Early*, *The Ball on Shipboard* and *Hush* present a unique picture of London society in the 1870s, a society in which Tissot was himself a great success

2

SOCIETY

'Never speak disrespectfully of Society, Algernon. Only people
who can't get in to it do that.'
Lady Bracknell in *The Importance of Being Earnest* by Oscar
Wilde

Painters of high life concentrated on the fashionable world at play – balls, concerts,
garden parties, theatre and opera, racing, riding to hounds, parading in Rotten Row,
and generally enjoying the season. However middle-class puritans might denounce these
worldly pleasures, the upper classes certainly managed to enjoy themselves. The puritan
revolution spread from the lower classes upwards, and there were some regions of the
aristocracy where it never seemed to penetrate at all. 'This damned morality will ruin
everything,' complained Lord Melbourne. Although there were many ideal Victorian
gentlemen, such as the first Duke of Westminster and Lord Shaftesbury, who earned
the respect of all classes for their devotion to public duties and charities, there were
other relics of the Regency, such as Lord Palmerston, who was caught corridor-creeping
at Windsor Castle, and Adeline, the pleasure-loving Countess of Cardigan, who wrote
in her memoirs, 'What woman does not appreciate having a thoroughly good time?'
The Swell Mob, led by the Duke of Hamilton, the Marquis of Waterford and the Marquis
of Hastings, devoted themselves to drink, women, gambling and debauchery with all
the reckless abandon of their Regency fathers. Yet the general tenor of the age was
restrained. You had to be careful, as the penalties for social misdemeanors were heavy,
even for an aristocrat. It was safer to keep a lady quietly in St. John's Wood than to
flaunt her in public.

As always, the strength of the aristocracy was its ability to move with the times. Most
of them attended to their duties, and tried to make themselves useful. They improved
their estates, and took an interest in their tenants' welfare. They sat on the boards of
companies and charities. They devoted themselves to politics, public service, the army
and the navy. They made judicious marriages with the mercantile and financial classes.
They led generally respectable lives and had family prayers. In spite of all the reforms
and social changes of the nineteenth century, the aristocracy carried most of its power
and prestige intact into the twentieth century. However Bright, the radical, might

18 JACQUES JOSEPH TISSOT (1836–1902) *Hush* Manchester City Art Gallery, 28 × 43¼in. (71·1 × 109·9cm.)
The last and most brilliant of Tissot's large society pictures, exhibited at the R.A. of 1875. Many attempts have been made to identify the party and the figures – the party is said to have been given by the Coopes and the violinist has been variously identified as Madame Neruda, Mlle. Diaz de Soria and Mlle. Castellan. Other people identifiable include Lord Leighton, Prince Dhuleep Singh, Arthur Sullivan, and in the doorway two of Tissot's friends, Ferdinand Heilbuth and Guiseppe de Nittis

denounce aristocratic wealth and privilege, most Englishmen had what Gladstone called 'a sneaking kindness for a Lord'. Victorians believed in the need for a governing class. In a democracy, wondered Matthew Arnold, 'who or what will give a high tone to the nation?'

It is ironical that the greatest painter of society life in Victorian times was not English but French – Jacques Joseph Tissot, or James Tissot as he liked to be known. Born in Nantes in 1836, Tissot was already a fashionable Parisian painter by 1870, when he was forced by the Commune rising to flee to London, like many other artists. He had already worked as a caricaturist for *Vanity Fair*, so it was perhaps natural that he should be attracted to London society as a subject for paintings. One of this first successes at the Royal Academy was *Too Early* (**17**), soon followed by *The Ball on Shipboard* (**19**), and *Hush* (**18**) which he sold to Agnews in 1876 for 1,200 guineas. Both pictures are typical of the elegance and style which Tissot brought to the English scene. He was the perfect society painter, because he painted society as it saw itself. Everyone in all three pictures looks distinguished, elegant and witty; even the rooms themselves are suffused with white, brilliant light from the chandeliers. They are ideal images of society, beautifully observed, free from social comment and free from the disturbing undertones which haunt many of Tissot's later pictures.

Above all, Tissot was a painter of Woman. He was obsessed by pretty, elegant women, and perhaps no one has painted them with such devotion. Every inch of his women's dresses are delineated with extraordinary fidelity, at a time when female dress was at its most elaborate, expensive and beautiful. He is an artist of the fashion plate. And like all models of any period, his girls have the same look – oval faces, large eyes, piled-up hair, and a vacuous, slightly disdainful expression. Tissot's other great love was the river, a taste going back to his boyhood in Nantes, and in London he was immediately drawn to the bustling life of the Thames. The result was many pictures of women on board ship, such as *The Last Evening* or *The Captain's Daughter* in which every detail of the ropes and rigging is drawn with an accuracy which a sailor could not fault. The titles of the pictures are unimportant, often enigmatic, and Tissot frequently changed them if a picture did not sell. He was painting an atmosphere, a style, a way of life. Although the influence of Degas and Manet, who he knew in Paris, is evident in his colour and grouping of figures, his discipline and tight technique seem to owe more to Gerôme and the academics.

Tissot himself was an enigmatic and strange figure. At first he was a great social success – 'a charming man', wrote the painter Mrs. Jopling, 'very handsome, extraordinarily like the Duke of Teck.' But about 1876 he met his *femme fatale*, in the shape of a beautiful divorcee, Mrs. Kathleen Newton. She became his mistress, and in his devotion to her, he spent more and more time in their large house in St. John's Wood Road, and gradually withdrew from society. His artist friends would occasionally call, but he kept Mrs. Newton hidden away. She appeared, however, in his pictures with increasing regularity, often with her two children. She is a typical Tissot beauty – petite, elegantly dressed, with a pretty face and a sad expression. When she died of consumption in 1882, Tissot fled the country in despair, having sold his house to Alma-Tadema. After a few more years in Paris he became a religious recluse and spent the rest of his life painting biblical subjects. An ironical end for the painter of fashionable society.

'Hyde Park at the height of the season; Hyde Park when the Four-in-Hand club is out in full force, is the best picture we can present to the stranger of the pride and wealth, the blood and bearing, the comeliness, beauty and metal of old England,' wrote Blanchard Jerrold in 1872. Very few artists, however, seem to have felt the scene worth painting, but we do have one record, a large picture of the Four-in-Hand Club in 1886, painted by two minor artists, Frank Walton and Thomas Walter Wilson (20). The whole of smart London society is there, led by the Prince of Wales in the carriage on the left.

Most Englishmen of the older generation agreed with Queen Victoria's low opinion of
Bertie and the Marlborough House set. But at least they brought a touch of gaiety to the
stuffiness of the late-Victorian epoch. And whatever else he may have been, Bertie was
not a humbug. He enjoyed women, low company and good food, and did not mind if
everyone knew it. His occasional illnesses brought brief outbursts of popularity, and
inspired the immortal lines attributed to Alfred Austin:

> 'Across the wires the electric message came,
> He is no better, he is much the same.'

But scandals like the Baccarat affair of 1890-1 outraged the middle classes, and a strong
prejudice against Bertie lingered in the hearts of most Victorians.

The same two artists, Walton and Wilson, painted an interesting companion picture
of *The Lawn at Goodwood* (21). Neither in this picture, nor in the one of Hyde Park,
have the artists included one feature which would have been much in evidence to any
observer at the time – the presence of the smart courtesans. An American journalist,
D. J. Kirwan, wrote a book about London called *Palace to Hovel* in 1870. He visited
Goodwood and called his chapter on the subject 'Scarlet Women'. He was horrified, or
affected to be for the benefit of his middle-class American audience, by the large numbers
of courtesans present, many in the most magnificent carriages and equipage, waited on
by crowds of admiring swells. He sneered at one such noble lord, 'a languid looking
fellow, who does not look as if he could fall to and saw a load of wood,' and watched
with approval an itinerant preacher set up his box, and begin to denounce them '. . .
you gaudy libertines, with your harlots and your women of Sodom . . .' The carriages
began to move off, the swells declaring the preacher to be 'a howwid little bore'. In Hyde
Park too, the courtesans, like Skittles and Mabel Grey, vied with society ladies for the
attentions of the gentlemen. The 'pretty horse-breakers' were often fine and dashing riders,
and their superb horses and carriages the envy of many respectable matrons and their
closely-guarded daughters. George Augustus Sala wrote in rapture 'The Danaes! The
Amazons! The Lady Cavaliers! The horse-women! Can any scene in the world equal
Rotten Row at four in the afternoon and in the full tide of the season?'.

Victorian entertaining was elaborate and formal. *Dinner at Haddo House* (22), an
interesting picture by Alfred Edward Emslie, shows us an aristocratic gathering, with
old family silver, old masters on the walls, distinguished guests, and a piper. They
appear to have reached the dessert course, the last hurdle of a Victorian dinner. To
start they would have had soup and fish, followed by the first remove, usually meat or
chicken. Then would come the flancs, smaller meat dishes sometimes placed at the
corners of the table. After this, an entrée, described by Alexis Soyer as 'the dishes upon
which . . . the talent of the cook is displayed.' The second part of the dinner was then
begun by the Roast, nearly always consisting of game. Then the second remove, a pudding
or soufflé, and finally, dessert, making a total of eight courses. Sir Henry Thompson,

19 JACQUES JOSEPH TISSOT (1836–1902) *The Ball on Shipboard* Tate Gallery, London, signed 13 × 51 in. (33 × 129.5cm.)

The second of Tissot's big society scenes, of a ball on board a yacht during Cowes week. The arresting composition, with the girl staring out of the canvas to the left, the empty area of deck, and the brilliant canopy of flags, all combine to produce a sunny, festive atmosphere, quite different from the drawing-room scenes. Several ladies, in particular the two by the railings in the centre, are wearing identical dresses, which would perhaps have caused embarrassment had it actually happened. The *Athenaeum* critic thought the women showy and ungraceful, and snootily asserted there was 'not a lady in a score of female figures'. How could he possibly know? It hardly matters; the picture remains a brilliantly subtle evocation of English Society Life – narcissitic, superficial, rather bored

19A JACQUES JOSEPH TISSOT (1836–1902) *Gentleman in a Railway Carriage* Worcester Art Museum, USA, 25 × 17in. (63·5 × 43·2cm.)
The identity of the sitter is unknown, but Tissot has created an image of opulence and luxury in what clearly must be a first–class carriage. The man's hand holding the strap also brilliantly conveys a feeling of the movement of the train

20 FRANK WALTON (1840–1928) and THOMAS WALTER WILSON (fl. 1870–1903) *The Four-in-Hand Club in Hyde Park 1886* Formerly Ralph Dutton collection; picture now destroyed, 36 × 60in. (91·5 × 152·4cm.)
Throughout the Victorian period, Rotten Row in Hyde Park was Society's parade ground. Every afternoon during the season the carriages of the rich, the fashionable, and the socially ambitious rolled up and down, vying with each other in the smartness of their dress, horses, and equipage. A particularly smart occasion was a meeting of the Four-in-Hand Club, a very exclusive sporting club whose main function seems to have been to show off their horses and carriages. 'Everybody belongs to the Four-in-Hand Club now,' said Lord Silverbridge to his disapproving father, the Duke of Omnium, in Trollope's novel *The Duke's Children*

21 FRANK WALTON and THOMAS WALTER WILSON *The Lawn at Goodwood 1887* (detail) From Goodwood House by Courtesy of the Trustees, signed, 36 × 60in. (91·5 × 152·4cm.)
The race-meeting at Goodwood, the private racecourse of the Duke of Richmond, was traditionally the last event of the London season, and a much more exclusive affair than the Derby. This picture, almost certainly painted from photographs, portrays the aristocracy out in force, led by the Prince of Wales once again, right in the centre of the picture, holding a cigar, with a sprinkling of celebrities, including Gilbert and Sullivan

22 ALFRED EDWARD EMSLIE (fl. 1867–1889) *Dinner at Haddo House 1884* National Portrait Gallery, London, signed, 14½ × 22¾in. (36·8 × 57·8cm.)

'Creatures of the inferior races eat and drink; only man dines. Dining is the privilege of civilisation,' wrote Mrs. Beeton. Here we see an aristocratic dinner party at Haddo House in Scotland. The lady with her back to us is the hostess, the Marchioness of Aberdeen. On her right is Gladstone, at that time the Prime Minister, and on one of his visits to his constituency of Midlothian and next to him is the Countess of Rosebery. On the left is Lord Rosebery, who was to become Prime Minister ten years later, and next to him is Lady Harriet Lindsay. Dessert is being served to the accompaniment of a piper in Highland dress, often the custom in grand Scottish houses. Over the fireplace can be seen a picture by Veronese; this was sold in Christie's in 1966, and made £42,000

23 SOLOMON JOSEPH SOLOMON, R.A. (1860–1927) *A Conversation Piece* By permission of Kensington and Chelsea Borough Council, Leighton House, London, signed and dated '84, 40 × 50in. (101·6 × 127cm.)

After dinner in a very heavy, bourgeois interior, also in 1884; time for songs at the piano and looking through the family photograph album. The room is a cushioned, padded, patterned fortress of middle-class respectability, but with arty overtones – potted plants, tiger skins, and some extraordinary objects on the piano, including an irridescent owl

24 SIR WILLIAM QUILLER ORCHARDSON, R.A. (1832–1910) *Mariage de Convenance I*
(detail) Glasgow City of Art Gallery and Museum
The most famous of Orchardson's upper-class social dramas. The *Art Journal* critic wrote, '. . . we are looking at a very fine picture – a sermon – and a dismal tragedy. At one end of the richly-appointed table sits the young wife – ambitious, disappointed, sullen, unutterably miserable. At the other end sits the husband – old, blasé, roué, bored too, and the more pitiable in that he has exhausted all his feelings and has only boredom left.' The model for the husband was Orchardson's fellow-painter, Tom Graham

25 SIR WILLIAM QUILLER ORCHARDSON, R.A. (1832–1910) *Mariage de Convenance – After*
(detail) Aberdeen Art Gallery, signed and dated 1886, 44 × 66in. (111·7 × 168·9cm.)
The sequel – the wife has fled, and the husband is left staring into the unswept hearth, the table behind him laid for one. By the 1880s, feeling against arranged marriages was mounting, in favour of love matches based on free choice

an amateur artist and noted host, called his dinner parties 'Octaves' – dinners of eight courses at eight o'clock for eight guests. The ladies then retired to the drawing room for coffee and the men remained for port, cigars and male talk for at least an hour, sometimes more. By the time the gentlemen finally re-appeared in the drawing room, they were often the worse for wear.

The guests in Solomon Joseph Solomon's picture, *A Conversation Piece* (**23**) have retired to the drawing room and are engaged in after-dinner occupations – looking through the photograph album, and songs round the piano. The room is heavy, padded, bourgeois and full of arty potted palms that would certainly not have been found in Haddo House. The two pictures form a nice contrast between the aristocratic and the bourgeois. In both, however, the men are squeezed into their white tie and tails, always *de rigueur* for evening parties. Sir Charles Eastlake in *Hints on Household Taste* (1878) wrote, 'our evening dress is in need of reform . . . in the existing state of society, Englishmen wear the same dress at any evening party and at a funeral.' But there was little sign of reform by the end of the century, except in the very advanced circles of aesthetes and 'passionate Brompton', who were considered by most people a huge joke and only good for du Maurier cartoons and Gilbert and Sullivan operas.

Finally, any picture of Victorian high society would be incomplete without mention of the master of the upper-class social drama – Orchardson. His two pictures *Mariage de Convenance I* and *Mariage de Convenance – After* (**24–5**) are perhaps the best-known of his many witty observations of society life, which have often been compared to the plays of Pinero. Certainly Orchardson's pictures of this type – *The First Cloud, Her Mother's Voice, A Social Eddy* – are very like stage sets, with wide, empty spaces, and the figures deliberately placed in isolation from one another. Pictures like this became the rage in the 1880s and 1890s. Their charm lay not only in the voyeurism of looking into the drawing rooms of the rich, but in speculating what was actually going on. This passion for psychological drama was carried to absurd lengths by later painters such as the Hon. John Collier and W. F. Yeames. *Defendant and Counsel*, painted by Yeames in 1895, showing a beautiful lady with her legal advisers, aroused such a furore of speculation the *Cassell's Magazine* actually offered a prize for the best explanation. *Mariage de Convenance* also repeats the familiar Victorian homily of the dangers of high living. The bored young wife and the old roué have absolutely nothing to say to each other, and stare in glum silence over the groaning board. In the second picture, we feel quite sorry for the poor old husband, his shirt front all crumpled, as he sits slumped in front of the drawing room fire. His wife has left him, and by this time, 1886, no one would have blamed her. The Matrimonial Causes Act of 1857 and the Married Woman's Property Act of 1870 had given wives a modicum of freedom and independence from tyrannical husbands. Divorce was expensive, and still socially undesirable, but at least the legal machinery was there should anyone want to use it.

3

THE RACE FOR WEALTH

'It's all very well to be handsome and tall
Which certainly makes you look well at a ball;
It's all very fine to be clever and witty,
But if you are poor, why it's only a pity.
    So needful it is to have money, heigh-ho!
    So needful it is to have money.'
                Arthur Hugh Clough, *Spectator Ab Extra*

The Victorians thought a great deal about money. Money meant security, respectability and the opportunity of 'getting on'. 'The eleventh Commandment', declared George Dawson, a Baptist preacher in Birmingham, 'is that thou shalt keep a balance sheet.' George Pontifex, the odious paterfamilias of Samuel Butler's *The Way of all Flesh*, much preferred his money to his children: 'his money was never naughty and did not spill things on the tablecloth at meal times, or leave the door open when it went out. . . . He never dealt hastily or pettishly with his money, and that was perhaps why he and it got on so well together.'

It was an age of spectacular fortunes, and equally spectacular collapses. The opportunities were enormous, and a determined and ambitious workman, with the Bible under one arm, and Samuel Smiles' *Self Help* under the other, could, and often did, become a rich man. 'To push on,' wrote Froude, 'to climb vigorously on the slippery steps of the social ladder, to raise ourselves one step or more out of the rank of life in which we were born, is now converted into a duty.' The mother of Daniel Gooch, the railway engineer, put it more succinctly: 'Ever remember, my dear Dan, that you should look forward to being some day manager of that concern.' Huge fortunes were made and lost by adventurers like Thomas Hudson, the railway king from Yorkshire. Before his collapse in 1849, he was regarded as one of the wonders of the age. But like many of his kind, he could not resist fiddling the books. As Clough wrote in *The Latest Decalogue*:

'Thou shalt not steal; an empty feat,
When 'tis so lucrative to cheat . . .
Thou shalt not covet, but tradition
Approves all forms of competition.'

37

26 WILLIAM POWELL FRITH, R.A. (1819–1909) *The Race for Wealth – 1. The Spider and the Flies* Baroda Museum, India, signed and dated 1880, 28 × 36in. (71·1 × 91·4cm.)

Here we see the corrupt financier, the Spider (in the centre with his thumb in his waistcoat), talking to prospective clients, who have come to invest in his companies. The figures include a widow, a man with a painting to sell, a country squire, and on the right, a clergyman examining a geological specimen, with a map of the mine open before him. Frith painted the scene in a stockbroker's office in the city. He could have had in mind the career of Baron Albert Grant, a notorious company promoter, who went bankrupt in the late 1870s to the tune of about £20 million. Among the countless companies he promoted were the Cadiz Waterworks, the Central Uruguayan Railway, the Labuan Coal Company, and the Emma Silver Mine

28 WILLIAM POWELL FRITH, R.A. (1819–1909) *The Race for Wealth – 3. Victims* Baroda Museum, India, signed and dated 1880, 28 × 36in. (71·1 × 91·4cm.)

The clergyman who we saw in the Spider's office examining a piece of rock is now seen with his family round the breakfast table. They have read in the paper that the company in which they invested their savings has collapsed; they are ruined. The poor clergyman and his family will obviously have to sell up and leave their comfortable rectory. Clergymen and widows were often the most gullible investors in speculative companies, and Baron Grant is known to have obtained lists of them, to send prospectuses of his new ventures

Frith's motive in painting *The Race for Wealth* series (**26**–**30**) was to expose this 'common passion for speculation'. An extraordinary literary parallel is the career of Auguste Melmotte in Trollope's novel *The Way we Live Now*, published five years earlier in 1875. Melmotte, a mysterious financier of reputedly enormous wealth, settles in London, buying a huge house in Grosvenor Square. Although suspected of dishonesty, he quickly establishes himself as an important financial figure and is courted by society. He becomes M.P. for Westminster and at the peak of his career gives a fantastic banquet for the visiting Emperor of China. In the end his fraudulent manipulation of his many companies is exposed, and the whole edifice tumbles down. Melmotte commits suicide, and his family flee abroad. Trollope intended the book as an attack on the materialism and corruption of the society of the 1870s, of which a glaring example was the career of Baron Grant, a real-life Melmotte who cheated a gullible public out of about £20 million.

27 (*left*) WILLIAM POWELL FRITH, R.A. (1819–1909) *The Race for Wealth – 2. The Spider at Home* Baroda Museum, India, signed and dated 1880, 28 × 36in. (71·1 × 91·4cm.)

Frith shows us the Spider entertaining in his picture-filled drawing-room. The interior was that of Frith's own house in St. John's Wood. On the left the Spider is boastfully showing off one of his pictures, while a young lady giggles behind her fan, obviously at the ignorance and presumption of her host. In the room beyond, the Spider's wife is receiving more guests. Many successful Victorian financiers, including Baron Grant, built huge houses in and around London, especially in Kensington Palace Gardens, for this reason known as Millionaires' Row. Grant also collected pictures, and after his collapse his collection was sold at Christie's in 1877

29 WILLIAM POWELL FRITH, R.A. (1819–1909) *The Race for Wealth – 4. Judgement* Baroda Museum, India, signed and dated 1880, 28 × 36in. (71·1 × 91·4cm.)
The scene in the Old Bailey, where the Spider is on trial for fraud and corruption. Frith painted this scene *in situ*, using several court officials as models. He also walked along the tunnel from Newgate to the Old Bailey, to see what a condemned man would feel like. The ruined clergyman is in the witness-box, and his wife is probably among the spectators on the right. In fact bankruptcy cases could drag on for years, and the unfortunate investors were unlikely ever to get their money back

30 WILLIAM POWELL FRITH, R.A. (1819–1909) *The Race for Wealth – 5. Retribution* Baroda Museum, India, signed and dated 1880, 28 × 36in. (71·1 × 91·4cm.)
The Spider has been sent to gaol, and is here seen in the yard of Millbank Prison. Frith obtained the permission of the Prison Governor to paint the Prison Yard, and also to use a warder and several prisoners as models. The picture is a unique record of Victorian prison life, the only other being Gustave Doré's famous illustration of Newgate Prison, which was the inspiration for Van Gogh's picture *The Prison Court-Yard*. Very few fraudulent financiers actually did go to prison; Baron Grant's bankruptcy dragged on for years, and he eventually died peacefully, of old age, in Bognor Regis in 1899

31 GEORGE ELGAR HICKS (1824–1914) *Dividend Day at the Bank of England 1859* The Governor and Company of the Bank of England, signed and dated 1859, $35\frac{1}{2} \times 53$in. (90·2 × 134·6cm.)

One of several modern-life subjects which Hicks painted in emulation of Frith. Dividend Day offered an ideal subject – a lively scene, full of figures of a wide range of social types. The *Art Journal* critic loftily remarked that the picture was 'very much like the place on the supposed occasion, only with somewhat more of fashion than is generally seen there.' Bank stock was the mainstay of many a Victorian middle-class family, and especially of widows who wanted to have their money in something safe. Hicks exhibited the picture with success at the 1859 Academy, and sold it for £250

32 GEORGE GOODWIN KILBURNE (1839–1924) *Poor Relations* Walker Art Gallery, Liverpool, signed and dated 1875, 30 × 42in. (76·2 × 106·7cm.)

Victorians who had made their pile lived in dread of their poor relations. As we see from this amusing picture, they kept turning up, making emotional appeals, and causing embarrassment. The paterfamilias is handing over a ten-pound note to his impoverished relation with grotesque reluctance, and glaring at his daughter for offering a glass of wine to the poor man's daughter, who is of course, very pretty. The resemblance between her and the wife on the left might tempt one to think that they are sisters, and that the old man is their father. The interior is a particularly good example of a Victorian middle-class drawing room

33 THOMAS FAED, R.A. (1826–1900) *They had been Boys Together* Durban Museum and Art Gallery, South Africa, signed and dated 1885, 43¾ × 60½in. (111·1 × 153.7cm.)
Begging letters from relations, schoolfriends, acquaintances or just hard-luck cases were a feature of Victorian life, from which anyone with money or public position suffered. In this case a boyhood friend, obviously once respectable but now fallen on hard times, has called on a solicitor or barrister at his office to beg for money. Appeals like this very often met with success, as the ups and downs of commercial life often put respectable men out on the streets. In the hearts of many Victorian businessmen lingered the thought that one day it might happen to them

The fact that Frith painted his series shows that Melmotte, Mr. Merdle, Sir Gorgius Midas, Ernest Ponderevo and others of their kind were established figures in the Victorian consciousness.

Money features in many other Victorian pictures. Hick's *Dividend Day* (31) shows a crowd of investors arriving to collect their money, and some are busy counting it. The banknote, like the letter, often makes an appearance, giving an economic twist to the narrative, as in Kilburne's *Poor Relations* (32), and Rankley's *Old Schoolfellows* (99). A banknote or a draft must be on the point of appearing in Faed's *They Had been Boys Together* (33), and perhaps the clerk is already writing one out.

4

THE ROAD TO RUIN

'Lord Hippo suffered fearful loss,
By putting money on a horse,
Which he believed, if it were pressed,
Would run far faster than the rest.'
Hilaire Belloc, *Cautionary Tales*

The Victorians had a horror of all forms of gambling. Even one so grandly aristocratic as Plantaganet Palliser, in Trollope's novel *Can you Forgive Her?* (1864), was furious when he found that his wife Lady Glencora had been gambling during their stay at Baden. 'Is it nothing,' he fumed, 'that I find my wife playing at a common gambling table, surrounded by all that is wretched and vile – established there, seated, with heaps of gold before her?' One artist who would heartily have agreed with him was Frith. He too visited Baden in 1843, and wrote, 'my first sight of the clustering crowd round the tables shocked me exceedingly. Instead of the noisy, eager gamblers I expected to see, I found a quiet, business-like unimpressionable set of people trying to get money without working for it. . . . Quite time, I thought, that a stop should be put to it.' But that did not stop Frith painting a picture of it (34). For all his moral indignation, Frith knew a good subject when he saw one. Also based on the gambling rooms at Homburg was Elmore's *On the Brink* (35) which carries the gambling saga one stage further. The critics as usual pooh-poohed the picture as 'somewhat sensational', but the crowds loved it.

Frith had more to say about gambling in his series *The Road to Ruin* (36–40), a set of five pictures which he exhibited at the Academy in 1878. Once again, they proved so popular that a guardian and a rail were necessary to protect them, a distinction accorded to many of Frith's pictures, from *Derby Day* onwards. In his *Autobiography* Frith records with pride each occasion this happened. He needed to justify himself, as the critics and his fellow-artists were invariably spiteful and not a little jealous of his popular success. 'There can hardly, we suppose,' wrote the critic of the *Art Journal* loftily, 'be a single country cousin who is not by this time familiar with the fact that these celebrated canvases are five in number and that they tell the tragic, and perhaps occasionally true, story of a young man etc. . . .' The same critic also objected to 'the inadequacy of the motive. A card party at college does not improve one's book learning, but it need not necessarily

43

34
WILLIAM POWELL FRITH, R.A. (1819–1909)
The Salon d'Or, Homburg (detail) Rhode Island
School of Design, $49\frac{1}{4} \times 102\frac{1}{2}$in. ($125\cdot1 \times 260\cdot4$cm.)
Frith has included himself and his wife, looking
suitably disapproving, in the middle standing
back from the table. With his usual thoroughness
Frith painted the room *in situ*, and also borrowed
the croupier's equipment to make studies from.
The picture was of course a great success. The
Victorian horror of gambling was combined with
a fascination to see what it was actually like, and
they would have enjoyed reading moral tales into
all the little incidents round the table

35
ALFRED ELMORE, R.A. (1815–1881) *On the Brink*
Fitzwilliam Museum, Cambridge, signed
and dated 1865, $45 \times 32\frac{3}{4}$in. ($114\cdot4 \times 83\cdot2$cm.)
Elmore gives the gambling saga a further twist. An
unhappy girl sits in the cold moonlight outside
the red glare of the gambling rooms at
Homburg, and an attractive man leans out to talk
to her. Elmore has used the detective novelist's
trick of deliberate vagueness, providing us only
with tantalizing clues. What is she on the brink
of? Gambling? Seduction? Or has she lost
everything and is contemplating suicide?
Unlike a detective novel, this thriller has no
ending, so we shall never know the answer

36 WILLIAM POWELL FRITH, R.A. (1819–1909) *The Road to Ruin – College* Private collection, Italy, 28 × 36in. (71·1 × 91·4cm.)

Frith greatly admired the work of Hogarth, and intended this series to be a Victorian 'Gambler's Progress'. This first scene shows the well-born young hero at an all-night card party in his rooms at college. It is early morning; one young man blows out a candle while another looks out at the dawn breaking. Frith visited an undergraduate's room at Cambridge to make studies for the setting; and had photographs taken to help him. The tower seen out of the window looks like the main gateway of Caius College, by Alfred Waterhouse

37 WILLIAM POWELL FRITH, R.A. (1819–1909) *The Road to Ruin – Ascot*, 28 × 36in. (71·1 × 91·4cm.)

Frith was inspired to paint this Hogarthian series when he saw the Royal Enclosure at Ascot, outside which illegal betting took place. Here we see the raffishly-dressed hero heading full-speed for ruin, placing his bets with the touts and bookies who cluster round him over the fence. An older man tries to restrain him, but to no avail. Among the fashionably-dressed ladies, the one on the extreme right looks like the gambler's wife

38

39

40

41 ROBERT BRAITHWAITE MARTINEAU (1826–1869) *The Last Day in the Old Home* Tate Gallery, London, signed and dated 1861, 42½ × 57in. (107·4 × 144·8cm)
Another moral tale of the feckless young blood who has gambled away everything on the horses, and is now drinking his last glass of champagne in the ancestral home. This is one of the best examples of a narrative painting that can be read like a book, as well as looked at. Almost every object in the room has significance – the pictures of horses, the lot numbers, the Christie catalogue on the floor, the newspaper open at the word 'Apartments', the old mother offering a five-pound note to the man with the keys – the observer becomes a detective assembling clues, forming his own conclusions as to the situation of all the characters

(facing page)

38 WILLIAM POWELL FRITH, R.A. (1819–1909) *The Road to Ruin – Arrest*, 28 × 36in. (71·1 × 91·4cm.)
The bailiff and his assistant have arrived with a warrant in the gambler's house. The gambler, languid and affectedly unconcerned in his dressing-gown, leans on the mantelpiece and stares arrogantly at the swarthy Jewish figure of the bailiff. The assistant casts a sympathetic glance at the surprised mother, and her two children, playing with their toys. The two servants in the doorway are discussing the affair in astonishment. In the fireplace lies a fashionable newspaper, *Bell's Life in London*

39 WILLIAM POWELL FRITH, R.A. (1819–1909) *The Road to Ruin – Struggles*, 28 × 36in. (71·1 × 91·4cm.)
The scene has moved to France, where the gambler sits, like Hogarth's Distressed Poet, trying to write a play, while his wife attempts to soothe the landlady, who holds a long bill in her hand. The wife has also been trying to earn money by painting in watercolours, as we see from the table on the left. The boy tries to comfort his father, while the little girl warms her hands before the fire. There is another young baby in a cradle behind the door

40 WILLIAM POWELL FRITH, R.A. (1819–1909) *The Road to Ruin – The End*, 28 × 36in. (71·1 × 91·4cm.)
Back to a garret in London for the final scene of the tragedy. The ruined man is locking the door before shooting himself with the loaded gun on the table. A letter on the floor reveals that the Theatre Royal, Drury Lane, have rejected his comedy, and the untidy squalor of the room testifies to the despair of his situation. The wicker cradle and broken toys on the floor remind us of the hardships that have doubtless come upon his wife and children. Frith found the furniture in junk shops in a poor quarter of London

end in suicide.' But Frith knew his market. The great majority of the self-righteous middle classes were genuinely horrified by gambling, and could quite believe Frith's story. One of the facts about the Baccarat Scandal which most aroused public opinion was the revelation that the Prince of Wales carried his own set of crested counters, to place on the baccarat tables of country houses.

Frith thought of the series as 'a kind of Gambler's Progress, avoiding the satirical vein of Hogarth, for which I knew myself to be unfitted.' The result is a very Victorian moral progress. Both the Bible and the Victorian novel taught the middle classes to believe that sin was followed by retribution. In Farrar's novel *Eric, or Little by Little*, the unfortunate Eric begins slipping into temptation while still at school. Bad language and cribbing lead to lying and stealing; smoking, gambling and even drinking follow, and before long Eric is on the inevitable death-bed, with agonizing pages of tears, confessions and forgiveness.

Although a friend of the Pre-Raphaelites, Martineau in his picture *The Last Day in the Old Home* (41) comes closer to the methods of Frith. Painted in meticulous, almost stifling detail, it shows a feckless aristocrat drinking his last glass of champagne in the ancestral home. Both the miniature case in his left hand, and the pictures of horses on the left, indicate that the turf has been his undoing. The upper-class rake was a stock figure in novels, particularly in the 1850s and 1860s. In Mrs. Henry Wood's best-selling *East Lynne* the wicked Sir Francis Levison commits every sin the author could think of, including seduction and murder, before getting his deserts and going to gaol. She even pursues him to his breakfast table, where he lounges 'unwashed, unshaven, a dressing-gown loosely flung on . . . these decked-out dandies before the world are frequently the greatest slovens in domestic privacy.'

HARD TIMES

'I am afraid there is more vice, more misery, more penury in this
country than in any other, and, at the same time, greater wealth.'
Charles Greville's *Diaries*

The glaring contrast between rich and poor was a constant source of anxiety and fear
in Victorian society. Serious-minded people, the harangues of Carlyle and Ruskin
ringing in their ears, their consciences disturbed by the dictates of their own religion,
earnestly desired greater social justice. Many worked hard to achieve it, but the problem
was too deep-rooted. The industrial revolution, born in a competitive atmosphere of
free trade, brought prosperity to many, and progress to Great Britain, but at the cost
of virtually enslaving the workers. Huge new industrial towns sprang up, undrained,
unpoliced and ungoverned, in which the labouring classes lived in conditions of appalling
squalor. The fluctuations of trade brought even greater hardship, bitter strikes, lock-outs
and riots. The machinery of local government was quite inadequate to cope and social
legislation was usually one step behind. The real work was done by professionals like
Chadwick, philanthropists like Lord Shaftesbury, and the charitable and voluntary
organizations. Conditions for the working man did improve gradually, but the problem
of poverty refused to go away. Many people despaired, and took refuge in the thought
that God had arranged these things for man's own good. Even as dedicated a reformer
as Herbert Spencer could write, 'The poverty of the incapable, the distress that comes
upon the imprudent, the starvation of the idle, and those shoulderings aside of the weak
by the strong, which leave so many in the shallows and in miseries, are the decrees of a
large, far-seeing benevolence.'

The Victorians strongly resisted the idea that poverty should be a subject for art.
Mrs. Gaskell might attempt in her novel *Mary Barton* to describe working-class life in
Manchester, but painting it was another matter. If poverty was to be painted at all,
then it should be converted into something agreeable and harmless, arousing a sympathetic
tear but not a desire for social revolution. Hence the endless pictures of pretty flower
girls, ragged children, and poor cottagers, resolutely cheerful and happy in their picturesque
rags. *The Knife-Thrower and his Family in a Garrett* by Gustave Pope (**42**) and *The
Poor, the Poor Man's Friend* by Thomas Faed (**43**) are typical of the type of picture popular

42 GUSTAVE POPE (fl. 1852–1910) *The Knife-Thrower and his Family in a Garret* Photo: B. Cohen and Sons, signed and dated '62, 27 × 36in. (68·6 × 91·4cm.)

Victorians liked their pictures of poverty to be picturesque, arousing a sympathetic tear rather than a desire for social reform. The swarthy knife-thrower and his garret combine the best of both worlds. Victorian travelling showmen had a precarious existence at best, and their living was gradually eroded by cheap theatres and the rise of the music hall

44 FRED WALKER, A.R.A. (1840–1875) *The Vagrants* (detail) Tate Gallery, London, signed with initials, 32¾ × 49¾in.
(83·2 × 126·4cm.)
Painted at Beddington in Surrey. The figure on the right was posed in the studio; the models for the other figures were
a family of gipsies. The Victorian fascination with gipsies is reflected in novels like George Borrow's *Lavengro*, and
Aylwin by Theodore Watts-Dunton. The gipsy beauty was often a femme fatale – Jane Morris, and Frederick Sandys'
mistress, for example

in the 1850s and 1860s. Frith painted a picture entitled *Poverty and Wealth* in 1888,
showing a rich lady in her carriage passing the door of a small shop outside which stands
the poor man and numerous ragged children. Frith was never a social reformer by
inclination, and his intention was doubtless sentimental rather than realistic.

It was only in the 1870s that anything like a school of social realist painters emerged.
The three pioneers were all young men – Luke Fildes, Frank Holl and Hubert von
Herkomer. They all produced illustrations for the *Graphic*, a magazine much admired
by the young Van Gogh, who came to England in 1873. He retained his admiration for
English illustrators to the end, and wrote to his brother, Theo, in 1882, 'For me one of
the highest and noblest expressions of art is always that of the English, for instance
Millais and Herkomer and Frank Holl.' Fildes, Holl and Herkomer were all admirers
of Fred Walker, whose blend of poetic landscapes and Millet-like peasants enjoyed a
tremendous vogue in the 1860s. *The Vagrants* (**44**), painted in 1868, is typical of his
romantic autumn landscapes, the figures with their wistful expressions and deliberately

43 (*left*) THOMAS FAED, R.A. (1826–1900) *The Poor, the Poor Man's Friend* (detail) Victoria and Albert Museum,
signed and dated 1867, 16 × 24in. (40·4 × 61cm.)
A typically sentimental treatment of the subject of poverty, converting it into something harmless and agreeable.
The fisherman and his family, although poor, are happy, and charitable enough to give money to a passing
blind beggar. The faded coat and battered hat of the beggar indicate that he is a respectable man fallen on hard
times, therefore one of the 'deserving poor'.

45 SIR LUKE FILDES, R.A. (1843–1927) *Applicants for Admission to a Casual Ward* (detail) Royal Holloway College, Egham, signed and dated 1874, 56×97½in. (142·2×242·6cm.)
One of the outstanding social realist paintings of the 19th century. It caused a sensation at the R.A. in 1874, but Fildes did not paint many more subjects of this type. He first used this subject as a drawing for the *Graphic* of 4th December, 1869. The figure of the woman carrying a baby on the left is strongly reminiscent of Fred Walker's *The Lost Path* of 1863, but the other figures were all based on real characters found by Fildes in nightly wanderings around London. When the picture was exhibited, Fildes added a quotation from Dickens: 'Dumb, wet, silent horrors! Sphinxes set up against the dead wall, and none likely to be at the pains of solving them until the general overthrow.'

monumental poses, which Ruskin called 'galvanised-Elgin' attitudes. But Walker died young in 1875, and his great rival in poetic landscape, George Hemming Mason, died in 1872. The first picture by the younger men to attract attention was Luke Fildes' *Applicants for Admission to a Casual Ward* (**45**) which caused a sensation when exhibited at the Academy in 1874. The English critics hailed Fildes as 'Hogarth's successor', and a foreign critic saw him as 'opening a new path in Art as Gustave Courbet had done in 1851 with his "Stonebreakers".' A private observer, Caleb Scholefield Mann, made an elaborate scrapbook of the 1874 exhibition to amuse his wife (now in the Ashmolean Museum). Deeply impressed with the *Applicants*, he wrote, '. . . a fable as forcible, as clear, and as awe-striking as an antique tragedy; that is, if the present ill-conditioned school of critics will condescend to admit that there is anything awful in sin, and misery, and disease, and impending death.' The ill-conditioned critic of the *Art Journal*, while acknowledging that the picture was 'the most notable piece of realism', considered that 'there is little in a theme of such grovelling misery to recommend it to a painter whose purpose is beauty.

... The state of things he represents to us ought rather to be removed than to be perpetuated, and its introduction into art which should be permanent is rather matter for regret.'

The critics were even less pleased by Fildes' next picture *The Widower* (**46**), exhibited at the Royal Academy in 1876. *The Times* warned that the subject 'was not happily chosen' and went on, 'The painter, we submit, is under a mistake who brings big, dirty boots, squalling and scrambling children, parental and sisterly love, into such contact. ... It is a great pity painters do not bear more in mind the fact that their pictures are meant to adorn English living rooms, and that intense painfulness, overstrained expression and great vehemence of momentary action or short-lived attitude are all qualities that make pictures unpleasant to live with.' The authentic voice of the Victorian philistine. Unfortunately for posterity Fildes took a short cut to fame and fortune – he gave up dirty boots for the calmer more profitable waters of portraiture and Venetian subjects in the manner of Eugene de Blaas. Royal commissions, a knighthood and a large Norman Shaw house in Melbury Road, Holland Park, were his reward. He died, rich and famous, in 1927, yet another victim of late Victorian and Edwardian official bad taste. After the celebrated *Doctor* (**102**) of 1891, he never painted another memorable picture.

The career of Hubert von Herkomer follows a similar pattern. He was born in Bavaria, the son of a woodcarver, who first emigrated to the United States, and finally settled in

46 SIR LUKE FILDES, R.A. (1843–1927) *The Widower* Gallery of New South Wales, Sydney, signed, 66½ × 98in. (168·9 × 248·3cm.)
The idea for this picture came from the labourer holding a child in his arms, in the centre of the 'Applicants for Admission'. The model was a man who used to bring the baby with him every time he came to Fildes' studio. 'One day he was resting behind a screen and my father, happening to look round it, discovered him nursing the child with the utmost tenderness. My father told him not to move, and taking paper and pencil made a study of the two of them just as they were.' (L. V. Fildes *Luke Fildes, R.A. A Victorian Painter*, 1968)

Southampton in 1857. Hubert entered the South Kensington Schools in 1866, and came under the influence of Fred Walker and Luke Fildes. Like them, he produced illustrations for the *Graphic*. Realizing that in England 'truth in art should be enhanced by sentiment' (concealed by sentiment would have been more accurate), he achieved success in 1875 with *The Last Muster, Sunday at the Royal Hospital, Chelsea*. In 1878 he followed this up with *Eventide* (**47**), a scene in the Westminster Workhouse for Women. At the time, the picture was seen as a female equivalent of *The Last Muster*. Although the figures are rather mawkish, the almost monochrome blackness of the colours and the huddled group of figures create a powerful impression of grimness and hardship. It was not until 1885 that he produced his next social picture *Hard Times* (**48**), the best of its type that he ever painted. Fred Walker had been dead ten years, but his influence on Herkomer can plainly be felt in the idealization of the figure of the workman, and the whole treatment of the subject. Herkomer wrote of the picture in his autobiography: '. . . [in 1885] hundreds of honest labourers wandered through the country in search of work . . . it was such a group, resting by the wayside of a country lane, that I depicted. The lane, with winding roadway and high trimmed hedges of hawthorn, lay on my very door at Bushey. It was named by the students "Hard Times Lane".' After this Herkomer only returned to social realism with *The First Born* (1887) and *On Strike* (**123**) (1890). Having

47 SIR HUBERT VON HERKOMER, R.A. (1849–1914) *Eventide* Walker Art Gallery, Liverpool, signed and dated 1878, $43\frac{1}{2} \times 78\frac{1}{4}$in. (110·5 × 198·7cm.)
This is practically the only Victorian picture of the dreaded Workhouse, and was based on observations made at the Westminster Workhouse in London

48 SIR HUBERT VON HERKOMER, R.A. (1849–1914) *Hard Times* Manchester City Art Gallery, signed with initials and dated '85, 33½ × 43½in. (85 × 110·5cm.)
Although agricultural workers got the franchise in 1884, the agricultural depression brought great hardships the following year. Scenes such as this were common all over England, and Herkomer painted the picture in a lane near his house at Bushey Heath. The students of his art school at Bushey christened the road 'Hard Times Lane'

known poverty in his youth, his desire for fame and riches gave him no rest, and led him inexorably down the primrose path to fashionable portrait painting. Honours were showered upon him – the C.V.O., a knighthood, even a German title from the Kaiser. He founded an art school at Bushey, built a monstrous Germanic house called Lululaund and a Wagnerian tower in Germany in memory of his mother, was Slade Professor, wrote operas, and lived to design both for the stage and the cinema. He died in 1914, a veritable pillar of the art establishment.

Frank Holl was the most interesting artist of the three, and the best painter, but his career was unfortunately the shortest. He died in 1888 aged only 43. He too became a successful and very good portrait painter, but his interest in social realism was more than just a passing phase. His first success was *The Lord gave and the Lord hath taken away*, 1869, a picture of a bereaved family praying round a table in a fisherman's cottage. Holl was awarded the Royal Academy's Travelling Prize for this, and went to Italy in 1869. He resigned it the following year and returned to England. Like William Morris, he genuinely preferred grey skies to blue, and he also felt that the study of old masters was irrelevant to his desire to paint subjects of modern life. In 1870 he exhibited another picture of fishing life, *No Tidings from the Sea* (**50**), which was bought by Queen Victoria. The widowhood theme obviously appealed to her as she had also tried to buy *The Lord*

49
FRED BROWN (1851–1941) *Hard Times*
Walker Art Gallery, Liverpool, signed and
dated 1886, 27½ × 35½in. (69·8 × 90·2cm.)
Another interpretation of Herkomer's theme,
showing a travelling labourer in a bar, where
he has stopped for a drink. The bundle on the
floor indicates that he is a farm worker or mechanic
'on the tramp' for work, a depressing and
dispiriting activity which was the lot of many
Victorian workers. The bareness of the interior,
and the little girl warming her hands before the
fire, add to the atmosphere of despair

50 FRANK HOLL, A.R.A. (1845–1888) *No Tidings from the Sea* Reproduced by gracious permission of Her Majesty the
Queen, 28 × 36in. (71·2 × 91·4cm.)
Queen Victoria admired Holl's work, and bought this from the R.A. 1870 exhibition. The dangers of a fisherman's
life, and the distress of their families, were subjects which made a strong emotional appeal to the Victorians, and
pictures of these subjects were common in the period 1880–1900. Holl witnessed this scene staying in a cottage in
Cullercoats, Northumberland. The figure of the kneeling woman foreshadows Frank Bramley's *Hopeless Dawn* of 1888

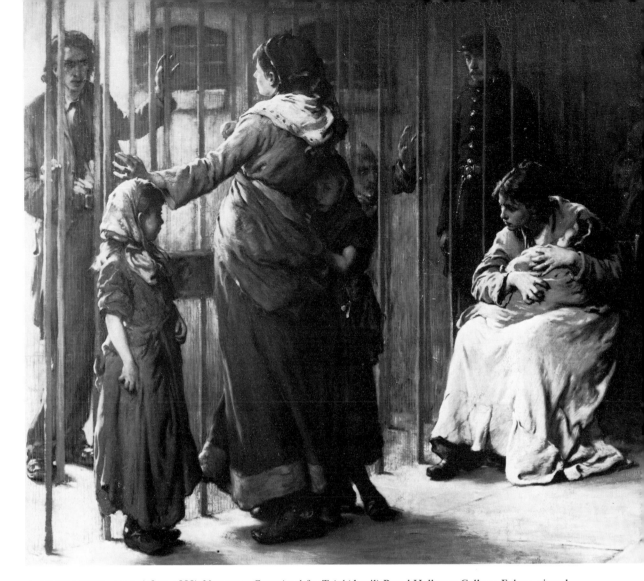

51 FRANK HOLL, A.R.A. (1845–1888) *Newgate – Committed for Trial* (detail) Royal Holloway College, Egham, signed and dated 1878, 61¼ × 84¾in. (155·5 × 215·2cm.)
Holl's masterpiece, and one of the outstanding examples of social realist painting produced in England. Again Holl based it on an actual scene he witnessed in Newgate Prison, when he saw a woman and her children coming to visit a prisoner for the first time. The models were clothed in real East End rags borrowed from pawnbrokers' shops and rag-and-bone men

gave in 1868. Dramas of life by the sea were popular in the 1870s and 1880s and artists often spent their summers painting in small fishing villages. In 1884 Stanhope Forbes founded his school at Newlyn in Cornwall, which became an important summer centre for artists. Here, too, life in the fishing village was the central theme. Many Victorian families spent their summer holidays by the sea, which perhaps explains the emotive appeal of this type of picture. The lost boat, the waiting women, the wreck and the life-boat became the stock-in-trade of many a successful hack artist.

In search of subjects, Holl prowled round the East End with another artist friend, C. E. Johnson. Seeing two policemen carrying a foundling baby, he turned this into *Deserted – A Foundling*, exhibited at the Royal Academy in 1874, but now lost. Visiting Newgate Prison, Holl witnessed another scene that was to result in his most famous picture, *Newgate – Committed for Trial* (**51**). What Holl saw was a bank clerk who had cheated his employers of a large sum, and had been sentenced to five years' penal servitude. In the final picture, Holl included other visiting wives to give the scene added interest. It is a large and moving picture. Holl's sympathy with social problems was genuine and sincere, and there is no forced sentimentality. The colours are gloomy and sombre, the use of light and dark dramatic; it is perhaps the masterpiece of English social realism.

Social realism as a movement in English art was brief, and never took root. Although the paintings of Walker, Fildes, Herkomer and Holl influenced many young artists, Van Gogh in particular, the results in England were disappointing. There was no Courbet in England to show how such subjects might be painted as simply and powerfully as possible. English artists were fettered by the bias towards narrative, the need to make every picture tell a story. Also the English buying public did not like this kind of picture. They were unsuitable for English living rooms, and what was worse, they smacked of French immorality, Republicanism, and the novels of Zola, all things most distasteful to the English mind.

𝕭

HOME SWEET HOME

'A tent pitched in a world not aright
It seemed, whose inmates, everyone,
On tranquil faces bore the light
Of duties beautifully done.'
Coventry Patmore, *The Angel in the House*

The home, and the family, were the central institutions of Victorian life. After battling all day in the market-place, the Victorian father wanted to come back to his own peaceful, private fireside, surrounded by dutiful children and an adoring wife (52–3). The very competitiveness of business life seems to have encouraged a corresponding elevation of home to a private temple of domesticity; for Ruskin it was 'a sacred place, a vestal temple, a temple of the hearth watched over by household Gods'. Presiding over the temple was the wife, 'the Angel in the House', dutiful, submissive, obedient, faithful, pure, and decorative. A woman's place was in the home:

'Man for the field and woman for the hearth;
Man for the Sword, and for the needle she;
Man with the head, and woman with the heart;
Man to command, and woman to obey.'

(Tennyson, *The Princess*)

Paintings of home and family life are the most common of all Victorian narrative pictures. The cosy room, the fireside, the children and the pets would feature in rows of pictures at the Royal Academy every year; small, sentimental, often exquisitely finished, and all extolling the joys of domestic happiness. Most of the homes depicted would be middle to lower class, but the cottage was the most popular symbol of homely domesticity (53). The feeling and the message are the same – rich or poor, family life is what makes for happiness. In an age of sweeping social change, the family provided continuity and security. It could be stifling, and it had many critics. Florence Nightingale knew 'nothing like the petty grinding tyranny of a good English family'. Samuel Butler went further: 'I believe that more unhappiness comes from the source of the family than from any other. The mischief among the lower classes is not as great, but among the middle classes it is killing a large number daily.' (*The Way of all Flesh.*) But we find

59

52 (*left*) JANE MARIA BOWKETT (fl. 1860–1885) *Preparing Tea* Photo: the late Mrs. Charlotte Frank (picture now destroyed), signed with monogram
A mother and two daughters are busy preparing tea in anticipation of the arrival of their father, whose train can be seen approaching out of the window. After the ruthless competition of Victorian commercial life, this was the kind of cosy domesticity which a man wanted to come home to. One little girl is making toast, while another brings daddy's slippers

53 (*right*) JOSEPH CLARKE (1834–1912) *The Labourer's Welcome* Sheffield Art Galleries, 30 × 21½in. (76·2 × 54·6cm.)
Instead of a businessman returning by train to the suburbs, here we have a farm labourer returning to his cosy little cottage. His wife is both pretty and domesticated, and keeps their cottage in a pleasing state of neatness and clutter. The grandfather clock tells us that it is five past six – the hour when most farm workers would return home. It is an idealized picture of what a relatively prosperous cottage might look like

few such criticisms in Victorian paintings. A family may meet with misfortune, certainly – death, sickness, loss of money – but this only seems to draw them closer together. It is what Ruskin rightly called the 'Art of the Nest', and criticized for 'Shallowness of Thought. To be quite comfortable in your nest, you must not care too much for what is going on outside. . . . As there is in the spirit of domesticity always a sanctified littleness, there may also be a sanctified selfishness.'

Within the family circle, family occasions were important events, each to be celebrated with the proper ritual. Births, deaths, christenings and weddings were the high points, but there was also the constant business of family correspondence, the round of visiting relations, and the reunions at Christmas and on birthdays. Frith has shown us in *Many Happy Returns of the Day* (**54**) what a middle-class family gathering looked like in 1856. He used many of his own family as models – his mother is the old lady on the left of the table, and the birthday girl in the centre is one of his daughters, later Lady Hastings. Frith himself sits at the head of the table holding a glass, a picture of the prosperous and respectable paterfamilias. The model for the old grandfather on the right was found by Frith in the Workhouse. Ruskin praised the picture, and detected signs of 'advancing Pre-Raphaelitism'. This irritated Frith considerably, as he had no wish to be associated with the still very controversial PRB. In his *Autobiography* he not only refuted Ruskin's charge, but excused himself even further by saying it was one of the worst pictures he ever painted. Ruskin also wrote that he was 'sorry to see any fair little child having too many and too kind friends, and in so great danger of being toasted, toyed, and wreathed

54 WILLIAM POWELL FRITH, R.A. (1819–1909) *Many Happy Returns of the Day* Harrogate Art Gallery, signed and dated 1856, 31½ × 44½in. (80 × 103cm.)
The family was the central institution of Victorian life, and all family gatherings were important dates on the calendar

55 ROBERT BRAITHWAITE MARTINEAU (1826–1869) *The Christmas Hamper* Alexander Gallery, London
35 × 50in. (89 × 127cm.)
'The unpacking of those hampers being an event of the most important and delightful nature possible . . . I do not
believe country cousins send hampers to town cousins nowadays . . . and I can but be sorry at the disappearance of a
good old custom.' (Mrs Panton, *Leaves from a Life*, 1908. Mrs Panton was a daughter of W. P. Frith.)

into selfishness and misery.' This is a typical Ruskinian moralistic outburst, which carries
the sentimental interest of the spectator too far, inviting him to invent a story where
none was intended.

Encouraged by royal example, the Victorians invented Christmas as we know it.
The whole paraphernalia of Christmas trees, presents, cards, holly, turkey, plum puddings,
carols and family gatherings was carried to a peak of cosy festivity. Martineau's *The
Christmas Hamper* (**55**) records an important prelude to Christmas, the unpacking of
the hamper, containing presents for all the family, letters, a hare, a pheasant and a large
turkey. An English Christmas is always a time for patriotic demonstration, and it is nice
to see a bust of the good Queen in the background and, above it, a picture of the widowed
Victoria and her children paying homage to the bust of dear, departed Albert.

7

CHILDHOOD

'I remember, I remember
The house where I was born'
Thomas Hood, *I remember*

Pictures of home life nearly always involve children. The Victorian raised large families, and were often strict parents, but in general they had great affection for their children. Babies were a particular object of worship, as they were too helpless and innocent to be subjected to parental discipline. Mothers who had little else to do but marry, raise a family, and run a household, felt special devotion towards their babies. Victorian painters brought a refreshing, secular atmosphere to the age-old tradition of the Madonna and Child, by then thoroughly moribund after centuries of repetition. All three pictures illustrated here, by Smith, Leslie, and Hicks (56–8) reveal a tenderness and depth of feeling which may surprise those who think of Victorian family life only in terms of repression and discipline. None of these painters normally painted this kind of subject, which perhaps accounts for their sincerity. Leslie was a painter of elaborate costume pieces from Molière and other literary sources; Hicks by 1870 had given up narrative scenes of modern life in favour of society portraits and generally insipid domestic scenes; George Smith was a specialist in small, intimate cottage scenes, but rarely achieved a feeling of such delicate and restrained tenderness as in *Fondly Gazing* (58). Although there are many pictures of motherhood, nowhere in Victorian painting is there any reference to pregnancy. Those unfortunate enough not to have children could follow the example of the elderly couple in F. B. Barwell's picture *Adopting a Child* (3).

Once the babies grew into children they would begin to feel the weight of parental authority. Parents considered it their moral duty to subject the wills of their children. In the words of Samuel Butler, 'At that time it was universally admitted that to spare the rod was to spoil the child, and Saint Paul had placed disobedience to parents in very ugly company.' Biographies of famous Victorians, among them those of Augustus Hare, Lord Curzon, and Kipling, contain hair-raising accounts of miserable, tortured childhoods. But there was another, more human side to Victorian family life. Within the strict limits of convention, families were often happy and united, and not stifling in their effect on the children. It is this benevolent side that is reflected in Victorian pictures of children.

63

56 CHARLES ROBERT LESLIE, R.A. (1794–1859) *A Mother and Child* Private Collection, 22 × 19in. (55·9 × 48·2cm.)
Victorians of all classes felt special affection for their children, and nowhere is this more tenderly expressed than in this
picture, which Leslie painted in 1846 for his patron John Gibbons. At the R.A. it met with universal praise: 'a passage
from the book of Nature which never can be more perfectly rendered'. (*Art Union*, 1846, p. 176.) Tom Taylor, who
edited the *Autobiographical Recollections of Leslie* (1860) thought that no mother could look at the picture without feeling maternal emotion, and praised the picture as 'free from all mawkishness' and for not 'trading in "deep domestic"
as a good saleable article for the market'

57 *(left)* GEORGE ELGAR HICKS (1824–1914) *New Hopes* Photo: Christie's, signed and dated 1870, 23 × 17½in. (58·4 × 44·4cm.)
Rich ladies like this one, who had very little to do but marry, raise a family and supervise a household, were likely to be especially devoted to their babies. A baby was too helpless and innocent to be subjected to parental discipline, although in a house with many servants it was difficult for a mother to be alone with her baby as much as she wished
58 *(right)* GEORGE SMITH (1829–1901) *Fondly Gazing* Photo: Phillips Ltd., signed and dated 1860 on panel, 15 × 13in. (38·1 × 33cm.)
There would not be any servants in this family, thus allowing the mother to gaze uninterruptedly at her baby, asleep in its wicker cradle and draped in a patchwork quilt. Most Victorian mothers gave their babies Godfrey's Cordial, which contained quite a high quantity of opium, causing them to sleep very soundly indeed

59
THOMAS WEBSTER, R.A. (1800–1886)
A Tea Party (detail) Harris Museum and Art Gallery, Preston, on panel, 19¾ × 24in. (50·2 × 61cm.)
In an age of large families, children were left to make their own amusements. These girls are having a make-believe tea party. The cottage is a humble one, but the children none the less have a few simple toys. Webster specialized in pictures of children, and after his retirement to Cranbrook in Kent in 1856, he gathered round him a group of fellow-artists, all painting similar subjects

60 CHARLES HUNT (1803–1877) *Bluebeard – Preparations for a Children's Pantomime* Photo: Sotheby's Belgravia, signed and dated 1865, $20\frac{3}{4} \times 29\frac{1}{2}$in. (52·7 × 75cm.)
Amateur theatricals were standard family entertainment in the 19th century. Almost all children took part in them, whatever their social background. These children appear to have rather elaborate costumes considering the humbleness of the cottage setting, but perhaps they are off to the village hall to perform

The great majority of them are of children's games (**59**). 'Old art waited reverently in the forum,' complained Ruskin, 'ours plays happily in the nursery.' In an age of large families, children were left to make their own amusements. Toys and games were manufactured for them; many of the great classics of childrens' literature were written for them, and great care was lavished on their production and illustration. This interest in the games, fancies, and thoughts of children is reflected in countless pictures. Artists like Thomas Webster and F. D. Hardy made a comfortable living painting nothing else. *Playing at Doctors* (**61**) and *The Young Photographers* (**62**) are typical of Hardy's work – charming, humorous, rarely over-sentimental and beautifully observed. The details of his interiors are always scrupulously accurate too, a wonderful source of information about Victorian interior decoration. There is of course, a certain rosy unreality about all these pictures. The children are never noisy, cruel, or sick, like the peasants of Brouwer and Ostade; they never fight, or break things, as children always will. But they remain, as Baudelaire found them, 'charming, intimate glimpses of home'.

62 (*right*) FREDERICK DANIEL HARDY (1826–1911) *The Young Photographers* Tunbridge Wells Library and Museum signed and dated 1862 on panel, 14 × 21in. (38·1 × 53·4cm.)
This scene takes place in the home of a portrait photographer, and his children are playing at their father's profession. Beyond can be seen the studio, complete with studio camera on a tripod and props – a chair, a balustrade, and a landscape background, the usual setting for Victorian carte-de-visite photographs. Outside in the street, the photographer is displaying examples of his work to two passers-by, and his wife sits with a baby on her knee, trimming photographs with a pair of scissors. The mantelpiece is also surrounded with portraits which look like daguerreotypes or ambrotypes

61 FREDERICK DANIEL HARDY (1826–1911) *Playing at Doctors* Victoria and Albert Museum, signed and dated 1863, $17\frac{5}{8} \times 24$in. (44·7 × 61cm.)
Interest in the games, fancies, and thoughts of children was one of the more enlightened aspects of the Victorian age. It found expression in an enormous number of pictures of children at play, in which Hardy was a specialist, being closely associated with Thomas Webster in Cranbrook. As with all Hardy's pictures, the interior is also charmingly observed, and full of authentic detail

63 GEORGE BERNARD O'NEILL (1828–1917) *The Children's Party* Richard Green Ltd., signed and dated
'71 30½ × 45in. (77·5 × 114·4cm.)
G. B. O'Neill was another artist associated with Webster in Cranbrook, and this party scene is typical
of his style. His children are always sweet, sentimental, and a little too good to be true, but this is a charming record of a Victorian children's party

64 (*above*) HARRY BROOKER (fl. 1876–1910) *Making a Kite* (detail)
Photo: Christie's, signed and dated 1902, 28 × 36in. (71·1 × 91·4cm.)
Children at play amid the typical clutter of a Victorian nursery. The boys are
in collars, boaters, and knee-breeches, and the objects in the room suggest that
they are in the schoolroom of a large house, middle or upper-class

65 (*right*) WILLIAM MAW EGLEY (1826–1916) *Military Aspirations* (detail) Holburne of Menstrie Museum, Bath,
signed and dated 1861, 24 × 18¼in. (61 × 46·4cm.)
Egley exhibited this picture at the R.A. in 1861, and intended it to be a triptych showing the life of a boy who wanted
to join the Army. Here he is busy tormenting his two sisters in the nursery. The relentless patterns of the walls and
carpet, the polished hardness of the furniture, and the neatness of the children's dresses all convey the claustrophobic
atmosphere of middle-class childhood

8

FOUNDLINGS

'Stay, Lady, stay, for mercy's sake,
And hear a helpless Orphan's tale:'
Amelia Opie, *An Orphan Boy's Tale*

Nothing stirred the Victorian conscience so deeply as deserted or neglected children. The streets of London swarmed with them, begging, stealing, sweeping crossings, shoe-cleaning, selling matches, scratching a living as best they could (**66–7**). All too often the social stigma of an illegitimate child forced mothers to abandon their babies, a melancholy subject which Frank Holl turned into a picture, *Deserted – A Foundling*. Sentimental pictures of ragged children were often called 'The Foundlings', to give them an extra emotional twist. G. F. Hicks explored this theme in even greater detail with his picture *The Infant Orphan Election* exhibited at the Royal Academy in 1865. Election was the usual method of entering most children to orphanages in the nineteenth century. Of course hospitals and charities were set up to support foundling children, one of the most famous being the Thomas Coram Hospital, founded in the eighteenth century and supported by many artists, including Hogarth. Still in the Coram Hospital collection are three fascinating pictures by Emma Brownlow, painted between 1858 and 1864. The first and best of them is entitled *The Foundling restored to its Mother* (**70**). The man in the centre is John Brownlow, the artist's father, who came to the hospital as a foundling himself, and eventually rose to the position of Secretary from 1849 to 1872. Emma Brownlow, later Mrs. King, was brought up at the hospital, and became a painter, mainly of domestic genre subjects, her work being exhibited at the Royal Academy from 1852 to 1867. Her pictures of life in the hospital are obviously based on accurate knowledge, which makes them a valuable documentary record. In addition, they are delightful narrative pictures. The emotion is not overstrained, and she doubtless witnessed similar scenes in the hospital herself.

Only illegitimate children under the age of twelve months were admitted during the nineteenth century. The official history of the hospital (by Nichols and Wray, 1935) states that also the petitioner (mother) had to be of good character 'previous to her misfortune', and the father had to have deserted his family. Quite how they ascertained the previous character of the mother is not stated, but each case was considered on its merits,

69

66 (*left*) WILLIAM DANIELS (1813–1880) *Children selling Matches at Night* Private Collection, signed and dated 1851, 18½ × 13½in. (47 × 34·3cm.)

Children of poor families were often sent out to beg or engage in one of the innumerable street trades. The streets of all the major cities swarmed with them. These two are selling matches by the light of a candle, and holding a notice to attract the sympathy of passers-by. It is only partly legible, but one can make out the words 'Benevolent kind . . . take pity . . . God.' Daniels was a Liverpool artist fond of using strong chiaroscuro effects, who must have felt sympathy for destitute children, as he often painted them

67 (*right*) WILLIAM MACDUFF (fl. 1844–1876) *Shaftesbury, or Lost and Found* Mrs. Viva King, signed and dated 1862 18½ × 16in. (47 × 40·6cm.)

Outside the window of Messrs. Graves, the print publishers, two shoeblacks are pointing to a portrait of Lord Shaftesbury (1801–1885) the great reformer and philanthropist who was responsible for the Mines Act of 1842 which stopped the employment of women and children under ten in coal mines, and for many other improvements in the laws relating to child labour. To the left of his portrait is a print of Millais' *Order of Release* and below it one of Faed's *Mitherless Bairn*. The paper on the ground is a notice of a meeting at Exeter Hall of the Ragged School Union, of which Lord Shaftesbury was President for 39 years. He also organized the 'Shoeblack Brigade' a boy's organization which had 306 members, and earned £12,000 in one year; the two boys in the picture are presumably members

68 EMMA BROWNLOW (fl. 1852–1869) *The Christening* Thomas Coram Foundation for Children, signed and dated 1863, 30 × 40in. (76·2 × 101·6cm.)

The children usually arrived on a Saturday, as the mothers were often domestic servants, and they were christened on the Sunday. Here we see the babies being christened in the Hospital Chapel, carried in by older foundling girls. Each baby had to have a sponsor – these are the two gentlemen on the right – and they were given completely new names. With a typical Victorian mixture of charity and severity, the identities of the children were lost to their parents, and a mother could only get in touch with her child by making a formal petition to the Governors. In the background hangs Benjamin West's *Christ presenting a little Child*. The parson is the Rev. J. W. Gleadall, morning preacher at the Hospital

and apparently most of the applicants were domestic servants. Housemaids were usually considered fair game for the young gentlemen of the family in the nineteenth century. Walter, that elusive Victorian Casanova, wrote that his first experience of sex was with a pretty maid employed in his parents' home. Babies were usually handed in at the Foundling Hospital on a Saturday, and they were baptized on the Sunday. The christening service was the subject of the next picture, which is set in the chapel of the hospital (**68**). Every baby was given a new name, its previous identity then being lost as far as the parents were concerned. After the christening, the babies were sent out to wet nurses all over the country, and then returned to the hospital at the age of five. Emma Brownlow's third picture *The Sick Room* (**69**) shows some of the older children being attended to by a

69 EMMA BROWNLOW (fl. 1852–1869) *The Sick Room* Thomas Coram Foundation for Children, signed and
dated 1864, 30 × 40in. (76·2 × 101·6cm.)
This scene shows some of the older foundlings in the sick room, attended by a doctor (Dr. Thomas
Wormald, Surgeon and Governor) and a nurse. By simply recording scenes she probably witnessed herself,
the painter has avoided the over-sentimentality which often mars Victorian paintings of children

doctor and nurse. For those lucky enough to get in, the Foundling Hospital seems to
have been a happy place, and these pictures reflect the humane and enlightened attitude
of the Victorians to the problem of unwanted children.

Dickens lived near the Coram Hospital in Doughty Street, and took a great interest
in it. He rented a pew in the Chapel, and attended services regularly. Foundling children
often figure in his novels, and there are obvious references to the Coram Hospital, about
which he also wrote an article in *Household Words*. In *Little Dorrit* Mrs. Meagles, whose
maid Harriet Beadle had been a foundling called Tattycoram, describes how she visited
the hospital chapel, 'oh dear, dear . . . when I saw all those children ranged tier above
tier, and appealing from the father none of them has ever known on earth, to the great
Father of all of us in Heaven, I thought, does any wretched mother ever come here,
and look among these young faces, wondering which is the poor child she brought into
this forlorn world, never through all its life to know her love, her kiss, her face, her
voice, even name!'

70 EMMA BROWNLOW (fl. 1852–1869) *The Foundling restored to its Mother* Thomas Coram Foundation for Children, signed and dated 1858, 30 × 40in. (76·2 × 101·6cm.)

The scene is set in the Secretary's room of the Foundling Hospital. The man at the desk is John Brownlow, the painter's father. A mother has come to claim her child, and her original receipt lies on the floor, with a box of toys she has brought for her baby. On the wall hangs Hogarth's *March to Finchley*, the portraits of Shakespeare and Ben Jonson, a tapestry of Salome after Guido Reni, a view of the Hospital, and part of *Elijah raising the Son of the Widow of Zarephath* attributed to Lanfranco, all of which are still in the Hospital collection

70A GEORGE ELGAR HICKS (1824–1914) *An Infant Orphan Election at the London Tavern* Private collection
signed and dated 1865, 35½ × 47½in. (90·5 × 120·6cm.)
This fascinating and rare picture records a now forgotten aspect of Victorian charity. Entry to most orphanages was
by election, and here we see sponsors and relatives of the children canvassing for each one, holding up placards with
the name of the child

70B ALFRED RANKLEY (1819–1872) *The Village School* Christopher Wood Gallery, London, signed and dated (with
monogram) 1855, 27½ × 35½in. (69.8 × 90.2cm.)
Victorian pictures of the traditional cottage or 'dame' school give a generally rosy image of rural education. Not all villa
schools can have been so warm and well-furnished as this, but the details of the interior are authentic

9

SCHOOL

'Fortunately in England, at any rate, education produces no effect
whatsoever. If it did, it would prove a serious danger to the upper
classes, and probably lead to acts of violence in Grosvenor
Square.'
Lady Bracknell in *The Importance of Being Earnest*
by Oscar Wilde

Lady Bracknell, like many Victorians of her generation, regarded the spread of general
education with deep distrust. Her dire prophecy about Grosvenor Square, at least, has
since proved all too true. The English in the nineteenth century took an almost philistine
pride in their lack of education, believing that character, moral fibre and energy were
more important than mere book learning. Even Dr. Arnold of Rugby would have agreed:
'What we must look for . . . is first, religious and moral principles; secondly, gentlemanly
conduct; thirdly, intellectual ability.' Tom Brown wanted to be 'A 1 at cricket and football, and all the other games . . . to carry away just as much Latin and Greek as will
take me through Oxford respectably. . . . I want to leave behind me the name of a fellow
who never bullied a little boy, or turned his back on a big one.' It is hardly surprising,
therefore, that the spread of general education was slow. Reform was also hampered
by religious prejudice, as non-conformist and Anglican could not agree over the question
of religious instruction. It was not until the Education Act of 1870, regarded by many
as a gross invasion of personal liberty, that Great Britain was provided with a system
of national schools. Previously schools had either been local grammar schools, private
schools, or those supported by voluntary organizations and charities. Dickens was the
most bitter critic of small private schools, attacking them in the shape of Mr. Squeers
of Dotheboys Hall and Mr. Creakle of Salem House. Although painters often took their
subjects from Dickens, only R. B. Martineau chose the subject of education for his
picture *Kit's first Writing Lesson* (71), an illustration to a scene in *The Old Curiosity Shop*.
Although Kit is a large lad, he is having great difficulty with his letters. He is lucky to
have Little Nell to teach him, as his local schoolteacher might not have been so sympathetic.
The conditions in most schools in poor town areas were appalling. Many children did
not attend them at all, and even those who did were often incapable of reading, writing
or doing arithmetic when they left. Understandably, these schools did not appeal to

71 ROBERT BRAITHWAITE MARTINEAU (1826–1869) *Kit's first Writing Lesson* Tate Gallery, London, 21 × 28in. (53·4 × 71·1cm.)

Although many artists used Dickens' novels for subjects, only Martineau chose an educational subject, Kit receiving a writing lesson from Little Nell, in Chapter 3 of *The Old Curiosity Shop*. '. . . he tucked up his sleeves and squared his elbows and put his face close to the copy-book and squinted horribly at the lines . . . from the first moment of having the pen in his hand, he began to wallow in blots, and to daub himself with ink up to the very roots of his hair.' In the background the clutter of the Old Curiosity Shop is painted with Martineau's usual precision. The picture was his first exhibited work, at the Academy of 1852, where it sold at once to Mr. Mudie of the famous library. Martineau was a pupil of Holman Hunt and he painted this picture in his studio, while Hunt was working on *The Hireling Shepherd*

artists as suitable subjects, but one interesting exception has recently come to light. Entitled *The Ragged School* (72) and painted in 1857, it depicts John Pounds, a crippled Portsmouth schoolmaster, teaching a group of unruly children in his cobbler's shop. Pounds was one of the pioneers of free education in England. Although the picture is not well painted, and the artist, John Barker, is unknown, it gives us a remarkably good idea of what these schools were like.

In the country conditions were usually better, although the standard of education might be equally patchy. The village school, or dame school, with its associations with homely rural life, proved a much more popular subject for painters. A good example out of many is William Bromley's *The Schoolroom* (73), a charming cottage scene. Flora

73 (*right*) WILLIAM BROMLEY (fl. 1835–1888) *The Schoolroom* Photo: Sotheby's, Belgravia, signed and dated 1863, 28 × 36in. (71·1 × 91·4cm.)

A delightful, if somewhat over-benevolent, view of the village, or dame, school, where most country children received their basic training in the three-R's – reading, writing and arithmetic. The details of the cottage interior are also authentic – the valance over the fireplace, Staffordshire china, sampler, birdcage, and geraniums in the window

72 JOHN BARKER *The Ragged School* Photo: Bearne's of Torquay, signed and dated 1857, $27\frac{1}{2} \times 35\frac{1}{4}$in. (69·8 × 89·5cm.)
One of the very few pictures to give us an accurate and unsentimental picture of a ragged school. The teacher is John
Pounds, a crippled Portsmouth cobbler and schoolmaster, who was a pioneer of free education. Lord Shaftesbury, the
philanthropist, was Chairman of the Ragged Schools Union for 39 years (see pl. 67). Although conditions must have
been bad in these schools, they at least provided education for children who would otherwise have received none

74

THOMAS FAED, R.A. (1826–1900) *The School Board in the Cottage* Sir Richard Proby, Bt. signed and dated 1892, 38 × 48½in. (96·5 × 123·2cm.)

Schools established under the Education Act of 1870 were administered by local, elected School Boards, who sent round Inspectors to supervise the schools and set exams for the children. This examiner is obviously not an Inspector, but a labourer testing his own children

75 (*below*) THOMAS WEBSTER, R.A. (1800–1886) *The Boy with many Friends* (detail) Bury Art Gallery, Lancashire, signed and dated (in monogram) TW 1841, 24½ × 35½in. (62·3 × 90·2cm.)

Webster was the inventor of the vogue for subjects dealing in a humorous way with the little dramas and trivial episodes of school life. This was one of his first successes, exhibited at the R.A. in 1841. Almost all the genre painters at some time tried their hand at school subjects. In them we find much good-humoured horseplay and scrapping ('After all, what would life be without fighting . . .?' wrote Tom Hughes) but any references to actual bullying and brutality are discreetly excluded. Before these pictures we reflect that boys will be boys, rather than remember Rugby or Dotheboy's Hall

Thompson in *Lark Rise to Candleford* describes her village school in Oxfordshire in the 1880s: 'even then, to an outsider, it would have appeared a quaint, old-fashioned little gathering; the girls in the ankle-length frocks and long, straight pinafores . . .; the bigger boys in corduroys and hobnailed boots, and the smaller ones in home-made sailor suits, or, until they were six or seven, in petticoats.' An event much dreaded at Flora Thompson's school was the arrival of the School Board Inspector, an official who went round the schools in his district, seeing that they were properly run, and setting exams for the children. Thomas Faed, who made a speciality of homely Scottish cottage scenes, painted one he called *The School Board in the Cottage* (**74**). Here we see not an Inspector, but more likely a farm labourer testing his own children at their lessons, while the mother sits nearby with two younger children. In remote country districts this was the way most children were educated. If there was no school, education was often left to the vicar and his family, or to the charitably-minded daughters of local gentry.

If it was Arnold who 'reconciled the serious classes to the public school' (G. M. Young, *Portrait of an Age*), he also seems to have reconciled the artistic world to the vogue for innumerable pictures of school life. The inventor of the genre was Thomas Webster, who made a comfortable living for over fifty years painting the little dramas of school. One of his first successes was *The Boy with many Friends* exhibited at the Royal Academy in 1841 (**75**). The bully in the centre recalls Flashman, but Webster's pictures never show

76 THOMAS BROOKS (1818–1891) *The Captured Truant* Mrs. S. Williams, signed and dated 1854, 28 × 46in. (71·1 × 116·8cm.)
Typical of hundreds of humorous Victorian pictures of school life

us any actual bullying, tossing in blankets, fagging, fighting or roasting, such as are described in *Tom Brown's Schooldays*. Over most Victorian pictures of schoolchildren hangs an atmosphere of deceptive benevolence. Brutality, if it appears at all, is turned into banality, with the aid of humour. There are no Squeers or Creakles here. The schoolmaster, as in Thomas Brooks' *The Truant* (76), is usually a figure of fun, myopic, shabby, and unable to impose discipline. His pupils are cribbing, whispering, turning the hands of the clock forward, and the truant is slipping a bird's nest to his accomplice behind his back.

In 1856 Webster retired to Cranbrook in Kent, where he gathered round him every summer a group of kindred spirits, all of whom painted children – F. D. Hardy, George Hardy, J. C. Horsley, A. E. Mulready and G. B. O'Neill. Webster was a disciple of Wilkie, and they share a common ancestry in the Flemish genre painters of the seventeenth century, especially Ostade and Teniers. Through Webster and the Cranbrook Colony, the Wilkie tradition of small, old-masterish scenes, usually painted on panel, was carried right through to the end of the century.

10

FOR BETTER, FOR WORSE

'But where is she, the bridal flower,
That must be made a wife ere noon?
She enters, glowing like the moon
Of Eden in its bridal bower.'
Tennyson, *In Memoriam*

The Victorians invented the white wedding as we know it, a romantic blend of religious pomp and secular splendour, although Jane Welsh Carlyle thought it 'something betwixt a religious ceremony and a pantomime.' (*Early Letters*, 1889) Most of the features of English weddings – the church packed with friends and relations, the bride in white dress and veil attended by bridesmaids, the nervous groom waiting with his best man, Mendelssohn's *Wedding March*, choral singing, the wedding breakfast with champagne, toasts and a cake, the presents on display, the honeymoon abroad – were established in the nineteenth century. And the bride in white floating veil is the perfect expression of the Victorian attitude to women. A Victorian husband liked his bride to be pure, innocent, faithful, and above all, ignorant. Tennyson, Ruskin, Coventry Patmore and most of the early Victorian writers put woman on a pedestal – an angel in white robes surrounded by lilies, too good for this world. Most Victorian girls, carefully sheltered from the realities of life, and absolved from the need to work by the abundance of domestic servants, had very little to do but hang around gossiping and embroidering, waiting for a brave knight in shining armour to carry them off to the altar. Most girls accepted their fate with resignation, but there were rebels. Florence Nightingale wrote angrily, 'why have women passion, intellect, moral activity – these three – and a place in society where no one of these can be exercised? . . . Marriage is but a chance, the only chance offered to women to escape and how eagerly it is embraced.'

Getting to the altar was not likely to be a simple matter. Although the Victorians paid lip service to romantic love, in reality most marriages were arranged. In 1854 G. R. Drysdale wrote, 'A great proportion of the marriages we see around us did not take place from love at all, but from some interested motive, such as wealth, social position, or other advantages; and in fact it is rare to see a marriage in which true love has been the predominating feeling on both sides.' The Victorian paterfamilias was a formidable figure, and often found some reason to object to the suitor who applied for his daughter's hand. The familiar picture of the suitor quaking on the study carpet while his future father-in-law asks demanding questions about his prospects was common in life as well as in fiction. The main problem was money; a man was not thought able to marry until he had established himself in a profession, or already had sufficient means to maintain a wife and children. The result was long engagements; usually a year or two, sometimes five or even ten years. Arthur Hughes' famous *Long Engagement* (**78**) has captured with tender pathos the plight of these unfortunate, dutiful children, forbidden by their parents to marry year after year. This poor young curate, whose meagre stipend is obviously quite inadequate, is waiting in hope of promotion to a living with a better salary. In *Lark Rise to Candleford* Flora Thompson describes one such sad pair known as 'Chokey and Bess'. Unable to get married, they walked out together every evening for about ten or twelve years, and did not finally marry until something like fifteen years had passed. As the century went on, the feeling against arranged marriages and protracted engagements grew stronger. Tennyson's poem *Locksley Hall* was an eloquent plea for romantic love:

> 'Cursed be the social wants that sin
>   against the strength of youth!
> Cursed be the social lies that warp us
>   from the living truth!'

Long engagements of course imposed a strain on everyone, and resulted in dispute, bitterness, jilting and breaking-off. John Cordy Jeaffreson, author of *Brides and Bridals* (1870), claimed that 'The Victorian miss enjoys greater liberty than the maiden of former time. She may retract any number of lightly given matrimonial promises; and after promising herself with interchangement of rings and holy close of lips to half-a-dozen suitors, she may become the wife of a seventh admirer, and ask her six jilted lovers to be spectators of her wedding.' This was a man's view, but of course there were men who jilted women too. The Breach of Promise laws acted as an effective deterrent against doing it too blatantly. Flirtation, jealousy and broken promises are the very stuff of Victorian novels, and also staple themes in genre paintings. Best-known is Calderon's classic *Broken Vows* (**79**). No one would want a picture of a jilted man, so of course the victim is a luscious keepsake beauty. Again there is ivy, frequently used to symbolize women in Victorian literature. Trollope in *Barchester Towers* echoes the masculine view of marriage: 'When the ivy has found its tower, when the delicate creeper has found its strong wall, we know how the parasite plants grow and prosper . . .'

Frith has left us two pictures of weddings, the first a royal one, *The Marriage of the Prince of Wales* (**80**). The wedding took place in St George's Chapel, Windsor, and the day declared a national holiday. Bertie wore the uniform of a General, and the Garter Robes. Lord Clarendon, the foreign secretary, thought the Prince 'looked very like a gentleman and more *considerable* than he is wont to do.' Princess Alexandra of Denmark,

77 WILLIAM POWELL FRITH, R.A. (1819–1909) *For Better, For Worse* Forbes Magazine Collection, signed and dated 1881, 60¼ × 49in. (153 × 124·5cm.)

Frith was inspired to paint this picture when he saw 'an almost identical realisation of it in Cleveland Square'. The house has not been identified exactly but the church is based on Christ Church, Lancaster Gate. The couple are leaving for their honeymoon, amid a shower of slippers and rice, heathenish customs which one imagines the puritanical Victorians would have deplored. It was also often the custom to scatter coppers for the boys in the street to scrabble for. The ironical title is perhaps a reflection on Frith's own domestic situation. In addition to his wife and family, he kept a mistress and another family in a house not far away in St. John's Wood

77A SIR SAMUEL LUKE FILDES, R.A. (1829–1907) *The Village Wedding* Manney Collection, USA, signed and dated 1883, 60 × 100in. (152.4 × 254.2cm.)

The most spectacular evocation of a country wedding painted in the Victorian period. After the success of *The Casual Ward*, and other gloomy social realist pictures, Fildes wanted to prove that he could also paint a happy picture. Although he painted it in 1883, Fildes has tried to recapture the spirit of the village as he remembered it in his boyhood. The setting is Aston Tirrold in Oxfordshire, and the models were mostly local people

78 (*left*) ARTHUR HUGHES (1832–1915) *The Long Engagement* Birmingham City Art Gallery, signed and dated 1859, $41\frac{1}{2} \times 21\frac{1}{2}$in. (105·4 × 54·6cm.)

Many dutiful Victorian couples were forced by their parents to undergo long engagements lasting several years. This picture shows a pathetic curate and his pining fiancée, who have been engaged so long that the ivy is climbing over her name 'Amy' carved on the tree. Hughes began the picture in 1853 as a Shakespearean subject, *Orlando in the Forest of Arden*, showing Orlando carving Rosalind's name on a tree. This picture was rejected by the R.A. in 1855. Hughes then painted out Orlando, put in the curate and his fiancée, and changed the name on the tree to Amy. In this form the picture was accepted by the R.A. in 1859. In true Pre-Raphaelite fashion, Hughes painted the landscape in the open and was tormented by heat, rain, and bees, and the difficulty of painting wild roses, the flowers of which close up when the sky is overcast

79 (*right*) PHILIP HERMOGENES CALDERON, R.A. (1833–1898) *Broken Vows* (detail) Tate Gallery, London, signed and dated 1856, $35\frac{1}{2} \times 26\frac{1}{2}$in. (90·2 × 67·4cm.)

The classic Victorian picture of the broken promise, a fate suffered by many young ladies of the period, and by young men too. To heighten the emotional appeal, the jilted girl, hand on throbbing bosom, is a luscious keepsake beauty, with impossibly large eyes and ringlets, rather prettier than what we can see of the girl the other side of the fence. As in *The Long Engagement* there is plenty of ivy, which the Victorians often used as a metaphor when referring to women. Her initials MH are carved on the fence, and on the ground lies a bracelet, doubtless a gift from the faithless lover

80 WILLIAM POWELL FRITH, R.A. (1819–1909) *The Marriage of the Prince of Wales* (detail) Reproduced by gracious permission of Her Majesty the Queen, 86 × 119¾in. (218·4 × 286·4cm.)

The marriage of the Prince of Wales and Princess Alexandra (Alix) of Denmark took place on 10th March, 1863 in St. George's Chapel, the first royal marriage to take place there since that of the Black Prince in 1361. Queen Victoria, like many Victorian mothers, closely supervised the weddings of all her children, and recorded most of them in pictures, and at length in her journal. Frith was commissioned to paint this one for £3,000, as the Queen admired his work, and already owned *Ramsgate Sands*. Nearly all the sitters went to Frith's studio; some portraits were painted from photographs, and the Duchess of Brabant from a description only. The picture was exhibited at the R.A. in 1865, and a rail was needed to protect it from the crowds. It is the best picture of a Victorian royal wedding, and reflects the contemporary taste for elaborate, sumptuous ceremonies, the expense of which must have caused many a Victorian father considerable alarm whose beauty captivated everyone, wore a white satin dress trimmed with orange-blossom and myrtle, and a long veil of Honiton lace. Royal brides in England, unlike other brides, are not allowed to cover their faces. It is curious that so blatant a fertility symbol as orange-blossom should have become *de rigueur* at Victorian weddings. Jeaffreson wrote sternly, 'Custom and romance have raised the chaplet of orange-blossom to un-merited respect. The white of the orange flower is an impure white, and the symbolism of the plant is a reason why some other flower should be adopted by the English bride.' None the less all the brides in the pictures in this chapter are wearing it. Princess Alix entered the chapel to Handel's March from *Joseph*; during the service Beethoven's *Hallelujah Chorus* was played, and *Albert's Chorale*, composed by Prince Albert, who had died only fifteen months earlier. At this point all eyes were on the widowed Queen, watching from her balcony, wearing a black dress and gloves, with the Star and Riband of the Garter. After a luncheon at Windsor Castle, the royal couple left for a brief honeymoon at Osborne. All over the country there were bonfires, banquets and rejoicings. Holman Hunt's picture *London Bridge at Night* records the festivities that took place in London that night.

Frith's other picture, *For Better, For Worse* (77), records an upper-class wedding in London. 'A crowd of another kind', wrote the *Art Journal* in 1881, such as collects in London on the smallest provocation within two minutes, line the path of the happy pair.' The model for the old Jewish man with the beard and top hat was an old-clothes dealer, who drove a hard bargain with Frith for his fee. Ten shillings for three hours was finally agreed, plus some old clothes thrown in for good measure. During the sittings the old Jew made strenuous efforts to persuade Frith to sell him his suit. Also among the crowd are a man with his family begging, a crossing sweeper, a performing monkey, a maid carrying a note and a policeman. The honeymooners are probably leaving for a Continental tour; the less well-off favoured Brighton or the Isle of Wight.

George Elgar Hicks, who had an even more mercenary eye than Frith for a good subject, painted two charming wedding scenes, *Changing Homes* (81) and *The Wedding Breakfast* (82). In the first, the bride is in white with a veil, now thrown back, and the inevitable orange-blossom. The groom is in a dark frock-coat, which had become standard by the mid-century. The room is crowded with little incidents and authentic detail – the bridesmaids in short dresses, shawls, bonnets, and holding baskets of flowers; the bride's mother looking tearful, helped by the other unmarried daughter; the relations shaking hands, the vicar, the old granny. On the right are the presents laid out for in-spection, and a bridesmaid stops a boy from carrying off a vase; in the next room is the elaborate wedding-cake.

The Wedding Breakfast (82) shows us a later stage of the proceedings; the bride and groom in their going-away clothes, in a dining-room where guests are seated, partaking of the so-called wedding-breakfast, or *déjeuner*. The necessity for this meal was the law forbidding marriages in church after midday, extended in 1885 until 3 p.m. So the guests

81 GEORGE ELGAR HICKS (1824–1914) *Changing Homes* Geffrye Museum, London, signed and dated 1862, 36 × 60in. (91·5 × 152·4cm.)
The bride and groom have returned after the ceremony to the drawing room of the bride's parents. The dealer Flatou commissioned this picture for £500

82
GEORGE ELGAR HICKS (1824–1914)
The Wedding Breakfast Photo: M. Bernard Ltd., on panel, 12 × 10in. (30·5 × 25·4cm.)
'After the ceremony, the world repaired to the mansion of Lord Culloden in Belgrave Square, to inspect the presents, and to partake of a dinner called a breakfast.' (Disraeli, *Lothair*.) The scale of the wedding breakfast varied according to the pocket and social standing of the bride's father. It was accompanied by champagne, toasts and speeches, frequently tearful, before the carriage was announced to carry the couple away for the honeymoon. The enigmatic lady in black is obviously a relation of the bride; perhaps she is newly-widowed, in mourning for her own husband, or for her father or mother? Hicks used the same model (Miss Perry) for the bride as in *Changing Homes*

83

JAMES CHARLES (1851–1906) *Signing the Register* Bradford City Art Gallery, signed, $93\frac{5}{8} \times 70\frac{1}{2}$in. (232·8 × 179·1cm.)
A humbler wedding, in contrast to the middle-class pretensions of Frith and Hicks. The old father and mother look on as their daughter signs the register. The father wears a traditional smock with a white favour, but does not seem to realize that both his stick and his boot are on the hem of the wedding dress. The bride wears a long veil and chaplet of orange-blossom; the bridesmaids are simply dressed in coloured dresses, reflecting not only economy, but a change of fashion

found themselves drinking champagne and large quantities of cold food in the morning and then having to wait until the evening, if there was a ball, when they would again have to consume a large meal. Many found this custom irksome. 'The man must combine the distinguishing characteristics of an alderman and a boa-constrictor, who can dine happily after the violent delights and cloying pleasures of a wedding-lunch,' wrote Jeaffreson. The nasty gap between breakfast and dinner was filled by walks in the shrubbery, afternoon naps, or if it was wet, the billiard-room.

The wedding scene continued to attract later painters who were more interested in painterly ideas than in narrative. James Charles chose the moment of the signing of the register for his picture (83) of a humble country wedding. John H. F. Bacon and Stanhope Forbes also preferred the simplicity and sincerity of country weddings for their pictures, *A Wedding Morning* (84) and *The Health of the Bride* (85). They both capture perfectly the excitement of the preparation before the wedding, and the quiet solemnity of the toast to the health of the bride. Although the Marriage Act of 1836, as well as legalizing Catholic and Dissenting marriages, set up the machinery for civil marriages, with registrars' offices, most brides ever since, whether believers or not, have preferred 'to think that marriage should be beautiful and hallowed with religious observances,' as Jeaffreson wrote in 1870.

84

JOHN H. F. BACON, A.R.A. (1868–1914)
A Wedding Morning Lady Lever Art Gallery,
Port Sunlight, signed and dated 1892,
46 × 64in. (116·8 × 162·5cm.)
It is the morning of the wedding, in a country
cottage, and the bride is putting the finishing
touches to her wedding dress. Like the bride in
Charles's picture, the white dress is very simple,
and she wears a long veil and orange-blossom.
Grandmother is helping her, and also another
girl at the table, perhaps the chief bridesmaid.
The other bridesmaids are arriving with flowers,
and their expressions of delight are unaffected
and natural; it is reminiscent of the wedding
scene in Thomas Hardy's *Under the Greenwood
Tree*

85 STANHOPE ALEXANDER FORBES, R.A. (1857–1947) *The Health of the Bride* (detail) Tate Gallery, London, signed
and dated 1889, 60 × 78¾in. (152·4 × 200·5cm.)
A magnificent picture, one of the outstanding realist paintings of the 19th century, and comparable with Courbet. The
scene was painted in the village inn at Newlyn, Cornwall, and the models were all local characters. Shortly after
completing the picture, Forbes himself married the painter Elizabeth Armstrong, to whom he had been engaged for
several years

THE SEVENTH DAY

'Remember the sabbath day, to keep it holy. Six days shalt thou labour, and do all thy work: but the seventh day is the sabbath of the Lord thy God.'

Exodus, chapter 20

To understand the Victorians it is essential to realise the extent to which religion dominated their lives. Although the Evangelical movement had its beginnings in the late eighteenth century, it gave Victorian England 'a creed which was at once the basis of its morality and the justification of its wealth and power, and, with that creed, a sense of being an Elect People. . . .' (G. M. Young, *Portrait of an Age*). The spirit of the age was the spirit of the middle classes, puritanical, earnest, sober, hard-working, who found in non-conformism, the gospel of work, the perfect way to combine piety with profits. Never since the seventeenth century had English people been so preoccupied with religious doctrine and church order. Religious debate was intense, and controversies like the Hampden case could convulse the nation, and even threaten a Government. Only the Victorian age could have produced a politician like Gladstone, who even treated foreign policy as a branch of religious affairs.

It was also an age of doubt. The evolutionary theories of Darwin, Huxley's natural laws, and Sedgwick's geological researches had put a time bomb under the very foundations of Victorian belief. Intellectuals like Ruskin, Tennyson and Clough were constantly tormented by the fear that their religion would not stand up to rational examination. Many followed the example of Charles Kingsley, and found relief from doubt in 'muscular' Christianity, with plenty of noisy observance, exercise, and good works, that left no time for thinking. But even agnostics like George Eliot, if she could not believe in God, none the less believed in the 'peremptory and absolute' call of Duty, substituting a personal code of conduct for religious belief.

Most middle-class families had family prayers (86) and by the mid-century most upper-class families had succumbed to respectability and adopted the habit. 'This evening at nine,' wrote Arthur Joseph Munby in his diary for Sunday, 9th October, 1864, 'we had prayers in the library as usual; my father sitting at the centre table and reading for the twentieth time one of those good, sincere old sermons, full of the simple Calvanistic

86 SAMUEL BUTLER (1836–1902) *Family Prayers* (detail) The Master and Fellows of St. John's College, Cambridge, 19½ × 15in. (40.5 × 38cm.)
Samuel Butler, author of *The Way of all Flesh*, was a bitter critic of the hypocrisy and repression of Victorian family life. Although he was not a professional painter, this picture, with the doll-like figures of the family and maids sitting primly upright, and the bare interior, admirably conveys the atmosphere of starched and stuffy morality which Butler so disliked. The scene is the drawing room at Langar, Butler's birthplace

87 THOMAS WEBSTER, R.A. (1800–1886) *Sunday Evening* Sir Richard Proby, Bt. signed and dated 1858, 23 × 36in. (58.4 × 91.5cm.)
The Victorians cherished the ideal of rustic innocence and piety, but this might be a not too fanciful picture of what cottage life might be like on a Sunday evening. Except for lawless groups such as navvies, most country people went to church or chapel, and read the Bible sometime later in the day. The Family Bible was a treasured possession, hand down from generation to generation, and often inscribed with the names and birthdates of all the family

Protestantism of thirty years ago.' Survivors of the easy-going days of the Regency found themselves out of place in a new, earnest, serious world. 'Nobody is gay now,' complained Lord Melbourne, 'they are so religious.' In every cottage in the kingdom, the family Bible was a treasured possession. In the evenings the head of the family would read to his children (87). Especially religious parents would often subject their children to too much religion at too young an age. J. A. Symonds, a child of religious parents, remembered having nightmares about the devil; so did Alton Locke, hero of Kingsley's novel of that name – 'I used to have accesses of terror, and fancy that I should surely wake next morning in everlasting flames.'

People of all classes, except the very poorest, went to church on Sunday, out of a sense of religious and social duty. Many went to both Morning and Evening service. During the rest of the day practically no activity of any kind was allowed except eating, walking, and reading the Bible, or some approved literature such as the *Sunday Book*. For children it was a day of paralyzing boredom. In *Lark Rise to Candleford* Flora Thompson recalled the tedium of afternoon service: 'the school-children, under the stern eye of the manor-house, dared not so much as wriggle; they sat in their stiff, stuffy, best clothes, their stomachs lined with heavy Sunday dinner, in a kind of waking doze, through which Tom's Amens rang like a bell, and the Rector's voice buzzed beelike.' Millais, and many other painters, turned children in church into sentimental pictures like *Her First Sermon* and *Her Second Sermon*. But there are other, more realistic pictures of Victorian congregations, two of the best being Walter Tyndale's *The Sermon* of 1888 (88) and James Lobley's *The Free Seat* (89). Sermons were an important part of any Victorian service.

88 WALTER TYNDALE (1855–1943) *The Sermon* (detail) Timothy Daniell, Esq., signed and dated '88, 17½ × 39½in. (44·5 × 100·4cm.)
A Victorian middle-class congregation, painted in St. Alphege's, Greenwich, the Hawksmoor church. The pews are numbered, as it was customary to rent your own place or family pew in the 19th century. The sermon was the most important feature of the service, and a church would always be packed for a well-known preacher

89 JAMES LOBLEY (1829–1888) *The Free Seat* Birmingham City Art Gallery, signed and dated 1869 on panel, 21¾ × 37in. (57·8 × 94cm.)

As most of the pews in churches were reserved by subscription for the use of individuals or families, it was customary to have a free seat for the poor at the back of the church. The artist has tried to enliven the scene by making the young man steal a look over his prayer-book at the pretty girl next to him. We are also reminded to 'Remember the Poor' by the notice above the Poor Box on the right. Lobley was a little-known artist, most of whose pictures are church interiors, painted in meticulous Pre-Raphaelite detail

90 THOMAS WEBSTER, R.A. (1800–1886) *A Village Choir* Victoria and Albert Museum, on panel, 24 × 36in. (61 × 91·4cm.)

Webster painted this in 1847, intending it to illustrate an earlier period, but it could well illustrate the easy-going eccentricity that survived in rural parishes, where the parson was a 'country gentleman in orders, who rode to hounds, and shot and danced and farmed, and often did worse things'. (Dean Church *Life and Letters* 1894). Orchestras continued to be used in many churches before organs were installed. Webster painted from experience, as he had been a Chapel Royal choir-boy in his youth

91 JAMES CHARLES (1851–1906) *Christening Sunday* Manchester City Art Gallery, signed and dated 1887, 62½ × 49½in. (158·1 × 125·7cm.)

A smart country congregation leaving church after a christening. The coachman on the right is perhaps waiting for the lady in the striped dress and veil. Sunday is still a traditional day for christenings, and as the woman in the veil on the left is also carrying a baby, there may have been more than one christening taking place. James Charles also painted a wedding scene, *Signing the Register* (see pl. 83)

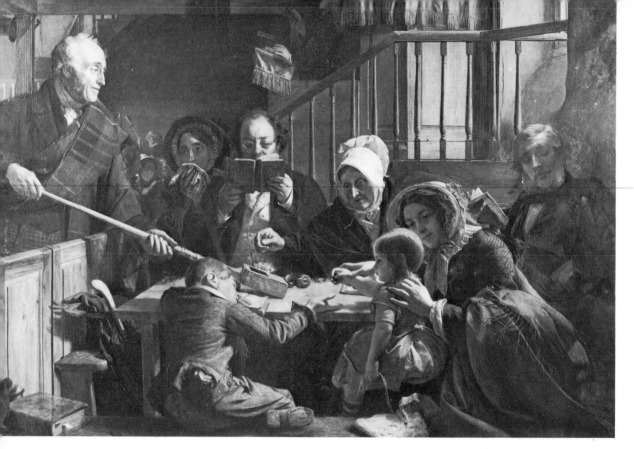

The most famous preachers were well-known throughout the country, and their sermons published and discussed with lively interest.

The bewildering number of denominations catered in the main for different social groups. The aristocracy and gentry remained solidly Church of England, or Roman Catholic, and the high Anglicans catered for those with ritualistic tastes; the middle classes were mainly Congregationalists, Unitarian or Methodist; and the lower classes Baptist or Primitive Methodist (Prim Ranters). In the country the lazy old ways of the eighteenth century lingered on much longer, under the paternal eye of the local squire and village parson. Most county families had their own pews, and these often had high enough partitions to enable the occupants to doze off. Arthur J. Ashton in *As I went on my Way* (1924) recalled a country squire who had his own fire in his family pew, and just before the sermon 'poked the fire, opened a cupboard, took out a glass, and then a bottle of golden wine, poured out a glassful of the elixir, drank it, sat down again and went to sleep.' Thomas Webster's *The Village Choir* of 1847 (**90**), although set in an earlier period, still records the atmosphere that must have existed in many village churches well into the nineteenth century. James Charles' *Christening Sunday* (**91**) shows how much more orderly and better turned-out a country congregation looked by 1887.

The Scottish Church seems to have inspired more pictures than the English, perhaps because of its strong nationalist tradition. John Phillip's *Collecting the Offertory in a Scottish Kirk* (**92**) depicts a quite cheerful side of the Presbyterian religion, whereas H. J. Dobson's *A Scottish Sacrament* (**93**) is redolent of the narrow, gloomy piety of 'the kirk'. John Phillip, who was fond of Scottish subjects before he discovered Spain, also painted *Presbyterian Catechising* (**94**), an interesting Wilkie-like picture of a minister listening to children reciting the Catechism in a cottage. Another aspect of the minister's work is shown in William Crosby's *The Pastor's Visit* (**95**) in which the figures and the cottage interior are painted with unusual fidelity.

A typical product of the age was the Temperance Movement, whose fanatical and noisy campaign for total abstinence attracted an enormous following, particularly in

93 HENRY JOHN DOBSON (fl. 1881–1900) *A Scottish Sacrament* (detail) Bradford City Art Gallery, signed, 33⅝ × 50¼in. (85·4 × 127·6cm.)
The cold greys and blacks of Dobson's picture and the bleakness of the interior convey something of the intense, funereal atmosphere of the Scottish church

94

JOHN PHILLIP, R.A. (1817–1867) *Presbyterian Catechising* (detail) National Gallery of Scotland, signed and dated 1847, $39\frac{5}{8} \times 61\frac{1}{4}$in. ($100\cdot6 \times 155\cdot5$cm.)
An earlier work by Phillip, much closer in style and subject to the village scenes of Sir David Wilkie. The minister is hearing a young girl recite her catechism, while her family and others look on

96 JOSEPH PATRICK HAVERTY (1794–1864) *Father Mathew receiving a repentant Pledge-Breaker* National Gallery of Ireland, 42⅛ × 54in. (107 × 137cm.)
Father Theobald Mathew (1790–1856), an Irish Franciscan, was one of the most celebrated Temperance preachers of the 19th century. His success in Ireland was prodigious; he addressed huge crowds, and was thought to have converted nearly half the adult population to total abstinence. His method was the familiar evangelical one of making a rousing speech, and then inviting converts to come forward and take the pledge. Here he is shown forgiving a repentant pledge-breaker, brought by his mother and son. Children were often made to take the pledge at a young age; the serious expression of the young boy indicates that he must have been an early convert

non-conformist areas such as the north, East Anglia, Wales and Cornwall. Temperance outings were also the foundation of the career of Thomas Cook, the first travel agent. But it is to the Temperance Movement in Ireland, of all places, that we owe the only picture of the subject – J. P. Haverty's *Father Mathew receiving a repentant Pledge-Breaker* (**96**). Father Theobald Mathew (1790–1856) was an Irish Franciscan who was persuaded to take the pledge in Cork in 1838, which he did with the words, 'Here goes – in the name of the Lord.' He rapidly became a celebrated speaker all over Ireland, and so many people took the pledge that duties on Irish spirits fell from about £1½ million in 1839 to £852,418 in 1844. In 1843 he came to London and Jane Welsh Carlyle attended one of his meetings. She was impressed by the orderliness and quiet of the crowd, and when one or two hundred came forward to take the pledge, she thought 'all the tragedies I have ever seen, melted into one, could not have given me such emotion as that scene did.'

95 (*left*) WILLIAM CROSBY (fl. 1859–1873) *The Pastor's Visit* (detail) Photo: Ian MacNicol Ltd., signed and dated 1863, 40 × 60in. (101·6 × 152·4cm.)
A Scottish family have been listening to 'the Word', the old man with the aid of an ear trumpet, and now the pastor is kneeling to say a blessing. Both the figures and the cottage interior are painted with unusual fidelity. The bottle of medicine on the left may indicate that one of the children is unwell – perhaps the reason for the pastor's visit. Crosby was a minor genre painter who lived in Sunderland, Co. Durham

97 JOHN THOMAS PEEL (1822–1897) *A Prayer for Health* (detail) Photo: Parke-Bernet, Ltd., New York City, signed, 31 × 43in. (78·7 × 109·2cm.)

Paintings dealing with the theme of sickness and ill-health, especially to do with children, had a strong emotive appeal for the Victorians. Sickness was dreaded by rich and poor alike, especially in the overcrowded, insanitary cities. This poor girl is in a cottage in the country, where the expectation of life was better, but medical treatment was likely to be rudimentary and painful. She trusts in God to restore her to health, rather than in the power of medicine

12

A PRAYER FOR HEALTH

'The annual loss of life from filth and bad ventilation are greater
than the loss from death or wounds in any wars in which the
country has been engaged in modern times.'

Edwin Chadwick, 1842

Sickness was a constant and very real threat in the nineteenth century. Sick pay did
not exist, and for a working man to fall ill could mean destitution for himself and his
family. Very few employers paid compensation for accidents either, and an injured man
would be largely dependent on the charity of his employer or his fellow-workers. Medicine
made enormous progress, but treatment could still be rudimentary and painful. Rich
and poor alike dreaded illness, and could succumb to diseases which modern medicine
has rendered harmless. The slums of the new cities, breeding-grounds for disease, were
frequently ravaged by cholera – an outbreak in 1848–9 killed 130,000 people in the
whole country. The smell of the Thames was so bad at that time that M.P.s were forced
to keep the windows of the Houses of Parliament shut. Of course, much was done to
improve the sanitation of the towns. Chadwick's famous *Report on the Sanitary Condition
of the Labouring Population* of 1842 was followed by the first of several Public Health
Acts in 1866, giving local councils compulsory powers. But in 1837 the expectation of
life in Manchester was only seventeen years for a working man, twenty years for tradesmen, and thirty-eight for professional people and gentry.

Sickness features in paintings in various ways. J. T. Peele turns it into an excuse for a
painting of a charmingly pretty girl praying to be returned to health, as she lies on her
cottage bed (**97**). W. L. Windus, a Liverpool follower of the Pre-Raphaelites, made
consumption the subject of his strange picture *Too Late* (**98**), an illustration to Tennyson's
lines from *English Idylls and other Poems* of 1842:

> 'If it were thine error or thy crime
> I care no longer, being all unblest;
> Wed whom thou wilt; but I am sick of time,
> And I desire to rest.'

A lover has returned to find that the girl he hoped to marry is dying of consumption –

98 WILLIAM LINDSAY WINDUS (1822–1907) *Too Late* Tate Gallery, London, signed and dated 1858, 37½ × 30in. (95·2 × 76·2cm.)
A lover has returned to find that the girl he hoped to marry is dying of consumption. She stands, pale and white, supporting herself with a stick, and the young man covers his face in despair. Both the *Art Journal* and Ruskin attacked this picture so vigorously that the artist virtually gave up painting, which was a pity, as he was one of the most interesting Liverpool followers of the Pre-Raphaelites

this is the story, which unfortunately the *Art Journal* critic attacked as 'the extremity of the "Pre-Raphaelite" manner' and 'hopelessly obscure'. Ruskin in his *Academy Notes* also gave the artist a severe lecture, warning him not to read too many 'melancholy ballads'. Windus, who was of a nervous temperament, was so shattered by these criticisms, and by the death of his own wife in 1862, that he gave up painting. Alfred Rankley, normally a painter of historical genre, turned sickness into a sermon on friendship in *Old Schoolfellows* (**99**), exhibited at the Royal Academy in 1854. The rich young man proffers the inevitable five pound note to his ailing schoolfellow, and on the floor, appropriately, lies a copy of Cicero's *De Amicitia*.

Inevitably, the sickness of children was the most consistently popular subject. Child mortality reached such horrific proportions, especially in the cities, that Disraeli was able to claim sarcastically in his novel *Sybil*, 'Infanticide is practised as extensively and as legally in England as it is on the banks of the Ganges.' The theme of the sick child recurs

99 ALFRED RANKLEY (1819–1872) *Old Schoolfellows* Sir David Scott, signed and dated 1854, 36¾ × 28in. (93·3 × 71cm.)
A young man, sick in a garret, tended by his wife (or sister?), is visited by an old schoolfellow. The picture was
exhibited at the R.A. in 1854, with a subtitle from *Proverbs*: 'A friend loveth at all times, and a brother is born for
adversity.'

100 THOMAS WEBSTER, R.A. (1800–1886) *Sickness and Health* (detail) Victoria and Albert Museum, signed and dated 1843 on panel, 20 × 32in. (50·8 × 81·3cm)
The sick child was the most consistently popular subject. Webster's treatment of it is typical of the 1840s' genre picture – sentimental rather than serious, contrasting the sick girl with her healthy sisters dancing to the barrel-organ. The girl on her pillow does not look very ill, anyway, and will doubtless soon recover

constantly in Victorian painting. In 1843 Webster exploited it in a typically early-Victorian sugar-sweet manner in *Sickness and Health* (**100**), contrasting the sick girl on her pillow with her healthy sisters dancing to the barrel-organ. Mrs. Farmer's picture of 1865, *An Anxious Hour* (**101**), strikes a much more serious note. The scene is simply and realistically handled, in a way typical of the more honest approach to modern-life subjects that developed in the 1850s and 1860s. The result is an effective and moving picture.

In 1891 Luke Fildes took up the theme, and created one of the most popular pictures of the century, *The Doctor* (**102**). The idea for the subject had been in his mind ever since the death of his own first child on Christmas Day, 1877, watched over by the family's doctor, Dr. Murray. Fildes' elaborate preparations for the picture are typical of the Victorian artist's search for authenticity. First he and his brother-in-law Henry Woods spent a week at Hope Cove in Devon sketching fishermen's cottages. Then a full-size replica of a cottage interior was built in Fildes' studio in Melbury Road, complete with rafters, walls, and the window on the right through which the dawn light was

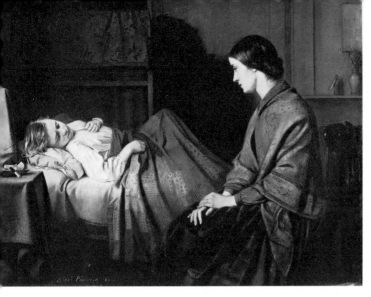

101
MRS ALEXANDER FARMER (fl. 1855–1882)
An Anxious Hour Victoria and Albert Museum,
signed and dated 1865 on panel, 12 × 16in.
(30·5 × 40·6cm.)
A simple but moving picture of an anxious
mother watching over her sick child, typical
of the more honest approach to modern-life
subjects of the 1850s and 1860s. The sickness,
and death, of children was one of the most
poignant themes in literature – those of Paul
Dombey, and Little Nell, for example, in the
works of Dickens

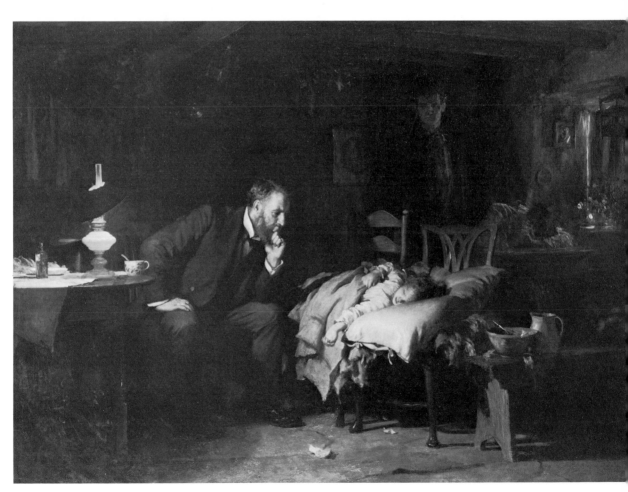

102 SIR LUKE FILDES, R.A. (1843–1927) *The Doctor* (detail) Tate Gallery, London, 64¾ × 96 in. (164·5 × 238·8cm.)
One of the most popular of all Victorian paintings. Over a million engravings of it were sold, and for years it was
one of the best-loved pictures in the Tate Gallery. In his search for authenticity, Fildes had a complete replica
of the interior of a fisherman's cottage built in his studio

to glimmer. When rumours reached the medical profession of Fildes' subject, he was inundated with requests from doctors to be allowed to sit for the principal figure. Fildes refused them all, and stuck to professional models. The picture was an instantaneous success at the Academy of 1891; engravings of it were sold in huge numbers, over a million in the United States alone, so it was thought. Sir Henry Tate, who had commissioned the picture for £3,000 in 1890, presented it to the nation, and for years it was one of the most popular pictures in the Tate Gallery. During the 1930s, however, it was the subject of bitter attacks from Roger Fry and other anti-Victorian critics, and was relegated to the basement. Since the war it has re-emerged, and now hangs once again in a prominent position.

13

THE CULT OF DEATH

'"For death is king of life", I cried;
"Beauty is but his pomp and state;"'
Ellice Hopkins, *Life in Death*

The Victorian cult of death is quite unique in English history. Never before or since have the English been so obsessed with the rites and rituals of death, funerals and mourning. A whole language of dress, objects and social formalities grew up around it, which will doubtless fascinate future generations of anthropologists. The most obvious manifestation of the death-cult was the desire for a good funeral. From highest to lowest, everyone wanted a decent send-off. 1852 was a good year for funerals – the Duke of Wellington's was the greatest funeral spectacular England has ever seen; the sixteenth Earl of Shrewsbury's funeral at Alton Towers was a High Catholic pageant, with a procession over a mile long. At the other end of the social scale, even the very poor contributed to Burial Clubs to ensure a respectable departure, and avoid the ultimate dread, a pauper's grave. A report of 1843 estimated that £4 or £5 million was 'annually thrown into the grave'. It was not long before the churchyards began to overflow. St. Martin's-in-the-Fields had a burial ground about 200 feet square, estimated to contain between 60,000 and 70,000 bodies. Cemeteries, and later cremation, provided the answer. The Victorians left their mark on the cemeteries of England, instantly recognizable by their pompous entrance gates in Egyptian, Classical or Gothic style.

The Victorians both thought and talked about death a great deal. It was quite *comme-il-faut* to discuss death or a funeral on social occasions. The twentieth century has brought a curious reversal of social habits – now death is taboo, but everyone talks about sex, whereas with the Victorians it was the other way round. Sex is the cliché of the twentieth-century novel; in the nineteenth century it was the deathbed scene. Only a Victorian painter would think of painting *For the Last Time* (**103**), and only a Victorian audience would have failed to find it morbid. The picture was well received at the Royal Academy in 1864, and mentioned in the *Illustrated London News*.

Neither were the Victorians squeamish about pictures of churchyards. A pretty girl in a graveyard was a favourite subject, of which Henry Bowler's *The Doubt* (**104**) is now the best known. The picture is memorable for two reasons; firstly, it is painted in beautiful

103 EMILY MARY OSBORN (fl. 1851–1893) *For the Last Time* R. K. F. Brindley, Esq., signed with monogram, 36×28in. (91·4×71·1cm.)

Two sisters, in full regalia of deepest mourning – black dresses, crape, jet jewellery – are going to look at the body of their dead father, or mother, for the last time. The blinds are drawn on the gothic windows, adding to the gloom. 'We often marvel', wrote the *Art Journal*, '. . . why artists choose the sad instead of the cheerful? But a wholesome lesson may be learned from such subjects.'

Pre-Raphaelite detail; secondly, by choosing to illustrate Tennyson's *In Memoriam*, the painter has tried to realize on canvas the religious doubts that lurked beneath the surface of mid-Victorian complacency. Science had brought the Victorians face-to-face with atheism; the possibility that there might be no God, no future life, no system, no truth. Tennyson's poem echoed the mood of the age:

> 'I falter where I firmly trod,
>   And falling with my weight of cares
>   Upon the world's great altar-stairs
> That slope thro' darkness up to God,
>
> I stretch lame hands of faith, and grope,
>   And gather dust and chaff, and call
>   to what I feel is Lord of all,
> And faintly trust the larger hope.'

Bowler's answer was the same, with '*Resurgam*' on the grave-slab, and a germinating chestnut. He too trusts in the larger hope, relying on faith rather than knowledge to overcome doubt. A churchyard picture of a more conventional type is Mann's *The*

Child's Grave (**105**). Although one or two of the children are a little tearful, in general they seem to be quite happy romping among the tombstones. Death has become a matter for sentimental reverie, not real emotion.

By contrast, Holl's *Firstborn* (**106**) is a genuine and moving cry of anguish. Many Victorians were struck by the difference between the elaborate funerals of the rich, which were so formal as to leave no room for genuine sorrow, and the simple but moving burials of the poor. 'Few pageants can be more stately and frigid than an English funeral in town,' wrote Washington Irving. Flora Thompson noticed the difference even as a child: 'Against the earth's spring loveliness the heavy black procession looked dream-like, like a great black shadow. . . . And, in spite of the lavish display of mourning, it did not touch her as the country funerals did with their farm-waggon hearse and few poor, walking mourners crying into their handkerchiefs.' William Morris deliberately rejected the hypocrisy of the age when he chose in 1896 a simple country burial at Kelmscott in Oxfordshire. His plain coffin, covered with flowers, was drawn to the churchyard by a farm horse and cart, and W. R. Lethaby wrote afterwards that 'it was the only funeral I have ever seen that did not make me ashamed to have to be buried.'

The death of children was a particularly emotional theme, as it was an experience suffered by almost every Victorian family. Infant mortality was high, and in the cities horrifying. In Manchester in 1840, 57 children out of every 100 died before the age of five. The empty cradle and the child's grave were a reality, not just a painter's fancy. La Thangue handled the theme with restrained pathos in *The Man with the Scythe* (**107**).

106 FRANK HOLL, A.R.A. (1845–1888) *Her Firstborn* (detail) Dundee Art Gallery, signed and dated 1876, 43 × 61¼in. (109·2 × 155·5cm.)
Much more genuine is Holl's moving picture of a simple country funeral. The background was painted in the churchyard at Shere, Surrey. At the R.A. of 1876 the picture was highly praised. 'Mr. Holl, we are sure, never painted better, or made the onlooker sadder.' (*Art Journal*)

107
HENRY HERBERT LA THANGUE, R.A. (1859–1929) *The Man with the Scythe* Tate Gallery, London, signed, 66 × 65½in. (167·6 × 166·4cm.)
A mother has come out of her cottage to find that her sick daughter has just passed away, propped up on a pillow in a chair; at the gate stands the symbolic figure of death, an old peasant carrying a scythe.

105 (*left*) JOSHUA HARGRAVE SAMS MANN (fl. 1849–1884) *The Child's Grave* Photo: Christie's, signed with initials, 39 × 49½in. (99 × 125·7cm.)
Whose child has died, and why the mother with a baby, the old widow, and all these children are in the churchyard is not at all clear, but the children seem quite at ease among the tombstones. A trip to the churchyard with the whole family was a regular feature of Victorian life, especially on anniversaries. Consequently they did not feel at all squeamish about pictures of churchyards, of which this is a typical sentimental example

108
GEORGE ELGAR HICKS (1824–1914)
The Death of a Child Photo; Christie's, signed
and dated 1890, 50 × 40in. (127 × 101·6cm.)
The cult of death had a romantic side – as this
father and mother crouch over the body of their
child, an angel in white is carrying its soul up to
heaven

The simple setting, outside a country cottage with a row of cabbages by the path, makes the symbolism of the forbidding figure at the gate doubly powerful. Parents were at least comforted by the thought that the souls of their little ones would go straight to heaven, carried by an angel (**108**). For all their materialism and belief in progress, the Victorians still believed in fairies and angels, and in communicating with the dead. Between 1850 and 1870 the vogue for fairy paintings was at its height. Spiritualism was rampant and took many forms – table-turning, séances, hypnotism, spirit photography, automatic drawing. In 1872 an enterprising manufacturer patented a party game called 'Gambols with the Ghosts'. In life, and in art, the Victorians had to find release from the sometimes intolerable pressures of organized religion, materialism, and a repressive social code.

14

THE WIDOW

'I had a home once – I had once a husband –
I am a widow, poor and broken-hearted!'
Robert Southey, *The Widow*

Another manifestation of the death-cult was the cult of widowhood. The burden of mourning fell mainly on women, and so the widow became a walking symbol of sorrow and bereavement. Custom demanded that she wear crape for at least a year after her husband's death. She then had to go into half-mourning, which meant dresses of grey or black only, for another six months. Trollope described the costume of a rich widow, Mrs. Greenow, in *Can you forgive her?*. 'The widow was almost gorgeous in her weeds. . . . The materials were those which are devoted to the deepest conjugal grief. As regarded every item of the written law her suttee worship was carried out to the letter. There was the widow's cap, generally so hideous. . . . There was the dress of deep, clinging, melancholy, crape. . . . There were the trailing weepers, and the widow's kerchief pinned close round her neck . . .' Different scales of mourning were laid down for children, parents, uncles, cousins, and even for relations by marriage. Servants had to go into mourning, too, if a member of the family died. In a large family the chances were that a woman might have to be almost continuously in some kind of mourning. It became an industry. Courtaulds founded their fortunes selling crape; Peter Robinson specialized in mourning clothes; there were other stores especially devoted to the sale of jet jewellery, black-edged letters, envelopes and visiting cards, black sealing-wax, and all the other paraphernalia.

Queen Victoria herself set an example of irreproachable widowhood for her subjects to follow. After Albert's death in 1861, she remained in mourning for over ten years, as we have seen, and to the end of her life she preferred to wear black. Her devotion to the memory of Albert was almost Egyptian in its intensity – she preserved his rooms intact at Osborne exactly as he had left them (rumour has it that hot water and towels were put out for him too); she built Albert Memorials wherever she could; she had herself photographed with her children around a marble bust of Albert; she was painted by Albert Graefle (**109**) in a similar pose. She made widowhood a way of life – she bought Frank Holl's pictures because their gloomy themes appealed to her; she enjoyed talking

109
ALBERT GRAEFLE (1807–1889) *Queen Victoria
as a Widow, 1864* Reproduced by gracious
permission of Her Majesty The Queen,
$52\frac{1}{2} \times 36\frac{1}{8}$in. (113·4 × 91·7cm.)
The widowed Queen sits beside 'the dear, dear
protecting head' of beloved Albert. She was also
photographed with her children round the same
bust. Victoria's obsession with widowhood went
far beyond the prescribed limits. She even set up
a stone to mark the spot where Albert shot his
last stag at Balmoral. Her ladies-in-waiting were
mostly also widows, and the court became 'a
sacred College of Vestal Widows . . . tending
the flame of their sorrow forever.' (Elisabeth
Longford, *Victoria R.I.*)

to other widows, of whatever class, and commiserating together. Many people thought
Victoria carried things too far; they never thought that much of Albert anyway. It was
only with difficulty that the Queen was persuaded to re-enter public life in the 1870s.
No country can remain loyal to a Queen in crape whom it never sees.

Such a powerful emotional symbol as the widow was not to be ignored by the painters.
One of Millais' models, a Miss Silver, who had sat for him for *The Gambler's Wife* in
1868, later came to him dressed in widow's weeds, pleading poverty, to enquire if he
could use her again. Millais asked her to return the next day, dressed as she was, and
the result was *The Widow's Mite* (110). In Victorian pictures, widows are nearly always
pretty (Leighton thought Millais' picture the best female head he ever painted). This
enabled the spectator to admire their beauty, and also to sympathize with their situation.
C. E. Perugini bravely painted an old widowed lady in *Faithful* (111). Although he was
not as stylish a painter as Millais, the result is a more honest and moving picture. Emily
Mary Osborn, who had a penchant for the heart-rending, gave the widow theme an
ingenious twist in *Nameless and Friendless* (112). The forlorn widow is trying to make
a living selling her pictures. From the poster the two gentlemen on the left are holding,
we learn that she was formerly a ballerina.

112 (*right*) EMILY MARY OSBORN (fl. 1851–1893) *Nameless and Friendless* Sir David Scott, 34 × 44in.
(86·4 × 111·7cm.)
This forlorn widow is trying to support herself and her son by selling her own pictures. The dealer is
scrutinizing it doubtfully, and does not seem keen to buy. On the left two gentlemen are holding a poster,
and looking at the widow as if they recognize her. Can she be the same lady as the ballerina on the poster?
There is a further subtlety in the fact that the widow is not wearing a wedding-ring, and is therefore in
mourning for her lover rather than her husband, which would explain why she is both 'Nameless and
Friendless'

110 (*left*) SIR JOHN EVERETT MILLAIS, Bt, P.R.A. (1829–1896) *The Widow's Mite* Birmingham City Art Gallery, signed with monogram and dated 1870, 46 × 30½in. (106·8 × 77·5cm.)
The widow was a symbol of helpless, suffering womanhood, and her appearance in paintings is therefore frequent. This widow, who is in full mourning dress, is making a contribution to the Hospital for Consumption, which was near Millais' house in Cromwell Place South

111 (*right*) CHARLES EDWARD PERUGINI (1839–1918) *Faithful* Walker Art Gallery, Liverpool, signed, 48 × 38in. (121·9 × 96·5cm.)
An old widow is laying flowers on her husband's grave. Many widows, like Queen Victoria, continued to wear black for the rest of their lives. Those of us who remember Victorian ladies living on into this century are mostly left with a memory of rustling black satin and bombazeen

A Victorian in possession of a comfortable income could imagine nothing more terrible than a visit to the pawnbroker. To have to pawn one's belongings meant that one had nearly touched rock bottom. All that was left after that was an arch under London Bridge. A widow in a pawnbroker's shop was therefore an even more powerful way of emphasizing her predicament – hence T. R. Lamont's *At the Pawnbroker's* (113). This poor widow is having to sell a miniature, which the broker opens to reveal a glimpse of a soldier in scarlet uniform. Even more grim is Arthur Brunton's *Extremity* (114). This widow stands outside the pawnbroker's hesitating before going in to sell her wedding-ring. Undoubtedly many widows were left badly provided for, and this, combined with

113 THOMAS REYNOLDS LAMONT (1826–1898) *At the Pawnbroker's* (detail) Private Collection, London, signed, 31 × 25in. (78·7 × 63·4cm.)
Another poor widow who is having to pawn a miniature, which the broker opens to reveal a portrait of a soldier in scarlet uniform – her late husband. The artist, Lamont, was a friend of du Maurier's in Paris, and is the original for the character of the Laird in du Maurier's novel, *Trilby*. Most pawnshops had partitions like this one, dividing the sales and pledge counters, so that customers could not see each other

114

ARTHUR D. BRUNTON *Extremity* Photo: Paul
Mellon Centre for Studies in British Art,
signed and dated 1886, 29 × 21 in. (73·6 × 53·3cm.)
The widow hesitates outside the pawnbroker's
before going in to sell her wedding-ring.
Unless a widow had money of her own, she
could often be left badly provided for if her
husband died unexpectedly. Although the
well-off might regard the pawnshop as the last
resort of the failure, to the poor it was part of life.
They would often pawn their valuables, including
the Sunday best, on Monday, and redeem them
again the following Sunday

115

RICHARD REDGRAVE, R.A. (1804–1888)
Throwing Off her Weeds Victoria and Albert
Museum, signed and dated 1846, 24½ × 30in.
(62·2 × 76·2cm.)
Not all widows remained in mourning for ever.
This attractive widow is throwing off her weeds
with relief, and preparing to put on a wedding-
dress. As Redgrave was a keen critic of
Victorian social habits, this may be taken as
a more balanced view of the cult of widowhood

the harsh blackness of their costume, made them irresistible symbols of helpless, suffering, womanhood.

Perhaps Redgrave should have the last word. His pretty widow in *Throwing off her Weeds* (**115**) is discarding her mourning clothes, and preparing to put on a wedding dress. Or so the critics thought in 1846, pointing to the orange-blossom and other objects on the table, the hat in the box on the floor, and the portrait of the late husband above the screen. Redgrave was keenly critical of the injustices and hypocrisies of Victorian society, and the implied sarcasm in this picture perhaps helps us to attain a more balanced view of the Victorian widow.

WORK

'Blessed is the man who has found his work'
Carlyle, *Past and Present*

God and work were the catchwords of the age. The Victorians' passionate belief in the gospel of work led them to despise idleness as a social and economic sin. And they worked incredibly hard, in both office and factory. Twelve hours a day, six days a week, was common for most workers, until Saturday half-days began in the 1850s. The doctrines of work, self-help, discipline and thrift were held to be the root of England's greatness, the justification of her position as the first and the greatest industrial nation in the world.

The gospel of work inspired two outstanding pictures – Ford Madox Brown's *Work* (116), and *Iron and Coal* by William Bell Scott (117). Both are remarkable in that they not only show people at work, but that they attempt to symbolize the industrial revolution and the new industrial society that emerged from it. Brown's picture was begun in 1852, and is set in Heath Street, Hampstead, not far from where he lived. Excavations were going on there, and he admired 'the British excavator, or navvy ... in the full swing of his activity', thinking him just as fit a subject for painting 'as the fisherman of the Adriatic, the peasant of the Campagna, or the Neapolitan Lazzarone'. Although it was recognized that the British navvy was the best in the world (he built most of the world's railways) no one had thought seriously of painting him. Even photographs of navvies at work are rare. Brown, however, found their costume 'manly and picturesque', and made them the centrepiece of his picture 'as the outward and visible type of *Work*'. The carpenter, with his bow-tie, fancy waistcoat and copy of *The Times*, represents the craftsman class, superior to the ordinary labourer. The other figures in the crowded composition are intended to symbolize the classes of Victorian society. In the background are a gentleman and his daughter on horseback, representing the leisured classes. The man (the model was the painter R. B. Martineau) is according to Madox Brown 'very rich, probably a colonel in the army, with a seat in Parliament, and fifteen thousand a year and a pack of hounds'. It was difficult for the artist to include the most vital element of Victorian society, the urban middle classes – industrialists, merchants and bankers. They are perhaps represented by the two crinolined ladies on the left, one of whom is entirely decorative, while the other distributes Temperance tracts, a favourite pastime of non-conformist ladies. The tract reads 'The Hodman's Haven, or Drink for Thirsty Souls'. The thirsty hodman in the centre is unrepentantly throwing back a pot of ale. The lady with the tracts was included at the request of Thomas Plint of Leeds, Brown's patron, and a fervent Evangelical. On the right, leaning on the fence, are the intellectuals, Thomas Carlyle, critic and prophet of the new society, and F. D. Maurice, Christian Socialist and founder of the Working Men's Colleges, a poster for which is on the wall to the left. Beside the poster is a girl flower-seller, ragged and barefoot; in the road to the right is an orange-seller and sandwich-board men; all representatives of that vast tribe of street traders so assiduously catalogued by Mayhew in his historic book *London Labour and the London Poor*. The sleeping tramps, the lounger leaning against the tree, the ragged children, even the pampered whippet eyeing a sleeping mongrel, are symbols of idleness. The whole picture is packed with moral innuendoes – it is the most intensely symbolic narrative picture of the Victorian period, as well as being Madox Brown's masterpiece. Even the frame is inscribed with biblical texts justifying the gospel of work: 'In the sweat of thy face shalt thou eat bread,' and, 'Seest thou a man diligent in his business? He shall stand before Kings.'

Iron and Coal (117) represents the busy industrial life of Victorian Newcastle. In the foreground are the ironworkers, known as 'Strikers', wielding hammers (the one on the left is a portrait of Walter Trevelyan's son, Charles, and the men were employees of Hawks, Crawshaw & Co. and Robert Stephenson's Works). Beside them on the right is a working drawing of a locomotive, and a newspaper dated 1861, which advertizes a panorama of Garibaldi's campaigns in Italy, a photographer, and Scott's own School of Design in Newcastle. The other objects in the foreground are the air-pump of a marine engine, an anchor, and the shell and barrel of an Armstrong gun, on which a girl sits with her father's dinner and a school-book. Behind the Strikers is a pit-boy, a 'driver' with his whip and Davy lamp. He is looking out over the quayside, which is bustling with commercial activity – fishwives, fishermen, milk-girls, porters, merchants and a photographer. In the background a train steams across Stephenson's High Level Bridge, and below a 'keel' laden with coal passes under the old bridge; overhead the telegraph wires and smoking factory chimney complete the picture of relentless industrial activity. Although the composition is rather awkward, and the colours livid in places, it is the only picture to record the Victorians' worship of the sheer force and power of the Industrial Revolution. Carlyle wrote of Manchester at five in the morning, 'the rushing-off of its thousand mills, like the boom of an Atlantic tide, ten thousand times ten thousand spools and spindles all set humming there . . . is sublime as a Niagara.'

Ford Madox Brown made few converts to his own brand of Pre-Raphaelite realism. He was a lonely man, embittered by his failure to achieve success and recognition. Associated with the Pre-Raphaelites, but never a member of the Brotherhood, he was neglected while Millais, Hunt and Rossetti, all younger men, became famous and success-

116 FORD MADOX BROWN (1821–1893) *Work* Manchester City Art Gallery, 53 × 77in. (134·6 × 195·6cm.)
The most intensely symbolic of all Victorian narrative pictures, glorifying the gospel of work, in all its forms. The crowded composition is packed with figures symbolizing different classes, forms of work, and moralistic contrasts between labour and idleness. Every detail makes a moral point, down to the posters on the wall, which advertize a Boy's Home, a Working Man's College, a reward for information, and a fragment enigmatically inscribed 'Money! Money! Money!' Brown also painted a smaller version (26½ × 38in.) now in Birmingham City Art Gallery

116A JOHN FINNIE (1829–1907) *Maids of All Work* The Geffrye Museum, London, signed and dated 1864–65, 24 × 18in. (61 × 45·7cm.)

The only job available to most women in the nineteenth century was domestic service. Although there were over a million female domestic servants in the mid-Victorian period, there are very few pictures of them. This one is surprisingly honest and realistic – and unusual in showing two servants gossiping on the doorstep, rather than at work indoors

117 WILLIAM BELL SCOTT (1811–1890) *Iron and Coal* Wallington, Northumberland, a property of the National Trust, 74 × 74in. (188 × 188cm.)

In contrast to Brown's *Work*, set in a London street, Scott's picture depicts the industrial life of Victorian Tyneside. It is the last of a series of eight scenes from Northumbrian history, painted for Sir Walter Trevelyan to decorate the inner courtyard of Wallington Hall, Northumberland. Scott must have had Madox Brown's picture in mind, particularly as the small version of *Work* belonged to a Newcastle collector, James Leathart

ful. Even now he remains the most consistently underrated of the Pre-Raphaelites. He made one surprising convert in the almost totally forgotten Thomas Wade, a self-taught Preston artist, a handful of whose works survive in the Preston Museum. *Carting Turf from the Moss* (**118**), an outstanding example of his work, has not only a landscape of ravishing Pre-Raphaelite detail, but an intense feeling of sympathy with poverty. As Wade lived near Preston, he could have seen the work of Ford Madox Brown and the other Pre-Raphaelites at the Liverpool Exhibitions.

Stonebreaking was regarded in the nineteenth century as the most degrading form of physical labour; it was a job often done by convicts and in workhouses. Courbet painted his *Stonebreakers* in 1849. Landseer had even painted the same subject, enlivened by a few terriers, as early as 1830. By an extraordinary coincidence, the two best-known pictures of stonebreakers, by Henry Wallis (**119**) and John Brett (**120**), appeared at the Academy in the same year, 1858. The two pictures form a total contrast. Wallis' picture, exhibited with a long fulmination from Carlyle's *Sartor Resartus* beginning, 'Hardly entreated, brother! . . .' is one of the most gloomy social realist pictures of the nineteenth century. In an evening landscape of haunting and melancholy beauty, the stone-

118 THOMAS WADE (1828–1891) *Carting Turf from the Moss* Harris Museum and Art Gallery, Preston, signed, 30 × 36½in. (76·2 × 92·7cm.)
Wade, a self-taught Preston artist, seems to have absorbed the message of Ford Madox Brown's Pre-Raphaelite realism. This painting combines a landscape of great beauty with a sincere sympathy for the hard life of the poor

119

HENRY WALLIS (1830–1916) *The Stonebreaker*
Birmingham City Art Gallery, signed and dated
1857 on panel, 25¾ × 31 in. (65·4 × 78·7cm.) Stonebreaking was for the 19th century a symbol of
degradation and poverty-stricken labour. Wallis's
and Brett's two pictures, which appeared by
coincidence at the R.A. in the same year (1858)
represent totally different approaches to the same
theme. As if to underline the social message,
Wallis exhibited his picture without a title, but
with an impassioned quotation from Carlyle

120 JOHN BRETT, A.R.A. (1830–1902) *The Stonebreaker* Walker Art Gallery, Liverpool, signed and dated 1857–8,
19½ × 26⅞ in. (49·5 × 68·2cm.)
Brett's stonebreaker, a boy with a dog, sits quite cheerfully at work in a landscape of breathtaking detail and beauty.
The scene was painted near Box Hill in Surrey, and a mile post records that it is 23 miles to London. The landscape
completely overshadows the social message, giving the picture a feeling of rustic innocence quite different from
Wallis's

121 WILLIAM PARROTT (1813–1869) *The Great Eastern under Construction at Millwall on the Isle of Dogs in 1857*
Private Collection; on loan to National Maritime Museum, 33 × 71in. (83·8 × 180·4cm.)
The great Victorian engineers led the world in the scale and daring of their achievements. Isambard Kingdom
Brunel's 'Great Eastern', in its day the largest ship ever built, was typical of both the man and the age. This rare
picture shows the ship on the mud flats on the Isle of Dogs, strangely out of place among the sailing ships and barges,
with Greenwich Naval College in the distance. After immense difficulties, the ship was finally launched on 31st
January, 1858, and moved to new moorings at Deptford, where she was inspected by Queen Victoria. The ship was
constantly dogged by ill-luck, explosions and financial problems, and ended her days laying cables all over the world

breaker lies dead on a heap of stones, seeming almost to blend into the earth itself, and a
stoat warily approaches his foot. Ruskin praised the picture, but reserved his enthusiasm
for Brett's version, which he thought 'simply the most perfect piece of painting with
respect to touch in the Academy this year'. He also made his celebrated exhortation to
the artist to paint the chestnut groves of the Val d'Aosta. Brett dutifully left for Italy
a month later. In Brett's *Stonebreaker* the accent is on the landscape rather than the
social message. With his geological interests, he obviously enjoyed painting the stones
more than the stonebreaker. The picture has an idyllic quality far removed from the
desolate gloom of Wallis

The great Victorian engineers were Napoleonic figures – dreamers, conquerors, com-
manders of huge armies of undisciplined navvies. Typical of the breed was the legendary
Isambard Kingdom Brunel, perhaps the only engineer remembered as a romantic hero.

His superb Great Western Railway can still be admired today as one of the most brilliantly self-confident feats of railway building. He also turned his restlessly inventive mind to the problem of iron steamships, building the historic *Great Western*, the *Great Britain* (recently rescued from the Falkland Islands) and finally, the stupendous *Great Eastern*, his last and most ambitious project, and the one which was to hasten his premature death. Who but Brunel would have had the sheer temerity and determination to build an iron steamship more than twice as big as any ship that had ever been built? Public interest in the ship was intense, but there are few pictures of it. Only William Parrott's picture (**121**) gives us an idea of what the leviathan looked like as it rose on the mud flats of Wapping.

Neither Brunel nor any of the engineers would have been able to realize their projects without Irish labour. Large numbers of navvies were Irish, and every year immigrants poured into Liverpool and the Welsh ports in search of jobs in railway gangs, building and farming. In the towns the Irish gravitated to the bottom of the social scale, creating some of the worst slums, while in the country, the Irish navvy gangs nearly always created trouble, mainly because of the hostile prejudice of Protestant workers. Erskine Nicol, a Scottish artist who lived in Ireland and painted many humorously observant pictures of the Irish, has left us an amusing and interesting picture of an Irish emigrant in 1841 (**122**). To the urchins on the quayside he is a figure of fun, and the boot-boy mockingly suggests that he polish his boots for him.

122 *(left)* ERSKINE NICOL, R.S.A. (1825–1904) *An Irish Emigrant landing at Liverpool* National Gallery of Scotland, signed and dated '71, $55\frac{3}{4} \times 39\frac{3}{4}$in. ($141 \cdot 7 \times 101$cm.)
'The rapid extension of English industry could not have taken place if England had not possessed in the numerous and impoverished population of Ireland a reserve at command.' (F. Engels, *The Condition of the Working Classes in England*, 1844.)

123 *(right)* SIR HUBERT VON HERKOMER, R.A. (1849–1914) *On Strike* Royal Academy of Arts, signed and dated '91, $89\frac{3}{4} \times 49\frac{3}{4}$in. ($228 \times 126 \cdot 4$cm.)
Herkomer painted this picture as his Diploma work in 1891, on attaining the rank of full Academician. The 1880s and 90s was a period of bitter strikes, and Herkomer may have had in mind the famous Dockers' Strike of 1889, when the London dockers, led by John Burns, won their battle for the 'docker's tanner'

Herkomer's *On Strike* (**123**), painted over twenty years later, presents quite a different picture from the happy-go-lucky Irishman. By the 1890s the threat of revolution had faded from the English consciousness. The great Chartist demonstrations were past history, and Engels' threat, 'the hangman stands at the door', had long been forgotten. There were sporadic outbursts of violence, such as the Hyde Park Riots of 1866, but they were usually connected with specific demands for reform. The new problem was labour relations. Parliament had recognized the rights of workers to collective bargaining, strike action and picketing, but it took time for employers to reconcile themselves to these changes. The result was a series of bitter strikes and lock-outs, reflected in the resolute attitude of Herkomer's Striker, for whom a strike will obviously mean hardship for himself and his family.

The Victorian age was still the age of the small craftsman. Although cottage industries were in decline, most of the new businesses in the towns were small family affairs, employing only a few people. One of the largest of these small trades was the boot and shoemakers, which numbered over a quarter of a million workers in 1851. Pictures of country shoemakers were popular with genre painters, as they combined sentimentality with familiarity. F. D. Hardy's *The Old Shoemender* (124) is typical of the type. Flora Thompson's Uncle Tom in Candleford was a shoemaker: 'His day was still that of the small business man who might work by his own methods at his own rate for his own hours, and afterwards enjoy the fruits of his labours and skill . . .' These skilled men formed a proud, independent class of their own, a cut above factory workers, miners and other labourers. Of course, they often went bankrupt, because of competition or the fluctuations of trade

124 FREDERICK DANIEL HARDY (1826–1911) *The Old Shoemender* Photo: Christies, signed and dated 1882, 18 × 24in. (45·7 × 61cm.)
Almost every town, every village, even every street had its boot and shoemaker. The 1851 census revealed that there were 274,000 of them – more than coalminers or factory workers. In an age when most people walked, the shoemaker was an important member of the community

125 (*left*) JAMES CHARLES (1851–1906) *The Knife-grinder* Manchester City Art Gallery, signed and dated 1887, 18 × 14½in. (45·7 × 36·8cm.)
'Needy Knife-Grinder! Whither are you going?
Rough is the road, your wheel is out of order –
Bleak blows the blast; – your hat has got a hole in't.
So have your breeches.'
　　George Canning, *The Friend of Humanity and the Knife-Grinder*

126 (*right*) GEORGE SMITH (1829–1901) *The Lacemaker* Photo: Christie's, signed and dated 1865 on panel, 26¼ × 19¾in. (67·7 × 50·2 cm.)
Lacemaking was an old cottage industry which went into decline during the Victorian period, but pictures of it continued to be popular

　　– the pages of Mayhew are littered with impoverished craftsmen. Proverbially hard up was the knifegrinder, beautifully recorded by James Charles in one of his most charming studies of country life (**125**). Blacksmith's and carpenters' shops occasionally feature in genre pictures, as they combined an interesting clutter of tools and objects with the pleasing spectacle of someone working for his living. Much more popular was lacemaking (**126**), mainly because of its happy associations with homely cottage life. Dickens once observed what fast friends picturesqueness and typhoid often were, but this never seemed to worry George Smith and the other painters of cottage idylls.

16

WOMEN AT WORK

'Oh God! that bread should be so dear,
And flesh and blood so cheap!'
Thomas Hood, *The Song of the Shirt*

In the Victorian scheme of things, only working-class women worked. For the women of the upper and middle classes, idleness was a mark of gentility. Charity work and Sunday School were thought proper, but actual work was taboo. For working-class women, the choice of occupations was limited, but they had to work just as hard as the men. The majority were domestic servants, but they could do farm work, factory work, dressmaking, or become shop assistants. Also many street traders were traditionally women, such as milk-girls and flower-sellers. Until Shaftesbury's Mines Act of 1842, women were also employed in coal mines. In the free-for-all atmosphere of Victorian commerce, exploitation of female labour was inevitable. Employers frequently preferred women and children because their wages were much lower. Harrowing tales leaked into the press; the conscience of the nation was aroused, and took its familiar Victorian shape – charitable organizations and volunteer groups. Before long the oppressed working-girl became a stock figure in the Victorian novel. Only one artist, Eyre Crowe, was brave enough to attempt a picture of factory girls – *The Dinner Hour*, *Wigan* (**130**). The picture received a mixed reception at the Royal Academy of 1874. The *Art Journal* critic was lukewarm in his praise, but admitted that it was 'a veracious statement, and in this quality alone it claims superiority over much of the work which surrounds it.' The *Athenaeum* thought 'it was a pity Mr. Crowe wasted his time on such unattractive materials,' – once again, the Victorian prejudice against too much real life in a picture. Caleb Scholefield Mann, a private observer, wrote, 'a photographer could have contrived as much; and possibly less realistic subjects would be more pleasant in paintings.' Mann also mentions another picture by Crowe in the 1874 exhibition called *A Spoil Bank*. 'We are here in the neighbourhood of a coal pit where grimy girls and children are gleaning fuel from one of the huge refuse heaps known as "Spoil Banks".' Tantalizingly, this interesting picture has now disappeared. So has another called *Shinglers* of 1869, showing iron-workers 'shingling', a part of the iron process. Although *The Dinner Hour* is unique as a subject in Victorian art, even Crowe found it necessary to idealize the scene for the Victorian

127 RICHARD REDGRAVE, R.A. (1804–1888) *The Seamstress* Forbes Magazine Collection, signed and dated 1846, 25 × 30in. (63·5 × 76·2cm.)

Redgrave's was the first picture to draw attention to the plight of the overworked and exploited seamstress. He painted two versions; the first, exhibited at the R.A. in 1844, shows the clock at 1.30 a.m., and there is a cup and bread on the table; in the second 1846 version, illustrated here, the clock is at 2.30 a.m., and the bread has been replaced on the plate by a magnifying glass

audience. The girls are prettier, neater and cleaner than the working girls in Munby's photographs. Compare them also with a contemporary account, from *The Life of John Arthur Roebuck* by R. E. Leader (1897), describing girls in a Glasgow cotton factory: 'The place was full of women, young, all of them, some large with child, and obliged to stand twelve hours each day. Their hours are from 5 in the morning to 7 in the evening, two hours of that being for rest. . . . The heat was excessive in some of the rooms, the stink pestiferous, and in all an atmosphere of cotton flue. I nearly fainted. The young women were all pale, sallow, thin, yet generally fairly grown, all with bare feet – a strange sight to English eyes.' By comparison with this, Crowe's picture is as harmless as a stage set for the first act of Carmen. Only one of his girls is barefoot; the rest wear solid boots and shoes, and the traditional shawls. They are cheerful enough to play ball, and one is giving money to a beggar.

Stitch, Stitch, Stitch!

The fate of the overworked and exploited seamstress was the one which seems to have attracted painters most. First to take up the cause was Richard Redgrave. *The Seamstress* (**127**), which he exhibited at the Royal Academy in 1844, was inspired by Thomas Hood's poem *The Song of the Shirt*, published anonymously in *Punch* in 1843. The poem, which caused a sensation, created Hood's reputation and is said to have trebled *Punch*'s circulation. Redgrave chose as a sub-title the classic lines:

> 'Oh! men with sisters dear,
> Oh! men with mothers and wives,
> It is not linen you're wearing out,
> But human creatures' lives.'

The picture seems to have had a powerful effect on Redgrave's contemporaries. A fellow artist, Paul Falconer Poole, wrote to him saying, 'I think it is the most powerful for truth and touching from its pathos of any picture I have ever seen. Who can help exclaiming "Poor Soul! God help her?" If any circumstance could make me wage war against the present social arrangements . . . it is the contemplation of this truthful and wonderful picture.' In 1847 Redgrave took up the cause of the distressed milliner, with *Fashion's Slaves* (**128**). The *Art Journal* describes the scene: 'Another philanthropic appeal on behalf of the poor workwoman, whom a young fashionable girl is chiding for not having brought home her dress at an earlier hour; the story is emphatically told, and the subject is put on the canvas with much elegance of composition and beauty of colour.' The poor milliner, like all Redgrave's heroines, has the air of oppressed gentility; she has known better days which makes her situation all the more pathetic. This is the implication of all Redgrave's social pictures; the first one, painted in 1840, *The Reduced Gentleman's Daughter*, provides a key to the rest.

Thomas Hood's *The Song of the Shirt* continued to provide inspiration for many

128 (*left*) RICHARD REDGRAVE, R.A. (1804–1888) *Fashion's Slaves* Private collection, 24 × 29½in. (61 × 75cm.) The second of Redgrave's pictures to highlight the plight of the working girl. Here a rich young lady, in her boudoir with her lady's maid, rebukes the milliner's girl for arriving late with her dress. The picture was painted in 1847 for Redgrave's patron John Gibbons, whose descendants still own the picture, and also the clock to which the lady points, the porcelain tea service and the urn on the same table

129
MISS ANNA BLUNDEN (MRS. MARTINO)
(1830–1915), signed and dated 1854,
$18\frac{1}{2} \times 15$in. ($47 \times 38\cdot1$cm.)
'*For only one short hour,*
To feel as I used to feel,
Before I knew the woes of want,
And the walk that costs a meal'
Private collection
Typical of many pictures of seamstresses painted
in the 1850s and 60s, inspired by Hood's poem.
This picture was featured in the *Illustrated*
London News as a part of a memorial to Thomas
Hood, who died in 1845. Miss Blunden developed
a crush on Ruskin, and pestered him with letters
asking for help and advice (recently published by
Virginia Surtees in *Sublime and Instructive*, 1972)

more pictures of poor seamstresses. Millais and even G. F. Watts painted the subject. In 1854 Anna Blunden, later Mrs. Martino, an artist much admired by Ruskin and other artists, illustrated another quotation from the poem (**129**). The girl clasping her hands and raising her eyes to heaven has distinct affinities with Redgrave's Seamstress of ten years earlier, although the view out over rooftops and chimneys gives it a more authentic setting. Still later Frank Holl, sensitive as always to social themes, returned to Thomas Hood with his *Song of the Shirt* (**131**). Holl's picture has none of the deliberately supercharged emotion of Redgrave or Miss Blunden, but its effect is, nonetheless, full of quiet pathos.

The Governess

'Wanted, in a highly distinguished family, a person as governess, to undertake the education of three young ladies of nine, seven and five. She must be of prepossessing appearance, of refined manners, and a perfect musician. She is required to instruct her pupils in French, Italian and English; geography and the use of globes, with music, drawing and dancing; in all which branches of education she is expected to be proficient. Equanimity of temper and cheerfulness of disposition, joined to uninterrupted health, are indispensable requisites. She must understand cutting out and making the childrens' dresses. Salary 25 guineas a year.' – From an advertisement.

130 EYRE CROWE, A.R.A. (1824–1910) *The Dinner Hour, Wigan* Manchester City Art Gallery, signed and dated 1874, 30 × 42½in. (76·2 × 108cm.)

A unique picture in Victorian art, showing a group of factory girls taking their dinner break outside a Wigan cotton mill. Crowe must have tried to idealize the scene a little – the girls are pretty, neat and cheerful, and there is no hint of any exploitation or misery – yet he was attacked by most critics for painting the subject at all. It was also to Wigan that Arthur Joseph Munby, the diarist and amateur sociologist, went to interview and photograph women coal-mine workers

130A JOHN AUSTEN FITZGERALD (1832–1906) *The Waitress* Christopher Wood Gallery, London, signed 24 × 20in. (61 × 50·8cm.)
A pretty and flirtatious young waitress takes a bottle of champagne and a glass to a customer, who is obviously a gentleman sitting behind the partition. Fitzgerald was better known as a painter of fairies, and modern life scenes by him are rare

This sums up neatly the difficult and ambiguous status of the Victorian governess. Although she might be well-born and educated, she was not one of the family for whom she worked, yet was superior to the other servants. She often ended up despised by both, and unable therefore to control the children. Katherine West in her excellent survey *A Chapter of Governesses* (1949) divides governesses in Victorian literature into six main types – the downtrodden, the valued friend, the strict instructress, the adventuress, the villainess and the snob exhibit. But although Victorian novels are thick with governesses – Clara Mordaunt, Jane Eyre, Becky Sharp, Emily Morton, Lucy Morris to name but a few – the iconography of governesses is rather sparse. Practically the only picture is Redgrave's celebrated *Poor Teacher* (**132–3**), of which I have illustrated two out of the four versions. The picture was a great success and the 1844 version was hung on the line at the Royal Academy and later engraved. Redgrave's son wrote in the biography of his father, 'All could feel touched by the representation of a young and pretty girl, just at the time when she would naturally rejoice in gaiety and merriment, immured in a vacant schoolroom to take her solitary tea, and left, when worn out with her day's work, to muse over and long for home-love and happiness.'

131 FRANK HOLL, A.R.A. (1845–1888) *The Song of the Shirt* Thomas Agnew and Sons, London, signed $18\frac{1}{2} \times 25$in. ($47 \times 63 \cdot 5$cm.)
Even when Holl chose to depict the sufferings of seamstresses, he too illustrated the same lines from Hood's poem as Redgrave had done over twenty years earlier

132 RICHARD REDGRAVE, R.A. (1804–1888) *The Poor Teacher* Shipley Art Gallery, Gateshead, signed and dated 1843, 24 × 29in. (61 × 73·6cm.)

Redgrave's moving plea for the unhappy lot of the governess was one of his most successful pictures, and the first of his social protest pictures to be painted in contemporary dress. He may perhaps have painted it in memory of his own sister Jane, who was sent away to work as a governess, pined, caught typhoid fever, and returned home to die in 1829. Redgrave painted four versions, of which this is the first

134
THOMAS BALLARD (fl. 1865–1877)
The New Governess Private collection,
19½ × 15½in. (49·5 × 39·4cm.)
Another forlorn governess, moving into her new
bedroom, which is obviously in the attic. Also
in black, she looks wistfully at a photograph,
perhaps of her father, or maybe the young man
she hopes to marry some day

Thomas Ballard's *New Governess* (**134**) is another of the downtrodden variety. She also wears black, and looks wistfully at a photograph of her loved one as she unpacks her cheap tin trunks. This is the only other known picture of a governess, which is surprising considering what an emotive figure in novels she was, and also considering the success of Redgrave's picture. Millais painted his wife Effie as *The Music Mistress* in 1862 (**135**). Although the music teacher did not live with the family, but came to the house, her wages were low and her profession a hard one.

Opinions still differ as to whether the Victorian governess had quite such a miserable time as the novelists would have us believe. Harriet Martineau thought that readers were fed up 'with the incessant repetition of the dreary story of spirit-broken governesses'. Lady Cardigan, widow of the notorious seventh Earl, who lived to write her memoirs as late as 1909, had some interesting observations to make about governesses, '. . . the Brontes are largely responsible for the fancied woes of the governess. In many of their novels she is a silly, colourless girl, who always fancies herself injured; the servants are rude to her; her employers are barely civil, and their friends ignore her. She is usually a clergyman's daughter, and as a reward for her persecuted life she sometimes marries

133 (*left*) RICHARD REDGRAVE, R.A. (1804–1888) *The Poor Teacher* Victoria and Albert Museum, signed and dated 1844, 28 × 36in. (71·1 × 91·4cm.)
John Sheepshanks, who commissioned this version in 1844, objected to the forlorn loneliness of the governess. Redgrave therefore added the girl by the door, and the two girls skipping outside; to the left he added the piano with the music of *Home Sweet Home*. The governess is still in black mourning dress, holding a black-edged letter, doubtless from her recently widowed mother. In 1845 Redgrave painted another version, and changed the title to *The Governess*

135 *(left)* SIR JOHN EVERETT MILLAIS, Bt. A.R.A. (1829–1896) *The Music Mistress* Private collection, signed with monogram and dated 1862 on panel, 13 × 8½in. (33 × 21·5cm.)
The lot of the music teacher, although not as unhappy as that of the governess, was also a hard and underpaid one, which is perhaps why Millais chose to paint his wife Effie as one, clutching *The Young Ladies Instruction for the Piano Forte*, as she trudges from house to house visiting her pupils

136 *(right)* FRANCIS PHILLIP STEPHANOFF (1790–1860) *Answering an Advertisement* Glasgow Art Gallery, 24½ × 29½in. (62·2 × 75cm.)
Victorian pictures involving servants are nearly always frivolous. In this one an elderly gentleman in his study is interviewing a pretty widow for the post of housekeeper; her predecessor stands by the door scowling

a curate. . . . This type of governess is always on the verge of tears and lamentations, and spends her time in writing long martyr-like letters to the dear ones at home in the creeper-clad parsonage. All I can say is, I never had a governess of this description and I don't think any of my friends had.' Dickens' only governesses were the proud and spiteful Miss Wade, and the dreadful Mrs. General (of papa, potatoes, poultry, prunes and prism fame), so perhaps the poor downtrodden governess was largely a figment of the Victorian imagination.

Servants

In contrast to the seriousness with which painters dealt with seamstresses and governesses, their attitude to servants seem to have been entirely frivolous. F. R. Stephanoff's *Answering*

an Advertisement (**136**) of 1841 is typical of their generally humorous approach to the
subject, and was exhibited with the full title, 'Wanted, a respectable female as housekeeper to a middle-aged gentleman of serious and domestic habits.' Stephanoff has
however bowed to convention and put the figures in earlier costume, which looks vaguely
eighteenth century. Perhaps the reason why painters did not feel strongly about servants
is that they were not an oppressed minority, like governesses; there were about a million
of them, and practically every Victorian household of any standing employed at least
one. The Victorians knew too much about servants. Middle-class houses had several,
and ducal establishments might have hundreds. Servants were taken for granted; they
were simply an inevitable part of their employers' lives, but they were background
figures. To marry a servant meant instant social disgrace. Lord Robert Montague, second
son of the Duke of Manchester, married a housemaid in 1862, and was ostracized by his
family and friends. Arthur Joseph Munby was married to a maidservant, Hannah Culwick,
for over thirty years, but managed to keep it a secret and go on living a bachelor life.

 The majority of Victorian pictures of servants deal in a lighthearted way with the
neglect of their duties. The maid in William Hay's *A Funny Story* (**137**) is reading a
novel when she should be dusting; in Mrs. Farmer's picture two maids have stopped work
to chuckle over a copy of *Punch* (**138**); George Smith's *Bootboy* is simply asleep (**139**).

137 (*left*) WILLIAM M. HAY (fl. 1852–1881) *A Funny Story* Mrs. Pamela Cavendish, signed and dated 1868, 24 × 20in.
(61 × 50·8cm)
To judge by pictures such as these, Victorian servants spent most of the time neglecting their duties

138 (*centre*) MRS. ALEXANDER FARMER (fl. 1855–1882) *Reading Punch, 1882* Photo: Sotheby's, Belgravia, 27½ × 21in.
(69·8 × 53·4cm.)
Two housemaids stop work to chuckle over a copy of *Punch*

139 (*right*) GEORGE SMITH (1829–1901) *The Sleeping Boots Boy* (detail) South London Art Gallery, 14 × 12in.
(35·5 × 30·5cm.)
As the boots boy's working hours might be from six in the morning until six at night, it is not surprising that he has
fallen asleep, in the scullery

140 THOMAS JOHN HUGHES (fl. 1879–1892) *Leaving Home* Photo; M. Newman, Ltd., signed, 24 × 20in. (61 × 50·8cm.)
A country girl prays before leaving home to go into service. Her mother comes in holding a Bible; a letter on the mantelpiece indicates that she is going to London

The only picture to strike a serious note is T. J. Hughes' *Leaving Home* (140) which shows a country girl about to leave home to go into service. The vast majority of female servants were country girls, who were usually sent to their first 'petty place' as a scullery maid at the age of twelve. 'After the girls left school at ten or eleven, they were usually kept at home for a year . . . then places were found for them locally in the households of tradesmen, schoolmasters, stud grooms, or farm baillifs. . . . The first places were called "petty places" and looked upon as stepping-stones to better things' (Flora Thompson, *Lark Rise to Candleford*).

17

THE FALLEN WOMAN

'Can the outcast retrace her steps?
Would any mourn with her although
She watered the earth with tears?'
        William Bell Scott, *Maryanne*

Sex was the Victorian bogey, but the full weight of the moral code fell more heavily on female offenders – unfaithful wives, unmarried mothers, mistresses and prostitutes. Although a man was free to do what he liked, provided he kept quiet about it, a lapse in a woman was thought of as a terrible thing. Mrs. Caroline Norton, a champion of womans' rights and herself the victim of a broken marriage, railed constantly against the double standards of morality: 'the faults of women are visited as sins; the sins of men are not even visited as faults.' The fate of these unfortunate women, literally social outcasts, aroused public sympathy, and in painting and literature the 'fallen woman' became a potent symbol of innocent suffering.

In painting, it was Redgrave once again who was first to draw attention to the plight of unmarried mothers. His picture *The Outcast* (**141**), painted in the 1840s, shows the classic scene of an angry father banishing his daughter and her illegitimate baby from the house. In an age of repression, seduction was rampant, and working-class girls were usually the victims. A seduced girl, especially with a baby, had little choice except prostitution. To find work was difficult if the facts of her life were known. In H. G. Jebb's *Out of the Depths*, a reformed prostitute's own story published in 1859, the girl describes the difficulty of finding respectable work. Even when she found it, she was often sacked as soon as her past was discovered. Mrs. Gaskell also explored the problem of seduction in her novel *Ruth*, published in 1853. The heroine of the book is an unmarried mother, and although a patently wronged and innocent woman, the novel aroused a furore of protest, and was hastily struck off Mudie's Select Library lending list. Redgrave's picture was painted as a diploma work, and given to the Royal Academy, so the public never had a chance to see it.

In the late 1840s, the social outcast found an unlikely supporter in the youthful G. F. Watts. After his return from Italy, he painted a number of realist pictures, including *Found Drowned* (**142**). Watts is said to have based the picture on a scene he actually

135

141 RICHARD REDGRAVE, R.A. (1804–1888) *The Outcast* Royal Academy, Diploma Gallery, signed and dated 1851, 31 × 41 in. (78·8 × 104·2 cm.)

A classic Victorian scene – the angry father banishes his erring daughter and her baby out into the snow. An incriminating letter lies on the floor, a picture with some suitable biblical reference hangs on the wall, and the family are in despair

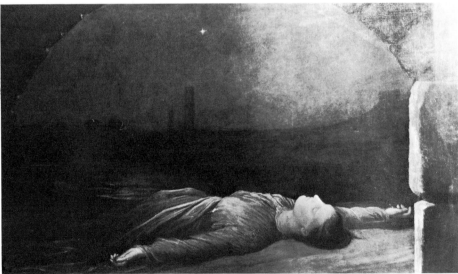

142 GEORGE FREDERICK WATTS, O.M., R.A. (1817–1904) *Found Drowned* Watts Gallery, Compton, 57 × 84 in. (144·8 × 213·3 cm.)

The body of a suicide lies washed up under an arch of Waterloo Bridge. One of a group of realist paintings by the young Watts around 1848–50; the others include *Under a Dry Arch*, *The Seamstress* and *The Irish Famine*

As he that taketh away a garment in cold weather,
so is he that singeth songs to an heavy heart.

143 WILLIAM HOLMAN HUNT (1827–1910) *The Awakening Conscience* The Trustees of Sir Colin and Lady Anderson, signed with monogram and dated LON 1853, $29\frac{1}{4} \times 21\frac{5}{8}$in. (74·3 × 55cm.)

The Pre-Raphaelites frequently discussed modern-life subjects, but Hunt was the first to tackle the theme of the kept woman, who has been stricken with conscience as she sits on her lover's knee at the piano, in their newly-furnished love-nest. To the theme of the damsel in distress, Hunt has brought his own intense symbolism of objects, almost every one of which adds detail to the story. Even the frame is carved with marigolds and bells, symbols of sorrow and warning. In order to lend religious seriousness to such a risqué subject, Hunt exhibited the picture with two religious quotations, and inscribed a third on the frame. This did not prevent most critics, except Ruskin, from attacking it as 'drawn from a very dark and repulsive side of domestic life'. (*Athenaeum*)

witnessed, but he might also have had in mind Hood's poem *The Bridge of Sighs* (1844):

'One more unfortunate
Weary of breath,
Rashly importunate,
Gone to her death.'

Hood was inspired to write the poem by reading in *The Times* of the attempted suicide of Mary Furley, a seamstress who made shirts at 1¾ pence each. Unable to support herself and her children, she threw herself and her youngest child into the Regent's Canal. She was rescued, but her child was drowned. Watts' drowned girl lies washed up under an arch of Waterloo Bridge; another of his realist pictures was called *Under a Dry Arch.* The arches of London bridges, and particularly the Adelphi arches, were the refuge of many of the destitute and homeless in Victorian London.

Redgrave painted a picture entitled *The Awakened Conscience* in 1849, a forerunner of Holman Hunt's elaborate moral fable of 1853, *The Awakening Conscience* (143). Hunt was moved by reading the description of Peggotty's search for Little Emily in *David Copperfield* but his intention was to paint a secular version of his own picture *The Light of the World*, 'representing in actual life the manner in which the appeal of the spirit of heavenly love calls a soul to abandon a lower life.' The model for the girl was Annie Miller, a good-time girl who Hunt himself tried to reform, with conspicuous lack of success. The reform of prostitutes was a favourite Victorian pastime – Dickens set up a home for them, Urania Cottage; Gladstone (known as Old Glad-Eye by the girls) embarrassed his political colleagues by his frequent nocturnal rambles in search of repentant Magdalenes. The Victorians failed to understand that many of the girls had no wish to be reformed at all. Successful courtesans, like Catherine Walters, the famous 'Skittles', lived into ripe and unrepentant old age in her own house in respectable Mayfair. Dr. William Acton, the only Victorian doctor to write intelligently about prostitution, realized that 'the better inclined class of prostitutes became the wedded wives of men in every grade of society, from the peerage to the stable.' He also pointed out that 'Prostitution is a transitory state, through which an untold number of British women are ever on their passage.' It is an extraordinary indictment of the age that even the enlightened Acton could write a book on sex, called *The Functions and Disorders of the Reproductive Organs*, without mentioning women at all. But very few people read Dr. Acton's books anyway, and the majority of spectators had difficulty in understanding what was going on in Holman Hunt's picture. Ruskin felt constrained to write his famous letter to *The Times* of 25th May, 1854, both explaining and praising the picture: 'The poor girl has been sitting singing with her seducer; some chance words of the song "Oft in the stilly night" have struck upon the numbed places of her heart; she has started up in agony; he, not seeing her face, goes on singing, striking the keys carelessly with his gloved hand.' Ruskin also explained the symbolism of the objects in the room: 'common, modern

vulgar, but . . . tragic, if rightly read.' The furniture, with its 'fatal newness'; the books
'marked with no happy wearing of beloved leaves; the torn and dying bird upon the
floor; the gilded tapestry, with the fowls of the air feeding on the ripened corn'; the
picture of the 'Woman taken in Adultery' over the fire place; even the hem of the girl's
dress led Ruskin to think, 'how soon its pure whiteness may be soiled with dust and rain,
her outcast feet failing in the street . . .' (He might also have mentioned the music on the
floor – Edgar Lear's music to Tennyson's *Tears Idle Tears*). This was for Ruskin 'painting
taking its proper place beside literature', confronting 'the moral evil of the age'.

Rossetti claimed to have begun his picture *Found* (**144**) as early as 1851, before Holman
Hunt's picture, but he only made a few drawings for it, starting the picture about 1854.
He continued to tinker with it for the rest of his life, but it was still unfinished when he
died, a striking testimony to his inability to paint modern-life subjects. The desire of the
Pre-Raphaelites to paint such subjects at all was symptomatic of a new attitude to social
problems. It began to be recognized that prostitution was the result of social and economic
pressures, not just bad women. Many female workers could not support themselves on
low wages, and were forced into part-time, or eventually full-time prostitution to supple-
ment their earnings. These girls were known as 'dollymops' or 'park doxies', as they often
hung about in the parks, especially Green Park, which was notorious after dark. 'A

144
DANTE GABRIEL ROSSETTI (1828–1882)
Found Wilmington Society of Fine Arts,
Delaware, 36 × 31½in. (91·4 × 80cm.)
Modern-life subjects were unsuited to Rossetti's
talents. He started this one in 1854, but left it
unfinished at his death. It shows a country
drover who has come to London recognizing his
former sweetheart, now a prostitute. In the
background is Blackfriars Bridge, and a symbolic
white calf enmeshed in netting is in his cart.
In his many drawings for the subject he also
included a churchyard with tombstones on the
left, one inscribed with a suitable quotation,
a rose in the gutter, and two birds building a
nest with straw from the drover's cart

145

146

147

sovereign would get any woman', recorded the informative 'Walter', author of *My Secret Life*, 'and ten shillings as nice a one as you needed.' There were plenty of hotels, boarding houses and restaurants which offered rooms to let, providing a discreet and cheap location for assignations. Walter's amazing memoirs, which fill eleven volumes and record in detail his relations with over a thousand women, give some idea of the incredible range and variety of sex available to the Victorian gentleman. His records of conversations with many of the girls about their life stories confirms Dr. Acton's claim that the majority were part-time prostitutes, who often married and settled down respectably later. But only gradually did the Victorians realize that the 'great social problem' was the responsibility of men as much as of women. 'As long as there are men to tempt, there are women who will be tempted and will fall', says the prostitute in *Out of the Depths*. But the great wall of prudery made any rational discussion of the subject impossible. Even as late as 1891 Hardy's novel *Tess of the d'Urbevilles* caused a tremendous outrage, and Mrs. Grundy was still strong enough to keep Shaw's *Mrs. Warren's Profession* off the stage until 1904.

Augustus Egg's triptych, now known as *Past and Present* (**145–7**), is a stern homily on the subject of adultery. The guilty wife is of course punished, and is seen in the third picture huddled under the arches of the Adelphi, 'the lowest of all the profound deeps of human abandonment in this metropolis'. (*Art Journal.*) The same critic praised Egg for choosing this location, but made the macabre suggestion that he should have included the rats which apparently infested the water's edge. The pictures abound in the symbolic clues we have already seen in the works of Hunt, Martineau and Madox Brown. Egg's pictures are exceptional in that they try to narrate a story over a period of years, filling in the details as would a novelist. Also very literary is the idea of depicting the last two scenes at the same moment, connecting people in different places. As Peter Conrad has written in *The Victorian Treasure-House*, Egg's pictures come nearest to transforming 'the Hogarthian moral progress into something like the three-volume novel'.

145–7 AUGUSTUS LEOPOLD EGG, R.A. (1816–1863) *Past and Present* (a set of three) Tate Gallery, London, signed and dated 1858, 25 × 30in. (63·5 × 76·2cm.)
Exhibited at the R.A. in 1858 with no title, but with the sub-title, 'August the 4th – Have just heard that B– has been dead more than a fortnight, so his poor children have now lost both parents. I hear she was seen on Friday last near the Strand, evidently without a place to lay her head. What a fall hers has been!' In the first picture the husband discovers his wife's infidelity; he holds the guilty letter and crushes a miniature of his wife's lover under his foot. The picture abounds with symbols – the apple, the children's house of cards collapsing, the pictures on the wall of the Expulsion from the Garden of Eden (labelled 'The Fall') and a shipwreck ('The Abandoned'). Once again, it was Ruskin in his *Academy Notes* who had to explain that the second and third pictures both take place at the same moment, five years later, after the death of the father. The children are now alone, and sit sadly at a window, thinking of their lost parents, watching the moon outside; the poor mother, with another baby, is watching the same moon from under the Adelphi arches. Posters on the wall advertize two plays at the Haymarket, *Victims* and *A Cure for Love*, and pleasure trips to the wicked capital of Paris. *Past and Present* is the title of a poem by Thomas Hood

148 JOHN O'CONNOR (1830–1889) *From Pentonville, looking West – Evening* London Museum, signed and dated 1884,
36 × 60in. (91·4 × 152·4cm.)
The artist has contrasted the romance and the drabness of the Victorian city. In the background the gothic towers of
St. Pancras Station rise out of the mist; in the foreground the trams, carriages, crowds, and small shops of a typical
London street. The classical church on the right is St. James's, Pentonville Road; the one further down is the Welsh
Congregational. At the foot of the hill rises the tower of King's Cross Station; beyond to the left are the tower of
St. Pancras Church (inspired by the Tower of the Winds in Athens) and the dome of University College

18

THE CITY

'So far from the smoke of London being offensive to me, it has
always been to my imagination the sublime canopy that shrouds
the City of the World.'
    Benjamin Robert Haydon, *Autobiography and Journals*

Although the social reformers – Ruskin, Morris, Carlyle – regarded the relentless
growth of the Victorian cities with alarm and horror, for artists and writers the city
was a place of romance, mystery and fascination. Haydon not only thought the fog and
mist of London a 'sublime canopy . . . hanging in gloomy grandeur over the vastness of
our Babylon', but found that it aroused 'feelings of energy such as no other spectacle
could inspire'. Similar feelings must have inspired John O'Connor to paint his remarkable view of Pentonville in 1884 (**148**). Against a red sunset sky, the gothic towers of St.
Pancras Hotel and the huge train shed behind it rise up out of the mists and smoke, a
fairytale contrast to the prosaic crowds and trams of Pentonville Road, and to the rubbish
piled on the roof in the foreground. 'I am not very fond of Milton,' wrote Samuel Butler
in *Alps and Sanctuaries* (1890), 'but I admit that he does at times put me in mind of
Fleet Street.' There was something Miltonic, something of John Martin, in London's
mist and smoke, out of which loomed towers, bridges and smoke stacks, giving the city
'a much more sublime and ideal effect, from the very inability to grasp the whole of its
literal reality', as Mayhew wrote. Lund's picture *The Heart of Empire* (**149**) reminds us
that the city was also a source of pride, 'the very symbol of civilisation, foremost in the
march of improvement, a grand incarnation of progress'. (*Chamber's Edinburgh Journal*,
1858.) The Victorians could justifiably claim to have invented the modern city as, by
1850, the population of the towns had overtaken that of the country, for the first time in
history. They watched in amazement as the great industrial cities expanded, seemingly
quite uncontrollable. 'It is the philosopher alone,' says Coningsby in Disraeli's novel of
that name, 'who can conceive the grandeur of Manchester and the immensity of its
future.'

But what attracted artists most was the busy street life of the cities, the endless crowds,
the contrasts, the bustle. David Masson, a visitor to London from Aberdeen in 1843,
wrote, 'Such an impression of vastness and populousness one never received before . . .

149 NIELS M. LUND (1863–1916) *The Heart of the Empire* Guildhall Art Gallery, London, 54 × 72in. (137·1 × 182·8cm.)
A panorama of the imperial city, taken from the roof of the Royal Exchange, looking down Queen Victoria Street and
Poultry, with the Mansion House on the left, St. Paul's in the centre, and on the right the Bank of England. Many
writers on London took as their starting-point the view from St. Paul's cupola. D. J. Kirwan, author of *Palace and
Hovel* (1870), wrote, 'In the civilized world perhaps such another sight cannot be witnessed, as that which greets the
eye from the great Cupola of Saint Paul's, when the view is taken on a bright summer morning . . .'

what an enormous aggregate of wakeful humanity.' A. B. Houghton's *Holborn in 1861*
(**150**) gives us a good impression of a London street in full flood. The pavements are
crowded; shoppers jostle with beggars and street urchins; to add to the confusion, two
navvies are digging up the road, and children are playing in the piles of earth; and two
overcrowded omnibuses are forcing their way through the crowds. The traffic in London's
main streets was extremely heavy, and possibly even noisier than the traffic of today.
Omnibuses and heavy carriages had iron-bound wheels, which made a considerable
noise, added to which there were the endless cries of innumerable street hawkers and
musicians. In Oxford Street, visitors to small shops had to shut the door in order to
make themselves heard.

Blanchard Jerrold published his *London – a Pilgrimage*, with the famous illustrations
by Gustave Doré, in 1872. It presents another romantic view of the city as a huge maze,
full of gothic mystery, populated with weird Dickensian characters. Doré's striking
illustrations, with their steep perspectives and menacing crowds, add to the impression.
Although Jerrold warns us that 'An English crowd is almost the ugliest in the world,
because the poorer classes are but copyists in costume, of the rich,' he recommends the
two great markets, Covent Garden and Billingsgate, as full of 'groups wonderfully tempting
to the artist's pencil'. George Elgar Hicks, whose picture of *Billingsgate* (**151**) was painted

150 ARTHUR BOYD HOUGHTON (1836–1875) *Holborn in 1861* The Trustees of Sir Colin and Lady Anderson, 12 × 16in. (30·5 × 40·6cm.)
A good impression of the noisy confusion of London's main streets. Holborn was in Victorian times a flourishing street full of shops and small businesses, although near it were some of the city's worst slums. An interesting group of street scenes by Houghton is in the Kenwood Museum, London

151 GEORGE ELGAR HICKS (1824–1914) *Billingsgate* Fishmongers' Hall, London, 27½ × 50in. (69·8 × 127cm.)
'The opening of Billingsgate Market is one of those picturesque tumults which delights the artist's eye.' (Blanchard Jerrold). The *Art Journal* critic praised this picture at the R.A. of 1861, especially the central group of the woman paying a porter, and the boy offering to carry her basket, as 'in action and expression not unworthy of Wilkie' but criticized the 'defective composition and unimpressive colour'. Hicks's picture seems to be the only one of this subject. He sold it to Vokins, a dealer, for £380

152 PHOEBUS LEVIN (fl. 1836–1878) *Covent Garden Market* London Museum, signed and dated 1864, 26⅛ × 43in. (66·4 × 109·2cm.)
Covent Garden at five in the morning, looking up from James Street towards the arcades built by the Dukes of Bedford, whose arms can be seen over the main arch. The glass domes of the flower market had not yet been built, and the cupola can be seen beyond, although this has now been taken down. On the left is the Tavistock Hotel, formerly the house of Sir Peter Lely and Richard Wilson; a Truman Hanbury and Buxton pub on the right offers gin, stout, and jellied eels

over ten years earlier, seems to have been the only artist to choose it as a subject. It is an amusing and interesting scene, in the Frith manner; the setting is obviously authentic, and the groups of figures based on sketches made on the spot. But compared to the rowdy confusion of Doré's version, it appears too composed, too orderly. Even the piles of fish seem to have been arranged with the deliberate care of a still-life. It is Billingsgate carefully tailored to meet the demands of the Royal Academy and the English drawing room. Phoebus Levin's *Covent Garden Market* of 1864 (**152**) gives a better impression of that 'picturesque tumult', although it too is carefully composed. Everyone is busy, everyone is doing something, and there is no suggestion that anybody might be starving in the gutter. Dickens' famous description of Smithfield in *Nicholas Nickleby* may remind us just how squalid and dirty the London markets really were.

For his three London street scenes, Frith set the first, *Morning* (**153**), in Covent Garden. He was commissioned to paint these by the dealer Gambart in 1862, for the incredible sum of £10,000. He painted the sketches only; the commission had to be cancelled because the Queen asked him to paint *The Marriage of the Prince of Wales* (**80**). Frith's

153–5 (*facing page*) WILLIAM POWELL FRITH, R.A. (1819–1909) *The Times of Day – 1. Morning – Covent Garden, 2. Noon – Regent Street, 3. Night – Haymarket* Private Collection, each 15 × 27in. (38·1 × 68·6cm.)
Sketches for three London street scenes, commissioned by the dealer Gambart in 1862. The large pictures were never completed, as the commission had to be cancelled. Frith's intention was to produce a Victorian equivalent of Hogarth's 'Times of Day'

1. Morning – Covent Garden

2. Noon – Regent Street

3. Night – Haymarket

intention was to produce a Victorian equivalent of Hogarth's *Times of Day*. In contrast to the bitter and cruel satire of Hogarth, Frith's scenes are orderly and composed narratives, full of incidents into which the spectator can weave his own interpretations. In *Morning* a detective arrests two burglars; two drunken swells tottering home accost a flower-girl drinking her morning cup of tea; homeless figures huddle on steps and in doorways. *Noon* (**154**) shows us Regent Street in the 'full tide of active life', full of coaches, shoppers, hawkers, and dog-sellers. In the foreground a blind beggar is helped across the street by his daughter and dog. The last scene, *Night* (**155**), is in many ways the most interesting, as it is set in the Haymarket, showing a party of theatregoers leaving the Theatre Royal. The Haymarket at night was one of London's most notorious haunts for prostitutes: 'Every hundred steps one jostles twenty harlots,' wrote Taine. Frith has included on the right, as he wrote in his *Autobiography* 'an over-dressed, and be-rouged woman, whose general aspect plainly proclaims her unhappy position; and by the expression on her faded though still handsome face, she feels a bitter pang at having lost for ever all claim to manly care or pure attention.' She gazes wistfully at the couple coming out of the theatre, the reverse of Hogarth, where an ugly old maid envies the rollicking couples emerging from a brothel and a tavern. In spite of Frith's high moral tone, the picture would surely have aroused a storm of protest had the finished version ever been exhibited. If a picture of a woman smoking a cigarette could cause a furore, how much more a prostitute in the Haymarket? In both painting and literature, the street-walker rarely makes an appearance, and when she does, she is a strange, outcast creature, like the mysterious woman who accosts Little Dorrit at dawn near London Bridge. '"I never should have touched you," she says, "but I thought that you were a child." And with a strange, wild cry she went away.'

It was at night that the city reached its heights of poetry and mystery. 'When the evening mist clothes the riverside with poetry,' wrote Whistler, 'the poor buildings lose themselves in the dim sky, and the tall chimneys become campanili, and the warehouses are palaces in the night.' In their different ways, Whistler, Atkinson Grimshaw and Henry Pether celebrated the romance of London at night, the docks full of ships and rigging, the gaunt outlines of warehouses, the gas-lit streets, the eerie squares under the cold moonlight. In a more narrative vein, A. H. Burr's *A Night Stall* (**156**) explores the same

156
ALEXANDER HOHENLOHE BURR (1835–1899)
The Night Stall National Gallery of Scotland, signed with monogram and dated '60, 20½ × 18½in. (52 × 47cm.)
Many artists – Whistler, Grimshaw, Henry Pether – were attracted by the poetry of the Victorian city at night. Most of the innumerable street traders worked at night, supplying the poor whose work might not finish until six or eight in the evening. The biggest street markets were held on Saturday nights

157 JOHN FAED, R.S.A. (1820–1902) *The Thirsty Customer* York City Art Gallery, signed, 53×44in. (134·6×111·7cm.) The busy life of the streets, and especially the street traders, seem to have attracted artists the most. Although the architecture and the newspaper on the right indicate that the scene is set in London, this water-seller, and one of the flower-sellers, wear Scottish caps, presumably because Faed himself was Scottish. The delivery van in the background is that of the Wenham Lake Ice Co. of 164a, The Strand

158 EYRE CROWE, A.R.A. (1824–1910) *Sandwiches* Photo: Fine Art Society, London, signed and dated 1881, 15½ × 24in. (39·4 × 61cm.)

Sandwich-board men in Trafalgar Square, 'taking their luncheon after the fashion of their tribe'. (*Athenaeum*.) The advertisements are for theatres, a 'Big Ourang Outang', and pictures by Gustave Doré and Millais. In the background are Morley's Hotel (now demolished and replaced by South Africa House) and the Grand Hotel (now Grand Buildings)

159
WILLIAM LOGSDAIL (1859–1944)
Saint Martin-in-the-Fields Tate Gallery, London, signed and dated '88, 56½ × 46½in. (143·5 × 118·1cm.)
A typical grey day in London, painted with unusual candour and fidelity. Logsdail hired a Pickford's van with a tarpaulin roof, and parked it outside Morley's Hotel. In it he spent several winter months painting the picture, his feet in straw for warmth. (*Logsdail MSS*)

theme. It was exactly at this time, 1861–2, that Mayhew published his now celebrated *London Labour and the London Poor*, a four-volume encyclopedia of the life and employment of London's 'submerged tenth'. With typical Victorian thoroughness he investigated and interviewed all the street traders he could find: 'I am informed that there are 18,000 itinerant and stationary street sellers of fish, vegetables and fruit in the metropolis.' He goes on to enumerate countless other trades, including cats' meat men, bone grubbers, old clothes men, play-bill sellers, turncocks and lamplighters, scavengers, concluding that about 30,000 adults were employed in these trades on the London street. It is these figures who feature most in narrative pictures – a waterseller in John Faed's *A Thirsty Customer* (**157**), flower-sellers in Logsdail's *St. Martin-in-the-Fields* (**159**) and Wilkinson's *Spring – Piccadilly* (**160**), sandwich-board men in Eyre Crowe's picture in Trafalgar Square (**158**), road-menders in Clausen's *Hampstead – Springtime* (**161**), a coffee-stall in Charles Hunt's picture (**162**). These pictures describe, in varying degrees of reality and sentimentality, the street life of the city. Some critics' comments help us to gauge con-

160 EDWARD CLEGG WILKINSON (fl. 1882–1904) *Spring – Piccadilly* Laing Art Gallery, Newcastle-upon-Tyne signed and dated '87, 37¼ × 54in. (92 × 137·1cm.)
Flower-sellers near Hyde Park Corner, with Decimus Burton's Hyde Park Screen on the left and Apsley House beyond. A flower-seller interviewed by Mayhew said she was sent out by her parents at the age of nine. They gave her money to buy flowers, and she got no supper if she 'didn't bring home a good bit of money'. Jerrold took a more hopeful view: – 'There is an affecting expression in the faces of some of these rough bouquetiéres, that speaks of honourable effort to make headway out of the lodging-house and the rents; . . .'

temporary reaction to them. Eyre Crowe's picture, one of the most realistic and un-sentimental, was praised by the *Athenaeum* for character, humour, and detail; a critic of the *Art Journal*, however, complained of another of Logsdail's London Pictures of 1890, *The Ninth of November*, showing the Lord Mayor's procession, 'need such a scene have been rendered at all? The hideous prose of modern life in a great city is only then a fit theme for Art when it goes to the root of things, and presents motives at once human and typical.' Quite how the painter is to go to the 'root of things' this critic does not explain, but his remarks about 'the hideous prose of modern life' make us realize how deep-seated was the Victorian prejudice against modern-life subjects, and how the painters therefore had to tailor their pictures to meet the demands of the Victorian public.

161 SIR GEORGE CLAUSEN, R.A. (1852–1944) *A Spring Morning, Haverstock Hill* Bury Art Gallery, signed and dated 1881, 40 × 53in. (101·6 × 134·6cm.)
Another London street in springtime, this time in Hampstead. In the background is St. Stephen's Church, by S. S. Teulon (1869)

162 CHARLES HUNT (fl. 1870–1896) *A Coffee Stall, Westminster* London Museum, signed and dated 1881, 24 × 36in. (61 × 91·5cm.)
Mayhew estimated that there were 200 coffee stalls in the metropolis. To the spectator of 1881, the effect of this picture might be nostalgic, as the artist has dressed the figures in the costume of about 1858–60

163 RICHARD ANSDELL, R.A. (1815–1885) *A Country Meeting of the Royal Agricultural Society of England at Bristol, 1842* (detail) Salford Art Gallery (on loan to the Royal Agricultural Society), dated 1843, 70 × 200in. (177·8 × 508cm.) The Victorian aristocracy and landed gentry at the height of their power and confidence. Nine dukes are present in this huge portrait group, which testifies to the interest which all landowners took in improving their estates by introducing modern methods of cultivation and stockbreeding. The machines in the foreground include such wonders as Cottam's Cycloidal Grubber, Wilkie's Swing Plough, a Turnip Cutter, and a Dynamometer

19

THE COUNTRY

'People were poorer, and had not the comforts, amusements or
knowledge we have today; but they were happier.'
Flora Thompson, *Lark Rise to Candleford*

In the nineteenth century, England changed from a rural society to an urban one, but
the Victorians clung to the vanishing ideals of country life. In art and literature the
feeling that 'Man made the Town, God made the country' lingered on; life in the country
was purer, healthier and more natural than in the smoky new cities. England remained,
and perhaps still does, patrician and rural in habit. Social prestige was associated with
the ownership of land. The man on horseback still dominated society as squire, J.P.,
and Member of Parliament. Money and trade were vulgar, and the Victorian new rich
hastened to kick over the traces and buy themselves country estates. Many of the great
Victorian country houses were built on new money, derived from biscuits to banking,
guano to ostrich feathers, as industrialists strove to achieve the dream of 'an estate in
the country, a glistening new country house with thick carpets and plate glass windows,
the grateful villagers, at the door of the picturesque cottages, touching their caps to their
new landlord, J.P., High Sheriff perhaps, with his sons at Eton and Christchurch and his
clean, blooming daughters teaching in the Sunday School.' (Mark Girouard, *The Victorian
Country House* 1971.)

Ansdell's huge portrait group of the *Royal Agricultural Society* (**163**) symbolizes the
power and confidence of the landed gentry at the beginning of Victoria's reign. The hungry
forties had reduced the price of land, enabling the big landowners to buy up and enclose
even larger estates. The men in Ansdell's pictures probably owned an enormous amount
of land between them, but at least they took an intelligent interest in estate management
and modern developments in cultivation and stockbreeding. James Lobley's squire (**164**)
reminds us that not all landowners, however, found farming quite so interesting. Pay for
agricultural workers was low, especially in the non-industrialized south and west, and
in winter many families did perhaps have to live on turnips. But in small villages, such as
Lark Rise in Oxfordshire, described by Flora Thompson, where the pattern of life had
not changed much since the Middle Ages, and contacts with the outside world were few,

164 ATTRIBUTED TO JAMES LOBLEY (1829–1888) *The Squire and the Gamekeeper* Sir David Scott, 29 × 24½in. (73·7 × 62·2cm.)

The exact meaning of this picture is not known, but it would appear that the gamekeeper is remonstrating with the bookish squire, who is more interested in his books than the rent which lies on the table, and complaining that he and his family have to live on turnips

people were happy and self-sufficient, like the family in A. W. Weedon's *Washing Day* (**165**).

The Victorian love of the countryside produced an avalanche of landscape pictures and rural scenes, to fill the parlours of the new middle class in their town villas and suburbs. Landscapes were the staple diet of the Royal Academy every year. So many of them were painted that they are still filling salerooms up and down the country every

165 AUGUSTUS WALFORD WEEDON (1838–1928) *Washing Day* Photo: B. Cohen and Sons, signed and dated 1845, 21 × 26in. (53·4 × 66cm.)
This country family are obviously poor but cheerful. The man may be a farm labourer, or perhaps a navvy, from the style of his dress

week even now. High honours and high prices were accorded to B. W. Leader, Vicat Cole, William Shayer, the Williams Family, and countless others who catered for the insatiable demand for pretty, idealized landscapes, peopled with contented, picturesque peasants going about their work or their rustic pleasures. It is difficult to resist the charge that most Victorian landscapes were machines for evasion. The majority of them are pleasant, competent, and harmonious; they display considerable artistry and industry; they succeed in their intention to please, but do not try and tell the truth. If, as Kingsley wrote, 'Picture galleries should be the townsman's paradise of refreshment', carrying him out of 'the grim city world of stone and iron, smokey chimneys, and roaring wheels, into the world of beautiful things', he did not want to be reminded of the unpleasant realities and hardships of country life. Mr. Millbank, the industrialist of Disraeli's novel *Coningsby* preferred 'a fine free landscape by Lee, that gave him the broad plains, the green lanes, and running streams of his own land.'

Among the welter of Victorian landscapes, one occasionally comes across one or two which depict in an honest and unvarnished way the life of farming people. G. R. Lewis'

166 WILLIAM DARLING MCKAY, R.S.A. (1844–1923) *Field Working in Spring – at the Potato Pits* National Gallery of Scotland, signed, 25⅛ × 38⅜in. (63·8 × 97·5cm.)
Farm workers, mostly women, are digging potatoes out of the pit. The grieve is then weighing them on the scales, before they are put into sacks. Women continued to do much of the farm work, especially in the north and in Scotland, until machinery, higher wages, and the agricultural depression of 1870–1900 drove them off the land

167 CHARLES RICHARDS HAVELL (fl. 1858–1866) *The Thatchers, Cutting Reeds* Photo: Sotheby's, 19½ × 30in. (49·5 × 76·1cm.)
A more sentimental picture of farm life, rather too full of rosy children, but interesting as a documentary record

harvest scene in Herefordshire, shown at the Tate Gallery's *Landscape in Britain* exhibition of 1974, tells us what a harvest of 1815 looked like, but most later artists followed the example of Vicat Cole, whose rosy and romantic harvesting scenes were popular at the Academy for many years. W. D. McKay's *Field Working in Spring* (**166**) is a refreshingly direct and straightforward observation of farm workers. Women still did a great deal of farm work, and in the north gangs of women called 'bondagers' could be hired by farmers. C. R. Havell's *Thatchers* (**167**) and T. G. Cooper's *Hop Picking* (**168**) are verging on rosy unreality, but are interesting as records of these two activities. But all these pictures are the exception rather than the rule. The Pre-Raphaelites, in particular Millais, Holman Hunt, and Madox Brown, produced many stunningly beautiful land-

168 THOMAS GEORGE COOPER (fl. 1857–1896) *Hop Picking in East Kent* Photo: M. Newman Ltd., signed and dated 1857, 20 × 28in. (50·8 × 71·1cm.)
Hop picking in Kent was a favourite summer job for the London poor, and continued to be so until well into this century

169 WILLIAM MAW EGLEY (1826–1916) *Hullo, Largess! A Harvest Scene in Norfolk* Mrs. Christopher Hussey, 48 × 72in. (121·9 × 182·9cm.)
This Norfolk custom was observed by Egley staying in Norfolk in 1860 with John Rose, who stands on the left with his children, horse and dog

scapes, but usually as backgrounds for historical and other subjects. In general the Victorian public seemed to want pretty landscapes in which the figures merely blend happily into the background. They liked a nice view, but did not want to be troubled with what the peasants were doing, or might be thinking. For preference they chose the well-mannered cows and sheep of Thomas Sidney Cooper, and the farmyards of John Frederick Herring junior, neat, orderly, well-manicured, with mud and manure well out of sight. 'Farmyard Friends' was a favourite title, and sums up all the picture-buying public really wanted to know about country life.

Country customs and festivals, although on the wane, made a picturesque and colourful subject. In *Lark Rise* Flora Thompson remembered the 'May Garland' ceremony still surviving in the 1880s. The garland, an elaborate wreath of flowers, was carried round the local villages and houses by the children, led by the May Queen. On a visit to Norfolk in 1860, William Maw Egley witnessed a local custom among the harvesters, and recorded it in *Hullo Largess!* (**169**). In his diaries, he explains the custom. If, during harvest-time, the farmer has a visitor, 'the head man among the labourers usually asks for a largess. They then collect in a circle, and "Hullo Largess!" is given as loud and as long as their

170 JACOB THOMPSON (1806–1879) *The Rush Bearers* Photo: B. Cohen and Sons, 34½ × 55½in. (87·6 × 141cm.) Thompson, a Cumberland artist who lived near Penrith, painted this local festival at Borrowdale Grange, near Derwentwater. The village and church in the background is called Morland. Many of the Lowther family, Thompson's patrons, are portrayed, as well as many local villagers

lungs will allow, at the same time elevating their hands as high as they can, and still keeping hold. This is done three times, and immediately followed by three successive whoops.' Jacob Thompson also recorded an interesting custom in his native Cumberland in *The Rush-Bearers* (**170**). Pictures like these of country life are unfortunately rare, and it was left to antiquarians and photographers like Sir Benjamin Stone to record the vanishing face of rural England, as it slowly succumbed to the pressures of the Industrial Revolution and the drift to the towns.

Flirtation

Pictures of flirtation in the countryside were much more suited to Victorian taste. They provided nature with romantic interest, and also an excuse for painting pretty girls in nice dresses. The Victorians loved nature and long walks; in a restricted society a country walk afforded a rare opportunity for a young man and a lady to meet and talk, without the inhibitions of parental supervision. Of course a chaperone was provided in the respectable classes, but there was nothing to prevent lovers meeting secretly in some quiet, out-of-the-way spot. The excitement of a secret rendezvous added glamour to

171 *(left)* JOHN CALLCOTT HORSLEY, R.A. (1817–1903) *Showing a Preference* Sir David Scott, 26½ × 20¾in. (67·4 × 52·7cm.)

172 *(right)* JOHN CALLCOTT HORSLEY, R.A. (1817–1903) *Blossom Time* Henry McIlhenny, Esq., 35 × 27in. (88·9 × 68·5cm.)

Flirtation and disappointment in the countryside – a favourite theme in Victorian pictures and novels. Horsley's recipe was 'sunshine and pretty women'. Both the men are sailors; one a junior officer, with one stripe on his arm, the other simply Jack Tar. *Punch* thought the lieutenant in *Showing a Preference* was 'showing a preference in a very indiscreet and decided manner. The very poppies hang their heads in shame. Let us hope, however, that he has made a fitting choice and that his charmer will become a mate before he is a commander.'

romance, and the seduction of village girls and servants usually began in this way. Arthur Donnithorne had secret meetings with Hetty Sorrel in *Adam Bede*; the seduced girl in *Out of the Depths* was a lady's maid who used to meet her lover by an old well not far from the big house.

Holman Hunt's *Hireling Shepherd* turned flirtation between a shepherd and his lass into an elaborate moral and biblical fable. As the couple flirt, the sheep are straying into the corn and eating green apples, symbolic of the church neglecting its flock. But most painters were content to follow J. C. Horsley's simpler recipe, 'sunshine and pretty women'. His *Showing a Preference* (**171**) and *Blossom Time* (**172**) are classics of the genre. Both his young swains are sailors, who often feature in these pictures. The Victorians seemed to look more kindly on their flirtations than they did on those of mere land-lubbers. 'The Sailor and his Lass' is always cropping up in genre pictures. Jacob Thompson's couple in *The Course of True Love* (**173**) seem to have temporarily run into one of those little difficulties which of course besets all true lovers. Thompson exhibited a larger version

173 JACOB THOMPSON (1806–1879) *The Course of True Love Never did Run Smooth* Sir David Scott, signed and dated 1854, $35\frac{1}{2} \times 27\frac{1}{2}$in. ($90 \cdot 2 \times 69 \cdot 8$cm.)

Lengthy courting and even lengthier engagements doubtless ensured that the path of true Victorian lovers rarely did run smooth. This picture is similar in spirit to Hughes' *The Long Engagement* and Calderon's *Broken Vows*, but predates both of them by several years at the Royal Academy in 1854, in which he introduced an angry lady, obviously the girl's mother, approaching over a stile, providing a more tangible interruption to the course of true love. More touching are the young lovers of Smallfield's *Early Lovers* (174), who hold hands over a stile, amid flowers and a landscape painted in lovely Pre-Raphaelite detail.

Showmen

In both town and country, travelling showmen were the only form of entertainment available to the poor. There are many pictures that record these now vanished entertainers, who were already beginning to die out in Victorian times. The travelling peep-show was popular with adults and children, as recorded by John Burr (175) and E. J. Cobbett (176). W. F. Witherington, who was one of the earliest nineteenth-century painters of village

176 EDWARD JOHN COBBETT (1815–1899) *The Showman* Walker Art Gallery, Liverpool, signed, 29½ × 39½in.
(75 × 100·4cm.)
Mayhew's peepshow-man found that 'theatrical plays ain't no good for country towns, 'cause they don't understand such things there. People is werry fond of the battles in the country, but a murder wot is well known is worth more than all the fights.' Other features of his show included The Dog of Montargis and the Forest of Bondy, The Forty Thieves, The Devil and Dr. Faustus, The Death of Lord Nelson, Napoleon at Waterloo, and 'Queen Victoria embarking to start for Scotland, from the Dockyard at Voolich'

174 (*left*) FREDERICK SMALLFIELD (1829–1915) *Early Lovers* Manchester City Art Gallery, signed and dated 1858,
30⅛ × 18⅛in. (76·4 × 46·1cm.)
Smallfield was mainly a watercolourist, but produced a few works under Pre-Raphaelite influence in the 1850s and 1860s, such as this delightful picture, a happy version of *The Long Engagement*

175 (*right*) JOHN BURR (1834–1893) *The Peepshow* Forbes Magazine Collection, signed, 30 × 25in. (76·2 × 63·5cm.)
In both town and country, the arrival of the travelling showman was an exciting moment for children. Mayhew interviewed a peepshow-man, who said that 'Before the theaytres lowered, a peep-show-man could make 3s. or 4s. a day, at least, in fine weather, and on a Saturday might about double that money.' He also observed that 'We takes more from children than grown people in London, and more from grown people than children in the country.'

177 WILLIAM FREDERICK WITHERINGTON, R.A. (1785–1865) *The Dancing Bear* Walker Art Gallery, Liverpool, 33 × 44½in. (83·8 × 113cm.)
Performing animals were common – in this picture there is not only a bear, but a monkey and a performing dog. Mayhew also records travelling showmen with performing fleas, birds and mice

life, has left us with a rare picture of a village being entertained by a dancing bear (**177**). The Punch and Judy show was a national favourite. Jerrold describes how the arrival of Mr. Punch in a London street would immediately bring all work to a halt and draw a large crowd. A. B. Houghton's *Punch and Judy* (**178**) concentrates on the audience, the wide-eyed children, the smiling street boys, a flower-girl and a soldier joining in the fun.

178
ARTHUR BOYD HOUGHTON (1836–1875)
Punch and Judy Tate Gallery, London,
14 × 10in. (35·5 × 25·4cm.)
'The barrel-organ is the opera of the street-folk: and Punch is their national comedy theatre.' (Jerrold.) Houghton has concentrated on the reactions of the audience; by the stall on the left is the man playing the pipes which accompanied the show

Fairs continued to be held in both town and country, and although they were primarily intended for the sale and exchange of goods, and the hiring of labourers, they also attracted the largest gatherings of travelling showmen, circuses, and entertainers of all kinds. The London fairs, such as Southwark, Greenwich, Saint Bartholomew's and Barnet Fair, became such notorious hotbeds of vice and disorder that Victorian propriety felt it necessary to suppress them. This was also the fate of Erskine Nicol's *Donnybrook Fair* (179), stopped in 1855. At fairs there was plenty of horseplay and good bucolic fun, but also plenty of pickpockets and other swindlers out to part the innocent countryman from his money. Another excuse for drunken revelry was an election, but few of these seem to be recorded on canvas. A rare exception is W. Sherwood's *Preston Bye-Election of 1862* (Harris Museum, Preston). The Victorians were perhaps ashamed of the fact that their elections were just as corrupt and disorderly as those of the eighteenth century, which is why no equivalent of Hogarth's election series was ever painted.

179 ERSKINE NICOL, R.S.A. (1825–1904) *Donnybrook Fair* (detail) Tate Gallery, London, signed and dated 1859, 42 × 83in. (106·7 × 246·4cm.)
Donnybrook Fair, near Dublin, was started by King John in the 13th century, but 'the noisy mirth and pugnacity with which the fair was conducted led to its suppression in 1855'. (L. R. Muirhead, *Ireland*, 1949)

180 GEORGE ELGAR HICKS (1824–1914) *The General Post Office at One Minute to Six* Richard Green Ltd., 35 × 53in. (88·9 × 134·6cm.)

The post effected a revolution in the lives of all classes, especially the poor. Hicks' picture catches the excitement and bustle of the big city post office just before closing time. The post office seen here is the General Post Office, St. Martin's-le-Grand, built by Sir Robert Smirke in 1812 and now demolished (see also jacket colour illustration)

20

THE POST

'What a blessing is the penny post!'
Trollope, *Phineas Redux*

Victorian painters brought the post into the service of art. Letters play an important role in narrative pictures and in novels, and the arrival of the post was a favourite subject for painters of domestic life. The penny post, introduced in 1840 by the reformer Rowland Hill, was a revolution in most people's lives. It was not only an enormous help to business, but enabled the less well-off to write to their relations and friends, anywhere in the world, for the first time in history. As a result, the Victorians became prodigious, almost pathological, letter writers. The post office rapidly became an important feature of life, in both town and country. G. E. Hicks' *General Post Office* (180) seems to be the only picture recording a big city post office. It is another of Hicks' carefully composed scenes in the Frith manner, but full of interest and incident, especially the newspaper department on the right, with parcels flying through the air. Witherington's *Village Post Office* (181), painted some years earlier in 1853, shows the arrival of the post by horse, in what must be a very small village. The post mistress, in her spectacles and mob cap, recalls the old-fashioned Miss Dorcas Lane, postmistress of Candleford Green, described by Flora Thompson, who ran the post office in part of her neat little cottage, next to the blacksmith's shop. She took great pride in her work, and especially in the telegraph machine; occasions for using it were rare and caused excitement in the village.

The uses to which painters put letters were endless. Charles West Cope's *Palpitation* (Victoria and Albert Museum) shows a big-eyed keepsake beauty with bosom heaving as her mother receives a letter from the postman outside. Letters from abroad were a popular subject; the best-known is probably Webster's picture in the Tate Gallery (183). James Campbell's *News from my Lad* (184) shows an old locksmith reading a letter from his son serving in India. Collinson's *Answering the Emigrant's Letter* (185) is of a family in a cottage replying to a letter from relatives in Australia.

Newspapers also effected a gradual revolution in the nineteenth century, especially with the rise of the popular press, but they do not feature so often in pictures, lacking the sentimental and narrative powers of letters. Haydon's *Waiting for The Times* was one of the first to make newspaper-reading a subject, but there are few other examples. Thomas Sword Good, a Scottish figure painter, made something of a speciality of men, usually ministers, reading newspapers.

181 WILLIAM FREDERICK WITHERINGTON, R.A. (1785–1865) *The Village Post Office* Photo; M. Newman Ltd., signed and dated 1853, 24 × 36in. (61 × 91·5cm.)
The mail arriving by horse-messenger in a small village. The post office rapidly became a centre of village life; before daily deliveries were organized in all areas, people called in to collect their letters personally

183 (*right*) THOMAS WEBSTER, R.A. (1800–1886) *A Letter from Abroad* Tate Gallery, London, signed and dated 1852, 16¼ × 20½in. (41·3 × 52cm.)
The post enabled poor people to communicate with their relations abroad for the first time in history. The postman is asking for extra payment on this letter, which does not seem to please the old lady

182 GEORGE SMITH (1829–1901) *The Morning Post* Photo: M. Bernard Ltd., signed and dated 1875, 33 × 45½in.
(83·8 × 115·5cm.)
The arrival of the morning post was an important event in family life. The hunting gentleman on the right is
receiving bad news, and his two dogs look at him sympathetically

184
JAMES CAMPBELL (*c.* 1825–1893) *News from my Lad* Walker Art Gallery, Liverpool, signed and dated 1859, 21⅜ × 19½in. (54·3 × 49·5cm.) An old locksmith receives a letter from his soldier son serving in India. The letter is dated from Lucknow, so the son must be fighting in the Mutiny, and it begins 'My dear old Daddy, I daresay you will read this in the old Shop . . . .'

185 JAMES COLLINSON (1825–1881) *Answering the Emigrant's Letter* Manchester City Art Gallery, signed and dated 1850 on panel, 27⅝ × 35⅛in. (70·2 × 89·2cm.)
A family in a cottage compose a reply to a letter from their relatives who have emigrated. The father holds the letter, and a map of Australia

21

DERBY DAY

'(The Derby) gives all London an airing, an "outing"; makes a break in our over-worked lives and effects a beneficial commingling of the classes.'
Blanchard Jerrold, *London – A Pilgrimage*, 1872

It was almost inevitable that Frith should choose the Derby as the subject of his second great panorama of modern life (**186**). The Derby was the great English carnival and every writer and sightseer in search of a panorama of English Society went to see it. Even Ruskin, who praised Frith's picture at the Royal Academy of 1858, thought it 'quite proper and desirable that this English carnival should be painted', but he found it 'difficult to characterise the picture in accurate general terms. It is a kind of cross between John Leech and Wilkie, with a dash of daguerreotype here and there, and some pretty seasoning with Dickens' sentiment.' Certainly there had been nothing quite like this in English art before. 'Oh, mama,' said one of Victoria and Albert's children, 'I never saw so many people together before.' Far more than in *Ramsgate Sands*, Frith has filled the picture with a complicated web of narrative incidents. On the left, near the Reform Club's private tent, a crowd gathers round a thimble-rigger's stand. Frith noted in his *Autobiography* that 'Gambling-tents and thimble-rigging, prick in the garter and the three-card trick had not then been stopped by the police.' The man taking a note out of his wallet is the trickster's accomplice. The wife of a rustic in a smock draws him away from temptation; nearby a boy with his hands in his pockets has been cleaned out by pickpockets. In the centre, the interest is concentrated on the acrobat and his boy, who looks hungrily at the picnic being laid out by a footman. On the right a flower-girl offers a posy to a swell, and a gipsy offers to tell the fortune of a lady in a carriage. Incidents of this kind are built up over the whole picture, giving it the appearance of 'a beautiful mosaic', which was Daniel Maclise's description. Although fascinating in detail, the overall effect is static and orderly and smacks too much of the studio. Frith used models for almost every figure; his patron Jacob Bell was tireless in producing pretty girls; the acrobat was borrowed from Drury Lane Pantomime; Tattersall's procured a jockey named Bundy, who posed on a hobby-horse, and found it much more tiring than riding a real one. The horse in the finished picture was painted by J. F. Herring. Frith has

173

186 WILLIAM POWELL FRITH, R.A. (1819–1909) *Derby Day* Tate Gallery, London, 40 × 88in. (101·6 × 223·6cm.)
The second of Frith's great panoramas of modern life, exhibited at the R.A. in 1858, where a rail was needed to
protect it from the crowds. Frith took 'fifteen months' incessant labour' to complete the picture, posing models for
every figure. He omits to mention in his *Autobiography* that he also asked Robert Howlett, the photographer, to
'photograph for him from the roof of a cab as many queer groups of figures as he could'. (*Journal of the Royal
Photographic Society*, 15th Jan., 1863)

imposed the history painter's detachment and calm on the rowdy, disorderly racecourse mob. An American clergyman, who visited the Derby in 1840 and wrote that 'there was here brought before me, in one concentrated and panoramic view, an exhibition of the world's varied allurements of sin', would not have felt the same had he seen only Frith's picture.

Frith's modern-life pictures inspired many imitators, but few rivals. One of the best was the little-known John Ritchie, a painter of historical pictures who made only a few attempts at Frith-type subjects. *A Summer Day in Hyde Park* (**187**) and *Hampstead*

187 (*above*) JOHN RITCHIE (fl. 1858–1875) *A Summer Day in Hyde Park* London Museum, signed and dated 1858, 30 × 51in. (76·2 × 129·5cm.)

Painted in 1858, the same year as *Derby Day*, and exhibited at the British Institution, where it does not seem to have attracted much attention. The view is from the Serpentine, looking towards Marble Arch, Connaught Place, Park Lane and Grosvenor House. Ritchie also painted a companion picture *A Winter Day in St. James's Park*, now lost

188 (*below*) JOHN RITCHIE (fl. 1858–1875) *Hampstead Heath* Private collection, signed and dated 1859, 32½ × 53½in. (82·5 × 135·9cm.)

Hampstead Heath was a popular place of entertainment in Victorian times. There were steam-driven roundabouts, side-shows and booths of every kind, and donkey-rides, which can be seen in the background

Heath (**188**) are now the only two known. The Hyde Park scene is full of narrative incidents in the Frith manner – the man on the left reading about the Indian Mutiny in his newspaper; the soldier talking to a lady on the bench; the visitor to London mopping his brow, with a map of London at his feet; the man on horseback raising his hat to a lady in a landau, much to the disapproval of her parents. It is interesting to contrast this more plebeian view of the park with Walton and Wilson's picture of the *Four-in-Hand Club* (**20**). Ritchie's picture of Hampstead Heath shows people walking or picnicking, with donkey-rides in the background; in fact, on Sundays and holidays the Heath was crowded with stalls, roundabouts, sideshows, and all the fun of the fair. On Whit Monday there were even 'marvels of instantaneous invisibility, Darwinism demented, flying heads, singing flowers, marvellous transmutations of plants and animals into Human Beings and startling transformations in Fairyland', for 1 shilling in the area, or 5 shillings in 'a sofa stall numbered and reserved'. Unfortunately Ritchie does not seem to have had much success with his modern-life pictures, and reverted to his normal history subjects. Another charming picture of the Victorians on holiday is J. W. Cole's view of the 1862 Great Exhibition (**189**), almost the only known work by this now forgotten artist.

189
JAMES WILLIAM COLE (fl. 1849–1882) *A Holiday – The International Exhibition of 1862* Private collection, $29\frac{1}{2} \times 24\frac{1}{2}$in. ($75 \times 62 \cdot 2$cm.) Increased leisure gave the Victorians time to visit exhibitions, which were both entertaining and instructive, and suitable for all the family. After the success of the 1851 Great Exhibition, the International Exhibition followed eleven years later. Another building was constructed in Hyde Park, similar to the Crystal Palace. Although overshadowed by the death of the Prince Consort in 1861, the second exhibition was as great a a success as the first

190 PHOEBUS LEVIN (fl. 1836–1878) *The Dancing Platform at Cremorne Gardens* London Museum, signed and dated 1864, 26½ × 43in. (67·4 × 109·2cm.)
Cremorne Gardens in Chelsea was the last of London's open-air pleasure grounds. It covered about twelve acres between the King's Road and the River, and the amusements included balloon ascents, acrobats, fireworks, cosmoramic pictures and a Stereorama, and dancing under the elaborate pagoda-style ironwork of the platform shown here. By the 1870s it had begun to decline, and was forced to close in 1877 due to pressure from local residents

During the 1860s and 1870s, Londoners in search of fun and entertainment went to Cremorne Gardens in Chelsea. It began as a starting-place for balloon ascents and other sporting events; later it expanded to include acrobats, fireworks, equestrian displays, ballet, clowns and music-hall. Although many contemporary writers mention Cremorne, Levin's picture seems to be the only visual record of it (**190**). Opinions about Cremorne varied. M. E. Perugini in *Victorian Days and Ways* (1936) remembered it as gay, entertaining and harmless: 'the main charm of the place was as a big open space, where a man could eat and drink, promenade and entertain his friends – and perhaps make new ones of a risqué character.' Both Dr. William Acton and Taine found it depressing. Acton observed that 'as calico and merry respectability tailed off eastward by penny steamers, the setting sun brought westward hansoms freighted with demure immorality in silk and fine linen.' He thought the dancers were mostly middle-aged men chasing illusions, as they 'paced round and round the platform as on a horizontal treadmill'. Later the Cremorne did deteriorate, and Derby nights were particularly noted for rowdyism and bad behaviour. The fun seems harmless enough in Levin's picture. Levin was yet another historical and religious painter who made only occasional forays into modern life. His others include *Covent Garden* (152) and *Life in the Hop Garden* (Towneley Hall Museum, Burnley).

Most of Tissot's pictures are to do with leisure, in one way or another, but he is at his most languorous and elegant in the superb picnic scene *Holiday* (191), painted in the garden of his house in Grove End Road, St. John's Wood. The picture was one of ten which Tissot exhibited at the opening of the Grosvenor Gallery in 1877. It is among the last of his elaborate social scenes, before his affair with Kathleen Newton began to have such a pervasive effect on his life and art. Perhaps the only English artist to approach Tissot was E. J. Gregory with his wonderful picture *Boulter's Lock* (192). The picture was exhibited at the Royal Academy in 1898, 'a picture for which his public have long been waiting'. (*Art Journal*.) Helleu and Sargent both admired it and one can see why. Although Gregory laboured for many years on the picture, making oil sketches for practically every figure and group, the result is amazingly lively and spontaneous. Quite rightly, the picture obtained for Gregory his election as a full Academician.

191 JACQUES JOSEPH TISSOT (1836–1902) *Holiday* Tate Gallery, London, 30 × 39⅛in. (76·2 × 99·4cm.)
'One of the pleasantest forms of entertainment is a well-arranged picnic (if only a fine day be selected),'
said Mrs. Beeton

192 EDWARD JOHN GREGORY, R.A. (1850–1909) *Boulter's Lock – Sunday Afternoon* Lady Lever Art Gallery, Port Sunlight, 84½ × 56¼in. (214·6 × 142·8cm.)
Gregory was the only English artist to rival Tissot with this wonderful picture of Londoners boating up the Thames on a Sunday afternoon

22

SPORT

'Play up, play up, and play the game!'
Sir Henry Newbolt, *Vitae Lampada*

Sport, and especially cricket, was for the Victorians part of the gentlemanly code. To play with a straight bat was a virtue both on and off the pitch, and 'not cricket' characterized anything mean, underhand and dishonest. The bloodthirsty pleasures of the Regency – prize-fighting, bear-baiting, ratting, cock-fighting – survived into the Victorian period, but were driven underground by a heavy blanket of disapproval, and eventually replaced by more civilized games – cricket, tennis, archery, croquet, football and cycling. This change is reflected in Victorian pictures of sport. There are practically none involving blood sports, whereas cricket, tennis and the other games became popular subjects.

'The true charm of cricket and hunting', wrote Tom Hughes, 'is that they are still more or less sociable and universal; there's a place for every man who will come and take his part.' This could be said to apply to cricket, but hunting remained the great sport of the aristocracy and gentry. The fashionable world moved to Melton Mowbray in winter to hunt with the famous Quorn, Pytchley, Cottesmore and Belvoir hounds. The size and splendour of these great hunts are recorded in the lively pictures of Ferneley, Alken, Herring, R. B. Davis, and Barraud, all of whom carried on the Regency tradition of sporting painting, quite independent of the mainstream of Victorian painting. Few of them bothered to exhibit; they worked entirely for private patrons, moving from house to house. Similarly, pictures of shooting and fishing were mostly private commissions, as were the racing and steeplechasing pictures of this type which record purely sporting affairs, far removed from Frith's *Derby Day*. John Charlton's picture of the Earl and Countess Spencer (193) at Althorp may serve as a typical illustration of a privately commissioned hunting scene.

Cricket was more genuinely democratic, as is shown by J. R. Reid's splendid *Country Cricket Match* (194). Although played at public schools and universities, it was also played on the village green, where anyone could join in. The County League began in 1873, and in 1877 the first Australian Test Match took place. As an artist, Reid has

193 JOHN CHARLTON (fl. 1870–1917) *Earl and Countess Spencer with Hounds in Althorp Park* Earl Spencer, signed and dated 1878, 29½ × 50½in. (75 × 128·3cm.)

Hunting remained the most popular sport of the upper classes, although anyone with enough money and a love of sport could join in, like Mr. Jorrocks: – 'Its the dash of the 'ound, the feathering for the scent, the picking it out, the challenge when it's found, the rush of the pack to the cry – the werry sight of the beauteous mottled intelligent h'animals is enough to set my werry blood boiling.' This picture shows the famous 'Red' Earl Spencer and his wife going out with the Pytchley; the building is the falconry in Althorp Park

195 CHARLES LEES, R.S.A. (1800–1880) *Skaters, a Scene on Duddingston Loch* Photo: B. Cohen and Sons, signed and dated 1853, $32\frac{3}{4} \times 49\frac{1}{2}$in. ($83 \cdot 1 \times 125 \cdot 7$cm.)
Skating, and roller-skating, enjoyed a vogue in the 19th century. Lees was a Scottish genre painter who specialized in sporting scenes. Duddingston Loch is near Edinburgh, and the castle can be seen in the background

194 (*left*) JOHN ROBERTSON REID (1851–1926) *A Country Cricket Match, Sussex* Tate Gallery, London, signed and dated '78, $42 \times 71\frac{1}{2}$in. ($106 \cdot 6 \times 181 \cdot 6$cm.)
'(Cricket) is more than a game. It's an institution.' 'Yes, the birthright of British boys old and young, as habeas corpus and trial by jury are of British men.' (Tom Hughes, *Tom Brown's Schooldays*.)

196
CHARLES LEES, R.S.A. (1800–1880) *The Golfers, a Match played over St. Andrew's Links in 1850 between Sir David Baird and Sir Ralph Anstruther against Major Playfair and John Campbell* (detail) Photo: Sotheby's
$15\frac{1}{2} \times 24\frac{1}{2}$in. (39·4 × 62·2cm.)
Except for a few enthusiasts, golf remained exclusively a Scottish sport for most of the 19th century, only achieving widespread popularity in the 20th. This lively scene shows a match in progress on the 15th green of the old course

affinities with the Glasgow School, but later he seems to have turned mainly to the seaside and fishing subjects so popular with the Newlyn painters. Another Scottish artist, who seems to have specialized in Scottish sports, was Charles Lees. His *Skaters on Duddingston Loch* (**195**) is an outstandingly attractive picture, and a splendid record of the Victorian love of skating. *The Golfers* (**196**), a sketch for a larger picture, is also interesting (golf however was little played outside Scotland until the twentieth century).

The great mid-Victorian social games were archery and croquet, both of which provided opportunities for flirtation and romance. The pretty Gwendolen first caught the attention of Grandcourt at an archery contest in George Eliot's novel *Daniel Deronda*. Frith wrote of his *English Archers* (**198**) that 'the girls are true to nature, and the dresses will be a record of female habilments of the time.' He has taken the trouble to get all the accessories correct; from the waist of the girl on the right hangs a large tassel for cleaning arrows, a greasebox (containing beeswax and lard into which the gloved fingers were dipped), two ornamental acorns, and an ivory pencil, probably for scoring. Hicks' lady playing croquet (**199**) is a sketch for a large picture of a croquet party which has unfortunately now disappeared. Jerrold wrote that 'Archery and croquet are two out-of-door amusements of fashionable London which no foreigner understands. They are conducted with a demureness and serious, business-like precision, that look more like performances of strict duty, than the *abandon* of pleasure . . .'

197 EDITH HAYLLAR (1860–1948) *A Summer Shower* Forbes Magazine Collection, signed and dated 1883 on board, 20 × 16¾in. (50·8 × 42·5 cm.)

Lawn Tennis, invented in 1874, rapidly superseded archery and croquet as a popular social game. Edith Hayllar, one of an artistic family, painted this delightful scene in the Hayllar's house, Castle Priory, in Wallingford, Berkshire, using her sisters and friends as models

197A HEYWOOD HARDY (1842–1933) *The Lady Gun* Private collection, signed and dated 1894, $25\frac{1}{2} \times 21\frac{1}{2}$in. (64·8 × 54·6cm.)

Ladies did not often shoot in the nineteenth century, so it is unusual to find a picture of such a young and elegant lady gun. The old gamekeeper seems distinctly nervous. Hardy was a well-known sporting painter, and this picture was almost certainly a commission, but the identity of the lady remains obscure

198 (*left*) WILLIAM POWELL FRITH, R.A. (1819–1909) *English Archers, 19th Century* Exeter Art Gallery, Devon, signed and dated 1872, $38\frac{3}{4} \times 32$in. ($98 \cdot 5 \times 81 \cdot 3$cm.)
'Who can deny that bows and arrows are among the prettiest weapons in the world for feminine forms to play with.' (George Eliot, *Daniel Deronda*.) The models were Frith's daughters Alice, Fanny and Louisa

199 (*right*) GEORGE ELGAR HICKS (1824–1914) *Croquet* O. and P. Johnson Ltd., signed and dated 1864, $24 \times 16\frac{1}{2}$in. ($61 \times 41 \cdot 9$cm.)
    'A luncheon despatch'd, we adjourn'd to croquet,
    A dainty, but difficult sport in its way.
    Thus I counsel the sage, who to play at it stoops,
    Belabour thy neighbour, and spoon through thy hoops.'
                – Frederick Locker-Lampson, *Mr. Placid's Flirtation*
Croquet was highly popular in the 1850s and 60s, before the craze for tennis. 'It may be said that a man is nearer the church-door when he has a mallet in his hand, than when to the strains of Godfrey, he has his arm round a lady's waist,' wrote Jerrold. Hicks's picture is a sketch for a large picture of a croquet party, now lost

The mania for tennis quickly swept the country after its invention in 1874. It was especially popular with the young, as it was more exciting than archery or croquet, and better exercise. Tennis parties rapidly became a feature of life in both town and country. The first Wimbledon Championships for men were held in 1877, and for women in 1884. Many artists and illustrators depicted tennis matches and tennis parties – Lavery, Mote, du Maurier to name a few – but perhaps most delightful of all is Edith Hayllar's *Summer Shower* (**197**), showing a tennis party taking refuge indoors during a shower of rain. The men are wearing knickerbockers and stockings; the ladies have tied their long dresses back with aprons, with pockets in them for spare tennis balls. When playing, they usually wore small straw hats. The picture is wonderfully redolent of an English summer afternoon, with sets of inconsequential tennis, lemonade, tea and cucumber sandwiches.

23

THE SEASIDE

'Oh I do love to be beside the sea-side,
I do love to be beside the sea.
I do love to walk along the prom-prom-prom,
With the brass band playing tiddley-om-pom-pom.'

Music-Hall Song

The Victorian passion for the seaside provided painters with a picturesque subject, and an opportunity to overcome what Frith called the 'drawbacks of unpicturesque dress'. Frith was the first to take the opportunity, with his great modern-life picture, *Life at the Seaside* (**200**), now usually referred to as *Ramsgate Sands*. He visited Ramsgate in 1851, to make sketches. He also tried to use photography, 'Talbotyping' he calls it, presumably meaning calotypes, but this was not a success. Instead he worked for nearly two years producing sketches, and hiring models for all the figures and groups. The man with the hare in the centre background was an exhibitor of performing animals; Frith got him to come to the studio, with his cages of cats, dogs, mice, rabbits and other animals, which caused great trouble. As the picture progressed, Frith worried about the possible impact such a modern-life picture might have at the Academy. Some of his fellow-artists were encouraging –Webster and Egg – but others scorned it as 'a piece of vulgar Cockney business'. His non-artist friends also disliked it. One said that 'the interest, which he could not discover, could only be local'. In fact, Ramsgate was a rather decorous, middle-class resort, quite different from its Cockney neighbour, Margate. It could boast some handsome buildings, seen in the background – the Clock House and obelisk by John Shaw, and Wyatt's Pier House with the copper dome.

In the end the picture was a great success at the Academy of 1854, and was bought by Victoria and Albert – a triumph for Frith, and a notable addition to the Queen's collection of Victorian pictures. Frith was encouraged to continue with modern-life subjects, and went on to even greater success with *Derby Day*. Other artists were quick to follow his lead. The clutter and paraphernalia of a Victorian beach was full of lively interest, and *Ramsgate Sands* contains most of the elements we find in other seaside pictures – crinolines and parasols, children paddling and building sand-castles, donkey-rides and other entertainments, musicians and bathing-machines. On the left is a group of minstrels; Jane Carlyle complained of the continuous music at Margate: 'a brass band plays all

187

200 WILLIAM POWELL FRITH, R.A. (1819–1909) *Life at the Seaside (Ramsgate Sands)* Reproduced by gracious permission of Her Majesty the Queen, 30 × 60½in. (76·2 × 153·7cm.)
Frith's first modern-life picture, exhibited at the R.A. in 1854. After a visit to Ramsgate in 1851, Frith decided he was 'weary of costume painting; I had determined to try my hand on modern life, with all its drawbacks of unpicturesque dress.' After working on the picture for two years, it was sold at the R.A. to a dealer named Lloyd for 1,000 guineas. Queen Victoria then bought it from him at the same price, although Lloyd retained the engraving rights

201 ARTHUR BOYD HOUGHTON (1836–1875) *Ramsgate Sands* Tate Gallery, London, signed 9½ × 11¾in. (24·1 × 29·8cm.)
One of the many seaside pictures inspired by Frith's *Life at the Seaside*

through our breakfast . . . succeeded by a band of Ethiopians, and that again by a band of female fiddlers! and interspersed with these are individual barrel-organs, individual Scotch bagpipes, individual French horns!' There are several people with telescopes on Frith's beach; Dickens commented on the elderly gentlemen at Broadstairs 'looking at nothing through powerful telescopes for hours, and when at last they saw a cloud of smoke, fancying a steamer behind it, and going home comfortable and happy.'

They might also be using their telescopes to watch ladies bathing. The bathing-machine, that cumbersome symbol of Victorian prudery, was an indispensable feature of the beach, with its 'modesty hood' at one end, invented by a Quaker in Margate. They were inconvenient and expensive, requiring horses and attendants, and of course drew attention to what they were attempting to conceal. Ladies' and gentlemen's bathing areas were segregated as men usually bathed naked. Ladies, in spite of their concern for modesty, were lifted from their machines into the sea by lusty male attendants. A visitor to Ramsgate in 1860 complained that 'bathers on the one hand, and the line of lookers-on on the other, some with opera-glasses or telescopes, seem to have no more sense of decency than so many South Sea Islanders.' The seaside offered exciting opportunities for flirtation, as we see in the pictures by Nicholls (**203**) and Muschamp (**207**).

Brighton was the biggest and most popular of all the south coast resorts. Thackeray wrote that it was 'a portrait of the West End of London *maritimized*', swarming with railroad directors, barristers, actors and actresses, dandies, city men, M.P.s, dragoons 'trotting up and down with solemn, handsome, stupid faces, and huge yellow mustachios; myriads of flies, laden with happy cockneys; pathetic invalid chairs . . .', all of which is borne out by Solomon's picture (**202**), where two very heavy swells, with Dundreary

202 ABRAHAM SOLOMON (1824–1862) *Brighton Front* (detail) Tunbridge Wells Library and Museum, 19 × 40in. (48·2 × 101·6cm.)
The Regency resort of Brighton retained its popularity into the Victorian era. Thackeray described it as 'London *plus* prawns for breakfast and the sea air.' This picture shows the crowded front near the Bedford Hotel

203 CHARLES WYNNE NICHOLLS (1831–1903) *On the Beach: a Family on Margate Sands* Scarborough Art Gallery (Laughton Loan), signed and dated 1867, 42 × 57in. (106·7 × 144·7cm.)
'One indiscriminate moving mass of cabs, cars, carts and carriages; horses, ponies, dogs, donkeys, and boys; men, women, children, and nurses; and, the least and biggest – babies and bathing-machines . . . little boys with spades; nurses with babies; mammas with sewing; young ladies with novels; young gentlemen with Byron, canes, and eye-glasses; older ones with newspapers, sticks and spectacles.' (Mrs. Stone, *Chronicles of Fashion*, 1845.) Margate was a gay, Cockney resort, rather more plebeian than its staid neighbour Ramsgate

204 JANE MARIA BOWKETT (fl. 1860–1885) *Folkstone* Private collection, signed with monogram JMB and dated 1875, 35½ × 71½in. (90·2 × 181·6cm.)
'Fashionable Folkestone' was one of the smaller, more respectable south-coast resorts

whiskers, can be seen leaning on the railing. Folkestone (204) was smaller, more select and middle-class. The railway of course played an important part in the development of all these resorts, particularly Brighton. Day trips cost only 3/6d, as recorded in Rossiter's well-known picture *Brighton and Back* (223), and local residents complained of 'those swarms . . . daily and weekly disgorged on its Steyne from the cancer-like arms of the railroad.' Victoria and Albert also found its crowds 'very indiscreet and troublesome' and never went again after 1843. The railway also created other resorts, such as Weston-super-Mare (205), connected to Bristol in 1841. Hopkins and Havell's charming picture still shows it as a relatively quiet resort. Two years later, in 1866, the line was doubled, and a new station built with a special excursion platform, hall and tea-room for trippers. The return fare from Bristol was 1/6d., and the result was a rapid expansion of the town.

There is something uniquely Victorian in the flavour of the seaside holiday with its piers and bathing-machines, donkey-rides and reading rooms, shrimps and German bands, which makes the pictures in this chapter a particularly valuable record of Victorian society. Still with us are the innumerable shell pictures, objects and bric-a-brac made of pebbles, seaweed and sand, taken home as souvenirs of a holiday by the sea.

205 WILLIAM H. HOPKINS (fl. 1853–1892) and EDMUND HAVELL (1819–1894) *Weston Sands in 1864*
Bristol Art Gallery, $24\frac{1}{4} \times 38\frac{1}{2}$in. (62·2 × 97·8cm.)
Weston-super-Mare remained a small resort until it was connected by rail with Bristol in 1841. Donkey rides were a great feature at most resorts; this one also has a goat-cart

206 FREDERICK IFOLD (fl. 1846–1867) *A Day by the Seaside* Private collection, $17\frac{1}{4} \times 23\frac{1}{2}$in. (43·8 × 59·7cm.)
Writing from Broadstairs, Dickens described the children as 'busy as bees . . . building impossible fortifications', attended by their 'mothers and aunts, and sisters, and cousins, and friends'

207 SYDNEY MUSCHAMP (fl. 1870–1903) *Scarborough Spa at Night* Scarborough Art Gallery, signed and dated 1879, 31 × 45in. (78·7 × 114·4cm.)
Scarborough was already famous as a spa in the 18th century, but after the arrival of the railway in 1845, it expanded to become the biggest resort on the north-east coast. String orchestras and brass bands were popular at all resorts

208
WILLIAM GALE (1823–1909) *The Convalescent* (detail) Photo: T. Agnew and Sons Ltd., on panel 12 × 18in. (30·5 × 45·7cm.)
Victorian doctors often recommended sea air as a cure for convalescents; many of the seaside towns were also spas, and others provided warm sea-water baths and other mineral baths for invalids

24

THE THEATRE

'The play is done; the curtain drops,
Slow falling to the prompter's bell;'
Thackeray, *The End of the Play*

Although music and the theatre played a lively part in the cultural scene, this is rarely reflected in Victorian pictures, being a more fertile field for cartoonists and illustrators. Holyoake's *Front Row at the Opera* (**209**) is one of the very few pictures of a Victorian audience, and the artist's prime concern seems to have been to paint a row of pretty girls. Grand Opera for the Victorians usually meant Italian opera – Verdi, Rossini, Donizetti or Bellini – and four star singers, whom not to have seen was social disgrace – Alboni, Mario, Giulia Grisi and Jenny Lind. Taste was conservative, and spectacle was important. Meyerbeer's historical extravaganzas, with casts of hundreds and lavish sets, were very popular, until the Wagner cult began to gather strength in the 1880s. English operas usually came to grief, although they produced a few memorable songs such as 'Home Sweet Home' (*Clari; or the Maid of Milan*) or 'I dreamt I dwelt in marble halls' (*The Bohemian Girl*). The nearest thing to a national opera were the comic operas of Gilbert and Sullivan, a quintessential part of the Victorian scene, and still very much part of English culture. Ballet was also largely a matter of star names – Taglioni, Cerito, Carlotta Grisi and Grahn. The cognoscenti and the righteous went to oratorios, but only the amazing conductor and impresario Louis Jullien could get the public to go to concerts, lured by such gimmicks as Beethoven's Fifth Symphony accompanied by three brass bands. Many of the greatest musicians performed only at small private concerts, such as that depicted in Tissot's *Hush* (**18**).

The theatre was a much more thriving and nationalistic affair. Victoria and Albert felt it their duty 'to revive and elevate the English drama', and their encouragement of Charles Kean and his wife Ellen did much to make the theatre respectable, and raise the status of the acting profession. By the end of the reign, many actors and managers were to receive knighthoods – Irving, Wyndham, Tree, Bancroft – and although re-spectable mothers might still shudder at the idea of their daughters going on the stage, the theatre had attained a new level of distinction and official recognition. Theatres became more comfortable; audiences were better behaved, as we see in J. W. Chapman's

209 WILLIAM HOLYOAKE (1834–1894) *In the Front Row at the Opera* Glasgow Art Gallery, 24¼ × 32in. (61·6 × 81·4cm.)
'Tonight we are going to the Opera in state, and will hear and see Jenny Lind (who is perfection) in *Norma*, which is considered one of her best parts.'

– Queen Victoria, letter to King Leopold of the Belgians

two pictures (**210–11**), even if a theatre queue could get out of hand, as Eyre Crowe's *Pit Door* (**212**) reveals. The standard of entertainment might not be high, but it is to the Victorians' credit that they revived and kept alive the Shakespearean tradition, despite the severe mauling he had suffered at the hands of Dr. Bowdler. Greater attention was paid to costumes, sets and scenery, and many artists such as Clarkson Stanfield, Telbin and Gordon Craig brought new standards of professionalism and artistry to the profession of stage designer. The last twenty years of Victoria's reign was a glittering theatrical period – the age of Irving, Ellen Terry, Gilbert and Sullivan, Wilde, Pinero and Bernard Shaw. Some idea of it is given in Stevens' evocative picture of *A First Night at the Palace Theatre* (**213**).

No account of the Victorian theatre would be complete without mention of that national and uniquely English phenomenon – the Music Hall, which burst on the stuffy Victorians 'like a loud woman in a raffish hat at a vicarage tea party', as Stella Margetson

210–11 JOHN WATKINS CHAPMAN (fl. 1853–1903) *A Private Box, Drury Lane;* and *The Gallery, Drury Lane* (a pair) Photo: M. Newman Ltd., both signed, 28 × 36in. (71·1 × 91·4cm.)
As with so many other things, the Victorians made the theatre respectable. These two pictures contrast the middle-class family in their box with the crowd in the gallery. Both are behaving decorously, although not all Victorian theatre audiences were quite so docile

212 EYRE CROWE, A.R.A. (1824–1910) *At the Pit Door* Harwood Gallery, Leeds, signed and dated 1873, 26¼ × 43½in. (66·7 × 110·5cm.)
'Again were struggling crowds early at the door; again were hats doubled up and dresses torn; and again was the throng of carriages, the clamour and conflict of coachmen, servants, policemen, mob, the same as of yore.' (Benjamin Lumley, manager of the Opera House, in *Reminiscences of the Opera*, 1864.) This crowd is queuing to see Miss Bateman in a play called *Leah*

213
ALFRED STEVENS (1823–1906) *A First Night at the Palace Theatre* Photo: Charles Jerdein, 44¾ × 32¾in. (114 × 83cm.)
All the glitter and elegance of a late-Victorian first-night. Some of the figures in the foreground are thought to be portraits of Lily Langtry, Joseph Conrad, and D'Oyly Carte

described it in *Leisure and Pleasure in the Nineteenth Century*. It was despised by prudes and purists, but attracted young bohemians like Sickert, whose early pictures form a fascinating record of the Music Halls (**214**). The singers – George Leybourne, Dan Leno, Albert Chevalier, the great Vance, MacDermot, Marie Lloyd, Katie Lawrence – were national heroes, and their songs, topical, cheeky, boisterous and catchy, swept through the land like wildfire. Even to recite their titles conjures up the unmistakable flavour of the gay 1880s and 1890s – 'Champagne Charlie', 'Oh, Mr. Porter!', 'My Old Man said Follow the Van', 'Bicycle made for Two', 'Daddy wouldn't Buy me a Bow-Wow', 'The Man who Broke the Bank at Monte Carlo', and, silliest and catchiest of all, Lottie Collins' 'Ta-ra-ra-boom-de-ay!'

214 WALTER RICHARD SICKERT, R.A. (1860–1942) *Noctes Ambrosianae, The Mogul Tavern* Nottingham Art Gallery, signed, 25 × 30in. (63·5 × 76·2cm.)
The music hall became part of the national culture in the late Victorian period, although despised by the high-minded as vulgar. Sickert was, as a young man, a great devotee of the music hall, and a friend of the singer Bessie Bellwood. The 'Mogul' was the Middlesex Music Hall

215 WILLIAM POWELL FRITH, R.A. (1819–1909) *A Private View at the Royal Academy in 1881* Christopher Pope, Esq., 40½ × 77in. (102·9 × 195·6cm.)
Frith's purpose in painting this collection of Victorian celebrities viewing the Academy exhibition of 1881 was 'to hit the folly of listening to self-elected critics in matter of taste, whether in dress or art', and also to record 'for posterity the aesthetic craze as regards dress'. He also writes with pride in his *Autobiography* that a rail was put up to protect the picture at the R.A. of 1883 for the sixth time in his career

25

THE ART WORLD

'I paints and paints,
Hears no complaints,
 And sells before I'm dry;
Till savage Ruskin
 Sticks his tusk in,
And nobody will buy.'

Punch

Frith's *Private View* (215) of 1881 gives us a splendid impression of the Royal Academy at the height of its power and prestige. In spite of continual criticism from young artists, in spite of the founding of rival exhibitions like the Grosvenor Gallery and the New English Art Club, the Academy remained the dominant force in the Victorian art world, under the olympian guidance of Lord Leighton (standing in the middle of Frith's picture talking to Lady Lonsdale seated on the ottoman). Among the other personalities in the picture are Gladstone, Browning, Trollope, John Bright, Baroness Burdett-Coutts, Oscar Wilde, Lily Langtry, du Maurier and Millais. The opening of the Royal Academy was an important event in the London Season. The merits of the 'pictures of the year' were hotly discussed in the press and at dinner parties. On the Sunday before the Academy opening, well-known artists would throw open their studios to friends, acquaintances and critics, providing them with a privileged preview of the year's pictures. The Victorian public, and the majority of the artists, never questioned the Academy's monopoly. They accepted that the Academy represented the heights of artistic excellence, and that an artist could aspire to nothing better than the coveted letters R.A. after his name. The Royal Academy could confer riches, fame and social position on its members.

Frith wanted to record the 'aesthetic craze as regards dress' and included on the left 'a family of pure aesthetes absorbed in affected study of the pictures.' The lady with the sunflower recalls Mrs. Cimabue Brown of du Maurier's cartoons, and next to them Frith placed, by way of contrast, the 'homely figure' of Anthony Trollope, in whiskers and top hat, marking his catalogue. Several ladies standing with their backs to us are also wearing long, aesthetic robes; the favourite colours were terracotta and sage green. The 'self-elected critics' who Frith wished to hit can only refer to Oscar Wilde, who stands with an orchid in his buttonhole, surrounded by admirers listening to his discourse in

216 GEORGE BERNARD O'NEILL (1828–1917) *Public Opinion* Leeds City Art Gallery, signed and dated 1863, 21 × 31 in. (53·4 × 78·7cm.)
This picture reflects the keen interest which the Victorian public took in art exhibitions, particularly the Royal Academy. A rail has been put up to protect the picture from the pressing crowds, which means they must be looking at 'the picture of the year'

aesthetic rapture. There are no other critics present, and Ruskin is conspicuously absent. Among the pictures on the walls are Millais' unfinished portrait of Disraeli, who died in 1881, and Collier's *Last Voyage of Henry Hudson*.

G. B. O'Neill's *Public Opinion* (**216**) shows a crowd gathered round one of the popular Academy pictures of the year, which has had a rail put up to protect it. Unfortunately this distinction was never achieved by any of the pictures of G. B. O'Neill. Victorian public opinion was very powerful, and did undoubtedly exert a strong influence on painters. There was a big demand for attractive landscapes, domestic scenes, genre (especially involving children) and still-life, and artists in search of a secure income willingly provided them. In the 1840s and 1850s, literary and historical subjects were all the rage, and Thackeray in exasperation suggested that a room be set aside at the Academy for pictures of the Vicar of Wakefield. This tradition was carried on by Marcus Stone and others, who painted romantic Regency figures with enigmatic titles – *Il y a toujours un autre* was one of his best-known. Henry James watched two ladies at the Academy studying a Marcus Stone with intense interest and furrowed brows; at last one of them whispered triumphantly, 'her mother was a widow'; they then moved on, happy at having solved the problem. The Victorian narrative picture had taught the public to read pictures like novels. The same standards of morality, propriety and sentimentality were applied to pictures as to novels; artists often took subjects and ideas from novels, and critics such as Ruskin positively encouraged the alliance between painting and literature. They became interchangeable – pictures look like novels; novels remind one irresistibly of narrative pictures.

Although the majority of Victorian collectors were solidly middle-class and middle-brow, there were some imaginative and dedicated collectors prepared to back their own tastes and ignore the critics. James Leathart of Newcastle, for example, bought the Pre-Raphaelites while they were still unfashionable. Most collectors, especially the Northern businessmen, preferred to buy off the Academy walls, or direct from the artist. Dealers were not highly regarded, and they seem to have been a rough crew, with the exception of Agnews, Gambart, Flatou, and a few others. Their galleries, however, were popular, as T. P. Hall's picture shows us (**217**), and some artists found it more profitable to exhibit

217
THOMAS P. HALL (fl. 1837–1867) *One Touch of Nature makes the whole World Kin*
Alex Jackson, Esq., signed and dated 1867, 25 × 30in. (63·5 × 76·2cm.)
A Victorian crowd gathers at a dealer's window. The artist has tried to represent all classes of society, from the dandy on the left to the omnibus driver in the hat, who seems to be keeping the omnibus waiting

a major picture with a dealer, especially in view of the lucrative sales of engravings. Frith, for example, sold *The Railway Station* (**220**), with the sketch and the copyright, to Flatou for £4,500. Flatou exhibited it in his gallery, and had 21,150 visitors in seven weeks.

Thomas Roberts' *Opinion of the Press* (**218**) was exhibited at the Society of British Artists in 1859, where it was noticed by Ruskin, who took the opportunity in his review of warning 'young painters against attaching too much importance to press criticism'. He maintained that 'an absolutely good painting is always sure of sale', and ended by

218 THOMAS E. ROBERTS (1820–1901) *The Opinion of the Press* Photo: M. Newman Ltd., signed, 24¾ × 29¾in. (62·9 × 75·6cm.)
Victorian critics could be outspoken, rude and vindictive, and they wielded considerable power. This young artist has read a bad review of his work. The rather unattractive picture of Prometheus on the easel suggests that his fate is not entirely undeserved

exhorting the young artist, 'Do your work well, and kindly, and no enemy can harm you.' This lecture is rather surprising considering Ruskin's own position as the virtual dictator of the art world. Perhaps he had forgotten his criticism of Windus' *Too Late* (**98**) the year before, which caused that unfortunate artist to give up painting? The *Punch* doggerel quoted at the beginning of this chapter must echo the feelings of many artists who suffered the lash of Ruskin's criticism.

But for an artist lucky enough to find favour with the public and the critics, the rewards could be tremendous. The huge artists' houses in Melbury Road are a striking reminder of an age which paid its artists well. What English artist before or since could boast Millais' incomes of around £30,000 or £40,000 a year? Landseer, Linnell, and even Sir John Gilbert died worth over £200,000, nearly millionaires in today's terms. Once an artist had found his niche, and became known for a certain type of picture, all he had to do was go on repeating the formula. Thomas Sidney Cooper went on repeating it up to the age of ninety-nine, and boasted to Orchardson that he painted two pictures every morning before breakfast. 'Even artists and men of letters,' wrote Froude, 'with here and there a brilliant exception, let the banker's book become more and more the criterion of their being on the right road.' There were of course exceptions – Watts, Rossetti, Burne-Jones, for example – who went their own way. But many put money before art, with the consequences that we see in the late work of Millais. Frith's *Sleepy Model* (**219**) shows

219 WILLIAM POWELL FRITH, R.A. (1819–1909) *The Sleepy Model* Royal Academy of Arts, London, 25 × 28in. (63·5 × 71·4cm.)
A self-portrait of Frith painting a model in his studio. The girl was a pretty Irish orange-seller who Frith persuaded to sit for him by becoming a 'large purchaser' of oranges. She told Frith that 'gentlemen is much greater blackguards than what blackguards is', and then fell asleep

us the successful Victorian artist at work in his studio. On the left is a suit of armour, a lay figure, and the other props of the historical painter. Victorian painters were nothing if not thorough. They were trained at the Academies – Sass's, Leigh's, Heatherley's, the Academy Schools – and received a thorough grounding in the techniques of painting and drawing. Even for his modern-life pictures, Frith adhered to the classical routine of drawings, sketches, and models for each figure. It is these drawings and sketches that often find more favour with twentieth-century collectors, being more spontaneous and fresh than the highly-finished Academy machines.

26

THE RAILWAY

'Railroad travelling is a delightful improvement of human life.
Man is become a bird; he can fly longer and quicker than a Solan
goose. . . . Everything is near, everything is immediate – time,
distance, and delay are abolished.'

Sydney Smith

The railway was the biggest single revolution of the nineteenth century. Within a generation it changed the face of England. 'We who lived before railways,' says a character in one of Thackeray's novels, 'and survive out of the ancient world, are like Father Noah and his family out of the Ark.' As the inventor and developer of the first railway system in the world, Great Britain was the first nation to experience its full impact on business and social habits. A railway station was a symbol of the new age. The huge Euston Arch 'with columns of gigantic girth opened a vista to the railway world beyond.' (Dickens, *Dombey and Son*.) And the railway world was exciting. To travel at speed was a new, dangerous experience. Charles Greville wrote of his first train journey, 'The first sensation is a slight degree of nervousness and of being run away with, but a sense of security soon supervenes, and the velocity is delightful. Town after town, one park and chateau after another, are left behind with the rapid variety of a moving panorama, and the continual bustle and animation of the changes and stoppages make the journey very entertaining.'

The station platform, as Greville observed, was a place of 'bustle and animation'. For the Victorians it had something of the glamour which now still faintly lingers at international airport terminals. Here was the perfect subject for painters of modern life. Frith's famous scene at Paddington Station (**220**) was by no means the first railway picture; almost all the others in this chapter were painted earlier, but as Frith's picture is the best-known, it is appropriate to discuss it first. Frith was doubtful about the subject, 'I don't think the station at Paddington can be called picturesque, nor can the clothes of the ordinary traveller be said to offer much attraction to the painter.' But the dealer Flatou liked the sketch, and agreed on a commission. So Frith as usual persevered, working hard for a year, modelling every figure. All classes of Victorian society are represented in the picture, including the criminal. Two detectives are arresting a man on the right, just as he steps into the train. The models were two well-known detectives of the day,

220 WILLIAM POWELL FRITH, R.A. (1819–1909) *The Railway Station* Royal Holloway College, Egham, 45½×98¼in. (115·5×244·6cm.)

The third of Frith's panoramas of modern life, after *Ramsgate Sands* and *Derby Day*, painted in 1862 for the dealer Flatou, for £4,500, including the sketch and copyright. The scene is Paddington Station

221 LEFEVRE J. CRANSTONE (fl. 1845–1867) *Waiting at the Station* (detail) Photo: M. Newman Ltd., signed and dated 1850, 26 × 42in. (66 × 107·7cm.)
The station platform appealed to many painters as a subject, and Cranstone painted this waiting-room scene as early as 1850, twelve years before Frith

Haydon and Brett. On the far left, a group of working-class people are heading for the third-class compartments. In front of them is a harrassed middle-class family, with a porter pushing their luggage on a barrow; perhaps they are going on holiday. Near them a family is seeing their two boys off to school. Mother embraces the smaller one, who holds a cricket bat; the elder boy looks on disdainfully, obviously too grown-up for all this maternal emotion. Both boys are probably at one of the newly respectable public schools, now reformed through the influence of Dr. Arnold, and acceptable to middle-class parents. In the centre of the picture, a dark-bearded man is arguing with a cabby over the fare. His dress, and binoculars slung over his shoulder, suggest that he is a rich man going to the races. The model for this figure was an Italian political refugee who gave Frith's daughters Italian lessons. Frith wrote that 'he was a nobleman, whose head was wanted in Venice to serve a very different purpose from that to which I put it in this country.' In the background a soldier kisses his very plump baby goodbye; further along to the right is a wedding-party, the ladies in crinolines, poke-bonnets and shawls. The man touching his hat to the bridegroom, and handing him a small case, is probably a butler or footman. Luggage is being stowed away on the roofs of the carriages. Even in 1862 the design of the railway carriage still bore a strong resemblance to the old stage-coach. L. J. Cranston's more rustic scene in a station waiting-room (**221**), which pre-dates Frith's picture by twelve years, is still in the Wilkie-Witherington tradition of village scenes. It has more affinity with earlier pictures of coaching inns, such as E. V. Rippingille's *Stagecoach Breakfast* (Elton Collection). F. B. Barwell's *Parting Words* (**222**) is a much more up-to-date picture, and anticipates many of the ingredients of Frith's picture of Paddington Station. As it was exhibited at the Royal Academy in 1859, it may even have given Frith the idea for his picture.

Charles Rossiter's *Brighton and Back* (**223**), also exhibited at the Royal Academy in 1859, is the only known picture to record the rigours of third-class travel. The carriage is open at the sides, whereas in Solomon's picture (**227**) there are at least sides and windows in the second-class compartment. The passengers are well wrapped in shawls and rugs, and equipped with umbrellas to keep out the rain. The first Brighton excursion took place in 1844. It started from London Bridge at 8.30 in the morning with forty-five carriages and four engines; went on to New Cross where six more carriages and another engine were added; then carried on to Croydon for another six carriages and yet one more

222 FREDERICK BACON BARWELL (fl. 1855–1897) *Parting Words, Fenchurch Street Station* The Hon. Simon Lennox-Boyd, signed and dated 1859, 31 × 52½in. (78·7 × 33·4cm.)
Pictures of the station inevitably involved the theme of parting; here the man saying goodbye to his wife in the fore-ground; on the right, parents seeing their boy off to school; both incidents which recur in Frith's picture, painted three years later. The Pickwickian gentleman on the left appears to be admiring the beauty of the young lady; why another lady is wearing an identical dress is not clear

223 CHARLES ROSSITER (fl. 1852–1890) *To Brighton and Back for 3/6d.* Birmingham City Art Gallery, signed and dated 1859, 24 × 36in. (61 × 91·4cm.)
The railway, and especially the cheap excursion, brought travel within the reach of the middle and lower classes. Excursion tickets were first tried to coincide with the Great Exhibition of 1851, and were so successful that they quickly became a feature on all lines, especially to the seaside resorts

224
AUGUSTUS LEOPOLD EGG, R.A. (1816–1863) *Travelling Companions* Birmingham City Art Gallery, signed, 25⅝ × 30⅛in. (64·5 × 76·5cm.)
Perhaps the most delightful of all railway pictures, and the simplest. It shows two girls, presumably sisters, in identical dresses, travelling in a railway carriage on the Continent. The landscape beyond is the Italian Coast near Mentone, and the picture was painted in 1862, when Egg was travelling in Europe for reasons of health

225 ABRAHAM SOLOMON (1824–1862) *First Class – The Meeting* (First Version) Photo: Ferrers Gallery, London, signed and dated 1854, 27½ × 38in. (69·8 × 96·8cm.)

226 ABRAHAM SOLOMON (1824–1862) *First Class–The Meeting* (Second Version) Southampton Art Gallery, 21½ × 30in. (54·6 × 76·2cm.)
Solomon exhibited the first version at the R.A. in 1854, where it was strongly criticized for showing a young man flirting with a pretty girl while her father is asleep. To soothe Victorian propriety, Solomon therefore painted a second version, in which the old man is woken up, the pretty girl moved to the window, and the young man changed into a naval officer – a typically Victorian example of morality influencing art

227 ABRAHAM SOLOMON (1824–1862) *Second Class – the Parting* Southampton Art Gallery, 21 × 30½in.
(53·4 × 77·5cm.)
Exhibited at the R.A. in 1854 as a pendant to *First Class*. The posters on the wall suggest that the boy may be
emigrating to Australia, but some critics thought he was a sailor boy going to join his ship

engine. This amazing 'steam caterpillar' arrived in Brighton not long after 1 p.m., dis-
gorging nearly two thousand passengers. Egg's delightful *Travelling Companions* (**224**),
by contrast, shows the luxury and comfort of a first-class compartment, with windows
and interior design still very similar to a stagecoach. Although foreign travel was still
the preserve of the rich, Thomas Cook's tours were beginning to make it available to
the middle classes, many of whom had probably never crossed the Channel before.

Abraham Solomon's *First Class* (**225**–6) and *Second Class* (**227**) are interesting for the
light they throw on Victorian attitudes to the railway, but also for the effect of Victorian
morality on art. The first version of *First Class* (**225**) was strongly criticized for impropriety. 'It is to be regretted', said the *Art Journal*, 'that so much facility should be lavished
on so bald – or vulgar – a subject.' The *Punch* reviewer thought 'The Young Lady looks

to me to be affected and the "Gent", I fearlessly assert, will maintain to be an arrant spooney.' Thackeray also saw the pictures at the Royal Academy, but did not comment on the morality issue: 'Here is Solomon in all his glory but he is not arrayed (RA'd) as one of these.' The reason for this rather heavy pun was removed in 1862, when Solomon was elected an A.R.A., but he died in Spain of heart disease the very day of the election, which must be a unique event in the history of the Academy. Anyway, Solomon bowed to morality and changed the figures in the second version (**226**), waking the old man up, and putting the girl out of harm's way by the window. There were no complaints about the *Second Class* (**227**) picture, and the same *Art Journal* reviewer of course thought it 'superior to the latter in everything. . . . The characters are well drawn and the story is pointedly told.' The contrast between the First and Second Classes is perhaps intended to imply, as Graham Reynolds suggests in *Victorian Painting*, 'that those who are rich enough to travel first class will move in an atmosphere of security and make interesting and useful friends; in the second class there is likely to be economic insecurity and distress.'

228 WILLIAM MAW EGLEY (1826–1916) *Omnibus Life in London* Tate Gallery, London, signed and dated 1859, $17\frac{5}{8} \times 16\frac{1}{2}$in. (44·8 × 41·9cm.)

Egley's picture was engraved by the *Illustrated London News*, who described it as 'a droll interior, the stern and trying incidents of which will be recognised by thousands of weary wayfarers through the streets of London. There crowded together higgledy-piggledy, is all the miscellaneous assemblage of old women, young misses, City swells, babies, baskets, crinolines, umbrellas etc. which ordinarily fill up the measure of these convenient vehicles; whilst the inexorable conductor peeps in through the door and announces "room for one more", a young lady is already ascending the steps with ample allowance of luggage to fill it.'

27

THE OMNIBUS

'Among the middle-classes of London, the omnibus stands
immediately after air, tea and flannel, in the list of the necessaries
of life . . . the Londoner cannot get on without it.'
                                                quoted in M. E. Perugini, *Victorian Days and Ways*, 1936

The omnibus was less glamorous than the railway, but equally necessary and equally a Victorian invention. Until the building of the first Underground in 1863, the omnibus was the only means of getting around, except for cabs and private carriages, and was much used by men going to work and ladies going shopping. For painters it offered the same opportunities as the railway to show different social types jumbled together; more so, as there were no first and second-class omnibuses.

One of the first, and now best-known, pictures of an omnibus was W. Maw Egley's *Omnibus Life in London* (**228**). Egley was a follower of the Pre-Raphaelites in the 1850s, and developed a distinctive style of his own, using hard, shiny colours, that glitter with an almost metallic surface. *Omnibus Life* was his first modern-life subject, and although the picture was a success, he continued to paint conventional historical and literary subjects for the rest of his career. Egley was an extraordinarily meticulous artist, and his notebooks are preserved in the Victoria and Albert Museum. They record that all the figures in the omnibus were painted from models, and that the interior was painted in a coach-builder's yard in Paddington. He also had a rough copy of it erected in his garden. The view out of the back of the omnibus is of Westbourne Grove, and was painted from a chemist's shop on the corner of Hereford Road. Egley also noted that the drawings for the picture took one and a half days, the picture forty-four days to complete, and that it was sold at the British Institution in 1859 for £80. Also pasted in to his notebooks are several reviews of the picture, including an unfavourable one in the *Daily Telegraph*, saying that the picture was 'utterly deficient in humour'. The *National Magazine* praised the picture, and thought the costume of the young men on the far left 'illustrates an amusing phase of young-London life'. The *Illustrated London News* also liked the picture enough to illustrate it. It was a pity Egley was not encouraged to paint more modern-life subjects.

T. M. Joy's lady with her dog (**229**) and John Morgan's *One of the People* (**230**) are

217

229 JOHN MORGAN (1823–1886) *One of the People – Gladstone in an Omnibus* Private collection, signed and dated 1885, 31½ × 42½in. (80 × 108cm.)
Quite why the artist chose to depict the Grand Old Man travelling democratically in an omnibus is not clear. Possibly he based it on some actual incident which he had read of in the newspapers. In 1885 Gladstone and the Liberals fell from power, but after a brief Conservative government under Lord Salisbury, the 'People's William' became Prime Minister once again in 1886

also amusing views of omnibus life from the outside and from the inside. Gladstone's omnibus is followed by a hansom cab, at that time 'the gondolas of London'. His fellow-passengers seem remarkably undisturbed by the great man's presence. George William Joy's *Bayswater Omnibus* (**231**) was painted ten years later, in 1895. In contrast to the happy extrovert pictures of Egley, T. M. Joy, and Morgan, the artist has introduced psychological subtleties more in keeping with the art of the nineties. Joy's own description was as follows: 'In the farthest corner sits a poor, anxious mother of children, her foot propped on an untidy bundle; beside her, full of kindly thoughts about her, sits a fashionable young woman; next to her the City man, absorbed in his paper; whilst a little milliner, band-box in hand, presses past the blue-eyed, wholesome-looking nurse in the doorway.' Joy's wife and daughter modelled for the group on the left, and the baby was borrowed from a policeman; a Miss L'Amy sat for the fashionable young woman, and Colonel Moutray Read for the City man; both the nurse and the milliner were taken from the same professional model. Like Egley, Joy also borrowed an omnibus from the London General Omnibus Company to paint the interior. Among the advertisements is one for Pear's Soap. It is a delightful picture, comparable to the boulevard scenes that were being painted at the same time in France by Beraud, Caillebotte and other Impressionist followers. But very few pictures of this type seem to have been painted in England. Joy's picture was obviously too prosaic for English taste, as it did not sell at the Academy of 1895, and his widow gave it on loan to the London Museum in 1929. The artist's daughter, Miss Rosalind Joy, who was the model for the little girl on the left, finally presented it to the Museum in 1966.

231 (*right*) GEORGE WILLIAM JOY (1844–1925) *The Bayswater Omnibus* London Museum, 48¼ × 69in. (122·5 × 175·2cm.)
A poor mother and her children, a fashionable lady, a City man, a nurse and a milliner on the Bayswater Omnibus as it passes Hyde Park or Kensington Gardens

230

THOMAS MUSGROVE JOY (1812–1866)
The Charing Cross to Bank Omnibus Photo:
M. Newman Ltd., signed with initials, 30×25in.
(76·2×63·5cm.)
A lady and her dog prepare to board a London
omnibus. The conductor points to 'Strand'
written on the back of the vehicle; perhaps this
is the lady's destination. This picture may be
'The Omnibus – One In, One Out', which Joy
exhibited at the British Institution in 1861

232 FORD MADOX BROWN (1821–1893) *The Last of England* Birmingham City Art Gallery, signed and dated 1855 on panel circular, $32\frac{1}{2} \times 29\frac{1}{2}$in. ($82 \cdot 5 \times 75$cm.)

The most famous, but by no means the only Victorian picture on the theme of emigration. Brown first had the idea of painting it when he went to Gravesend to say farewell to his friend Thomas Woolner, the sculptor, who was emigrating to Australia. The picture was begun in 1852, finished in 1855, and exhibited at the Liverpool Academy in 1856. The models for the two figures were the artist and his wife Emma

28

THE LAST OF ENGLAND

'I awoke once more and on my way I went,
And my heart was overflowing with a deep content:
In the dear homeland, far across the sea,
They had missed me and they loved me,
And they prayed for me.'
The Emigrant's Dream (anonymous)

Between 1850 and 1900 about ten million people emigrated from the British Isles. The majority went to the United States, with Canada and Australia next in popularity. Emigration was a topic frequently discussed in Parliament and in the press. Politicians and reformers encouraged it as a cure for social problems. 'Are none of you going to emigrate?' wrote Kingsley in *Town Geology* (1873). 'If you have courage and wisdom, emigrate you will, some of you, instead of stopping here to scramble over each other's backs for the scraps, like black beetles in a kitchen.'

The emigrant, forced by economic pressures to leave his homeland, was an emotive figure, and appealed to many painters of social subjects. Emigration was at its height in the 1850s, but it was a personal experience which caused Ford Madox Brown to paint his now famous *The Last of England* (**232**). Brown wrote of it, 'This picture is in the strictest sense historical. . . . Absolutely without regard to the art of any period or country, I have tried to render this scene as it would appear.' To our eyes the picture is of course unmistakably Pre-Raphaelite, but it has a directness and honesty that makes it one of the most moving of all Victorian narrative pictures. Brown went to incredible lengths to achieve authenticity: 'To insure the peculiar look of light all round, which objects have on a dull day at sea, it was painted for the most part in the open air on dull days, and when the flesh was being painted, on cold days.' His wife Emma had to sit for the picture out-of-doors, in all weathers, even with snow on the ground. So painstaking was Brown that the red ribbons on the bonnet took him four weeks to paint. He worked on the picture for three years. None of the other Pre-Raphaelites took up the emigration theme, except for James Collinson, briefly a member of the Brotherhood, mainly because of his engagement to Christina Rossetti, and noted for his tendency to fall asleep at their meetings. His pictures of *The Emigration Scheme* (**233**) and *Answering the Emigrant's Letter* (**185**) are more in the mainstream of Victorian domestic genre painting, although

221

233 JAMES COLLINSON (1825–1881) *The Emigration Scheme* Private collection, 22¼ × 30in. (56·5 × 76·2cm.)
A family in their cottage listen to a boy reading the *Australian News*. The title of the picture suggests that they are considering emigration. Collinson painted another picture in similar vein, *Answering the Emigrant's Letter* (185)

Pre-Raphaelite influence is faintly detectable in the detail and colouring.

Collinson's pictures are charming, but lack of the intensity of *The Last of England*, or the emotion of Redgrave's *Emigrant's Last Sight of Home* (**236**). Redgrave seems to have concentrated on the landscape, the finest he ever painted, as if to emphasize the sadness of the emigrants at having to leave it. Ruskin commented on the 'beautiful distance', and the *Art Journal* also remarked that Redgrave had applied himself to the landscape 'with a fervency of devotion rarely witnessed'. The figures are well painted also, but it is the beauty of the landscape that sticks in the memory, not the fact that the picture is about emigration.

Herkomer's large and powerful *Pressing to the West* (**234**) is by contrast very much about emigration, its sufferings and hardships. Herkomer began the picture in New York in 1883, but based it on his own boyhood memories of emigrating from Germany to New York, over thirty years before. The voyage from Germany took six weeks. The passengers lived mainly on salt beef, and few families survived without the death of at least one of its members. On arrival in New York, no accommodation was provided for the emigrants until they were ready to 'press to the west', and they were temporarily billeted in an old concert hall. Herkomer wrote of the picture, 'the extraordinary medley of nationalities interested me; but the subject touched me in another way that was more personal – here I saw the emigrant's life and hardships – conditions in which my parents found themselves when they left the Fatherland for his Land of Promise.' It is the only Victorian picture to depict honestly and realistically the unpleasant side of emigration. Ruskin found it much too strong for his taste, and criticized the artist for being 'content to paint whatever he is in the habit of seeing.... Mr. Herkomer, whose true function was to show us the dancing of Tyrolese peasants to the pipe and zither, spends his best strength in painting a heap of promiscuous emigrants in the agonies of starvation.'

Pathos verging on sentimentality is the keynote of most emigration pictures, the majority of which treat of the fate of the unfortunate Scottish Highlanders, ruthlessly

234 SIR HUBERT VON HERKOMER, R.A. (1849–1914) *Pressing to the West* Leipzig Museum, signed and dated '84, 56¾ × 86in. (144 × 215cm.)

Herkomer's picture is the only one to deal realistically with the sufferings and hardships endured by emigrants. It shows a group of emigrants billeted in an old concert hall, Castle Gardens, in New York. Herkomer had a personal reason for painting the subject, as his own family had emigrated from Germany to New York in 1851, when he was only two years old. His father Lorenz Herkomer, a woodcarver, was unable to make a living in the United States, and the family moved to England in 1857, settling in Southampton

cleared away by the first Duke of Sutherland and other landlords to make way for more profitable sheep farms and sporting estates. So much ink has already flowed on the heated topic of the 'Highland Clearances' that I have no desire to add fuel to the flames. Whether the real extent and nature of the clearances was exaggerated or not hardly mattered to the painters. They accepted that the Highlander was an oppressed figure, forced against his will to leave this beloved country. This is the implication of Thomas Faed's large and moving *The Last of the Clan* (235), Watson Nicol's tearful *Lochaber No More* (237), and Herdman's *Landless and Homeless* (238). All three pictures are by Scottish artists, and Faed's is as much a lament for the passing of a way of life as an

235 THOMAS FAED, R.A. (1826–1900) *The Last of the Clan* Photo: Fine Art Society, signed and dated 1865, 57 × 72in. (144·8 × 182·9cm.)
The fate of the Highlander forced to emigrate as a result of the notorious 'Highland Clearances' was the most common theme in emigration pictures

236 RICHARD REDGRAVE, R.A. (1804–1888) *The Emigrants' Last Sight of Home* Roy Miles Fine Paintings Ltd., signed and dated 1858, 27 × 39in. (69·5 × 99cm.)
Painted at Leith Hill, near Abinger, in Surrey, where Redgrave had a house, and exhibited at the R.A. in 1859.
Although not as intense as Redgrave's social pictures of the 1840s, it is one of his most beautiful works, unknown until its recent re-appearance at an auction sale in London

236A THOMAS FALCON MARSHALL (1818–1878) *Emigration – The Parting Day* Christopher Wood Gallery, signed and dated 1852, 36 × 60½in. (91·4 × 153·6cm.)
Unlike most other painters of emigration scenes, Marshall has made this emigration seem almost a happy event, suggesting that a better life awaits them overseas

236B THOMAS BROOKS (1818–1891) *Relenting* McCormick Collection, USA, signed and dated 1955, 34 × 46in. (86.4 × 116.9cm)
A bailiff and his agent have come to inspect the lodgings of a poor widow and her children, clearly with a view to evicting them. The title implies, however, that he is relenting, and that humanity will prevail. All the details of the room emphasize the widow's plight – the late husband's portrait and army sword, the empty watchcase, the medicine bottles, the sewing, the empty bird-cage

237
JOHN WATSON NICOL (fl. 1863–1924) *Lochaber No More* Photo: Fine Art Society Ltd., signed and dated 1863, size unknown
'The foot that quits its native glen
    with half unwilling motion,
Shall mount with dauntless courage then
    The bark that braves the ocean.'
            – Anon., *The Emigrant Highlander's Wife*

238
ROBERT HERDMAN, R.S.A. (1829–1888)
Landless and Homeless – Farewell to the Glen
Photo: Christie's, signed with monogram and dated 1887, $54\frac{1}{2} \times 44\frac{1}{2}$in. (138·4 × 113cm.)
'Ah we must leave thee and go away
    Far from Ben Luibh,
Far from the graves where we hoped to lay
    Our bones with our fathers.'
            – Walter C. Smith, *Glenaradale*

emigration scene. There can be little doubt that the artists were sincere in their desire
to draw attention to a social evil, but it is interesting that all three could not resist introducing animals in order to heighten the pathos – Faed's white pony looks positively
mournful, as do both the dogs in the other pictures. O'Neil's *Parting Cheer* (**239**) is
more cheerful and hopeful, and recalls the famous emigration scene in *David Copperfield*,
where the Micawbers, Mr. Peggotty, Emily and Martha depart for Australia.

Although there are many pictures of Scottish emigrants, there are surprisingly few
of the Irish, who emigrated in even larger numbers after the terrible famines of the
1840s. G. F. Watts painted a large, gloomy, and now almost invisible picture of the
Irish potato famine (Watts Gallery, Compton), but the only emigration picture appears
to be Erskine Nicol's (**240**) of a poor Irish couple waiting at a railway station. To end
on a more cheerful note, it should be remembered that some emigrants came back.
Thomas Woolner, whose departure inspired Madox Brown's picture, returned after
only a few years. So did the Australian emigrant in G. B. O'Neill's picture (**241**).

239 HENRY NELSON O'NEIL, A.R.A. (1817–1880) *The Parting Cheer* Private collection, signed with monogram and
dated 1861, 17½ × 25½in. (44·5 × 64·8cm.)
'As the sails rose to the wind, and the ship began to move, there broke from all the boats three resounding cheers,
which those on board took up, and echoed back, and which were echoed and re-echoed. My heart burst out when I
heard the sound, and beheld the waving of the hats and handkerchiefs.'

Charles Dickens, *David Copperfield*

240
ERSKINE NICOL, R.S.A. (1825–1904)
The Emigrants Departure Tate Gallery, London,
signed and dated 1864, 18 × 13¾in. (45·7 × 35cm.)
Nicol, although a Scottish artist, specialized in
Irish subjects, so this may depict a poor
Irishman and his wife emigrating to America.
Nicol was described by an *Art Journal* reviewer
as 'painter in ordinary to the Irish peasant'

241 GEORGE BERNARD O'NEILL (1828–1917) *The Return from Australia* Photo: Fine Art Society, 21¼ × 25¼in.
(54 × 64·1cm.)
Not all emigrants left for good; this one has come back from Australia, with a bush hat, and a stuffed baby
kangaroo in a glass case

242 LADY BUTLER (1846–1933) *The Roll Call (Calling the Roll after an Engagement, Crimea)* (detail) Reproduced by gracious permission of Her Majesty the Queen, 36 × 72in. (91·4 × 182·8cm.)
Perhaps the most famous picture of the Crimea, but not painted until twenty years afterwards. Exhibited at the R.A. in 1874, it created a sensation, which made the artist, then Miss Elizabeth Thompson, famous overnight. The picture was bought by Queen Victoria

29

WAR

'Their's not to reason why,
Their's not to make reply,
Their's but to do and die.'
Tennyson, *The Charge of the Light Brigade*

During the Victorian period England was only involved in two major wars, the Crimean Campaign and the Boer War. The remainder were entirely small colonial wars and expeditions, the most serious being the Indian Mutiny. Hardly a year of Victoria's reign went by without some kind of action somewhere; Bond in *Victorian Military Campaigns* (1967) lists 72 separate campaigns. The only two to have an appreciable impact on painting were the two most traumatic, the Crimean War and the Indian Mutiny.

The Crimea

Lady Butler's *The Roll Call* (242) is perhaps the best-known picture of the Crimea, much reproduced in engravings and history books, but it was painted in 1874, nearly twenty years after the war was over. Patriotic memories, however, were easily stirred, and the picture was the success of the season. Even the Royal Academy hanging committee, led by J. R. Herbert, gave it three cheers. The public response was equally enthusiastic, and a policeman was needed to protect the picture from admiring crowds. Caleb Scholefield Mann, a private viewer at the Academy, wrote that 'The Roll Call . . . is surrounded from morning to night by a dense mob of ardent admirers, who go in exstasies over the painted bearskins and grey gaberdines of the Grenadiers; who declare that the sergeant's orderly book is a miracle of still life painting.' Mann obviously thought the fuss rather exaggerated, but Queen Victoria, with her soft spot for soldiers and happy memories of awarding Victoria Crosses, thought otherwise and bought it. Florence Nightingale also had the picture sent round to her bedside, to re-live Crimean memories. Miss Elizabeth Thompson, as the artist then was, became famous overnight. Nearly a quarter of a million photographs of her were sold. The idea of a young woman painting a picture of soldiers caught the popular imagination. Like all good Victorian artists, Miss Thompson did her homework. The sergeant was a Crimean veteran, who advised on details, such as the correct lettering on haversacks. The uniforms were culled from pawnbrokers' shops. A controversy arose over the movement of the horses' legs; Miss Thompson replied that she had worked it out by crawling on all fours round her studio, and advised her critics to do the same. The picture is undoubtedly striking, and one can understand why it made such a strong dramatic and patriotic appeal. If she had lived today, Miss Thompson would have made a good film director.

The horrors and blunders of the Crimean War are also too well-known to need repeating here. One of the few good things to emerge from it was Florence Nightingale. Although 'the lady with the lamp' became a national heroine, there are few pictures of her. Jerry Barrett, after his great success with *Victoria and Albert visiting the Crimean Wounded* (14), visited the Crimea in 1856 to make sketches. The result was *The Mission of Mercy* (243), not finished until 1858, showing Florence Nightingale receiving the wounded at the entrance to the notorious hospital at Scutari. Both pictures were enormously popular through engravings.

Another contemporary picture was J. D. Luard's *The Welcome Arrival* (244), exhibited with great success at the Royal Academy in 1857. The man standing smoking a pipe was

243 JERRY BARRETT (1814–1906) *The Mission of Mercy – Florence Nightingale receiving the wounded at Scutari, 1856.* Prviate collection, 55 × 83in. (139·7 × 210·8cm.)
After his great success with *Victoria and Albert visiting the Crimean wounded* (14), Barrett painted this picture of Florence Nightingale in 1858. The picture is based on sketches made in Scutari in 1865, and many of the figures in the picture later sat to Barrett in London, including Miss Nightingale herself, who stands on the left below the window. The figure looking out of the window is Barrett himself, and other portraits include Alexis Soyer, Mr. and Mrs. Bracebridge, and Lord William Paulet. A sketch for the picture is in the National Portrait Gallery

244 JOHN DALBIAC LUARD (1830–1860) *The Welcome Arrival* National Army Museum, dated 1857, 29⅞ × 39⅜in. (76 × 100cm.)
Three soldiers at Balaclava in 1854 unpacking a gift box from England. The one on the right is holding a pair of mittens; on the left another is looking at a photograph or miniature. Two of the men sport beards and pipes, both of which later became fashionable in England as a result of the Crimean campaign. The picture was exhibited at the R.A. in 1857, a year after the war ended

the artist's brother, Richard Amherst Luard, and the officer beside him Captain William Gair of the Carabiniers. The cat was called Tom, and belonged to Captain Gair. Tom died at Sebastopol on 31st December, 1856, and his body was brought back to England, stuffed, and preserved in the National Army Museum, where it is displayed beside the picture. Luard was a friend of Millais, and they shared chambers for a time, but Luard died aged only 30 in 1860. Millais' *Peace Concluded* of 1856 is also on the theme of the Crimean War, but shows a wounded soldier back in England with his family.

Surprisingly, there is no good picture of the famous Charge of the Light Brigade. At Deene Park, Lord Cardigan's house in Northamptonshire, there are pictures of it by A. F. de Prades and G. H. Laporte, but they are really only equestrian portraits devoted to the greater glory of Lord Cardigan. Several artists, such as William Simpson and E. A. Goodall, were sent out to cover the war for the *Illustrated London News*, but their work is of historical interest, not great artistic merit. By far the best records are the photographs of Roger Fenton and the dispatches of Russell, *The Times* correspondent. But few people at the time saw Fenton's photographs. Pictures like *The Roll Call* and *The Mission of Mercy* fulfilled the desire of the public to get some strong pictorial idea of what the war was actually like; a need that is now provided by war films.

245
HENRY NELSON O'NEIL, A.R.A. (1817–1880)
Eastward Ho! August 1857 Sir Richard Proby,
Bt., 53½ × 42½in. (136 × 108cm.)
Soldiers leaving to serve in India during the
Mutiny say goodbye to their wives. The picture
was exhibited at the R.A. in 1858, while the
Mutiny was still in progress, and aroused
tremendous patriotic enthusiasm as well as
critical praise

The Indian Mutiny

The Mutiny seems to have inspired many more pictures than the Crimea. The horror
of the Cawnpore Massacre and the sufferings of English women and children at Lucknow
must have made a profound impression on the British public. The bravery of the women
and children was the subject of most pictures, but the most popular were O'Neil's *Eastward Ho!* (**245**) and *Home Again* (**246**). O'Neil had been a member of the Clique, a group
of young Victorian rebels against the Academy in the 1840s, and his intention was to
paint striking incidents which appealed to the feelings. He certainly succeeded with
these two pictures, which were a tremendous popular success. The compositions are
strikingly effective, and both pictures sum up mid-Victorian attitudes to war – a combination of patriotism, pluck and sentimentality. An *Art Journal* reviewer, who saw
both pictures at the International Exhibition of 1862, wrote that 'this school of pictorial
art is emphatically English . . . because we in England are daily making to ourselves a
contemporary history, . . . Britain is a land of action and of progress, trade, commerce,
growing wealth, steadfast yet ever changeful liberty; a land and a people wherein a contemporary Art may grow and live, because in this actual present hour we act heroically,
suffer manfully and do those deeds which in pictures and by poems, deserve to be recorded.' As narrative painting applied to current events, O'Neil's pictures are outstandingly
good examples.

246 HENRY NELSON O'NEIL, A.R.A. (1817–1880) *Home Again, 1858* Major William Spowers, signed and dated 1859, 53½ × 42½in. (136 × 108cm.)

So great was the success of *Eastward Ho!* that O'Neil followed it up with a sequel, showing the troops returning home. The soldiers are re-united with their wives and families – one proudly waves a medal to his old pensioner father; the wounded sergeant has to be helped ashore; others receive good and bad news from the wives. Several of the same faces re-appear from *Eastward Ho!*

Edward Hopley, normally a painter of fairy subjects, portrays a man and two women, one with a small baby, alarmed at night during the Mutiny (**247**). Goodall's *Jessie's Dream* (**248**) shows the besieged defenders of Lucknow sighting the column of the relief force, with Jessie realizing the truth of her dream. Solomon's *Flight* (**249**) depicts English women and children fleeing from Lucknow after the siege was over. Noel Paton's *In Memoriam* (**250**) commemorates the bravery of English women, especially at Cawnpore. The *Art Journal* critic wrote that 'any mere allusion to these fiendish atrocities cannot be borne without a shudder', but praised the 'Roman virtue' of the woman praying and holding her Bible. Paton must have decided that the picture was too painful, so he changed the figures of sepoys, bursting in to murder the women, into kilted highlanders coming to rescue them. This concession to public taste was strongly attacked by Ruskin, who saw it as symptomatic of the weakness of Clemency Canning, then Viceroy of India, and others who favoured mild treatment of the rebels. A French writer, Ernest Chesnau, in *The English School of Painting* (1891), also justly criticizes Paton's modifications: 'A pleasant but a decidedly commonplace conclusion, by which the work is both enfeebled and stunted; all the terror therein depicted is a mere delusion, and the drama terminates in the happy and paltry manner of a trashy three-volume novel.'

247 EDWARD WILLIAM JOHN HOPLEY (1816–1869) *An Incident in the Indian Mutiny* Jeremy Maas Gallery, dated 1857, 24¾ × 30¼in. (62·8 × 76·9cm.)
A British family alarmed at night during the Mutiny. The scene is probably intended as Lucknow, because the music on the piano to the right is *The Campbells are Coming*, a possible reference to Sir Colin Campbell, who relieved Lucknow on 14th November, 1857

248 FREDERICK GOODALL, R.A. (1822–1904) *Jessie's Dream* Sheffield Art Galleries, signed and dated 1858,
31⅝ × 48in. (80·4 × 121·9cm.)
The defenders of besieged Lucknow sight the column of the relief force. Jessie Brown, the girl who stands up pointing,
was the wife of a corporal in the 78th Highlanders, who at the height of the siege had a dream in which she heard the
bagpipes of the Scottish troops coming to relieve the city

249
ABRAHAM SOLOMON (1824–1862) *The Flight*
Leicestershire Museums, signed and dated 1858,
24 × 18in. (61 × 45·7cm.)
After a siege lasting nearly six months,
Lucknow was finally evacuated between 14th and
18th November, 1857. Solomon's picture shows
the women and children fleeing from the
burning city

250 SIR JOSEPH NOEL PATON, R.S.A. (1821–1901) *In Memoriam* engraving after Paton by W. H. Sammons
Private collection, 34 × 27in. (86·4 × 68·6cm.)
The picture by Noel Paton, which has now disappeared, was exhibited at the R.A. in 1858. Both the picture and the engraving were 'dedicated to commemorate the Christian Heroism of the British Ladies in India during the Mutiny o 1857, and their ultimate Deliverance by British Prowess'. In the original version, sepoys with fixed bayonets were bursting through the door, to murder the women and children; because of criticism Paton changed the sepoys into highlanders, yet another example of the influence of Victorian morality on art

The Volunteers

The Volunteer Movement, which began in 1859, arose out of widespread fears of the supposed ambitions of Napoleon III. Although the fears may have been largely illusory, young men all over the country flocked to join. In 1863 a grand parade of 20,000 Volunteers was held at Brighton. The Volunteer Movement offered exercise, dashing uniforms, good company, and patriotic service, and was understandably popular. Their activities are reflected in several pictures. Houghton's *Volunteers* (**251**) is primarily a lively street scene, but it shows what a popular distraction the Volunteer parades were in the 1860s.

251 ARTHUR BOYD HOUGHTON (1836–1875) *Volunteers* Tate Gallery, London, 12 × 15½in. (30·5 × 39·4cm.)
The Volunteer Movement, which began in the 1860s, inspired a number of pictures, of which this is the best known. It has affinities with Houghton's *Holborn in 1861* (150), and the artist was obviously primarily interested in a lively crowd scene, enlivened by humorous incidents – the girl looking between the Volunteer's legs, the woman on the right driving her pram into an old gentleman

Sam Bough's picture of 1860 (252) seems to be the only one to record the splendour and display of a grand Volunteer parade. H. T. Wells' large and impressive group (253) shows Volunteers at shooting practice. It includes portraits of the Hon. W. Colville, Lord Elcho, Henry Halford, Captain Drake R.E., Captain Horatio Ross, Captain Heaton, Stewart Pixley, Martin R. Smith, and Edward C. Ross. Wells built a glass shed in which to pose his sitters, so as to be sure of getting an outdoor effect. The *Art Journal* praised 'the manly bearing of the heroes . . . altogether patriotic and English. Taken for all in all, the picture is noble; and we are not surprised to learn that its merits won for Mr. Wells the honour of Associate.' The Volunteer Movement continued to flourish, fed by invasion fears aroused by books like Chesney's *Battle of Dorking* (1871), and by the 1890s there were over 200,000 Volunteers, but the subject seems to have had no further appeal to artists.

252 SAM BOUGH, R.S.A. (1822–1878) *The Royal Volunteer Review, 1860* National Gallery of Scotland, signed and dated 1860, 40½ × 70⅝ in. (118·1 × 179·4cm.)
Volunteer parades were a great public spectacle and attracted large crowds. This one takes place just outside Edinburgh, near Arthur's Seat and St. Margaret's Loch

254 (*right*) GEORGE BERNARD O'NEILL (1828–1917) *Manning the Navy* National Maritime Museum, 30 × 46in. (76·2 × 116·8cm.)
The young man in the centre has been taking part in a regatta, and is still in his rowing uniform. A recruiting party is trying to persuade him to 'take the Queen's Bounty', but he is restrained by a pretty girl, and his old widowed mother

253 HENRY TANWORTH WELLS, R.A. (1828–1903) *Volunteers at Firing Point* Royal Academy, London, signed and dated 1866, $73\frac{1}{4} \times 114\frac{3}{4}$in. ($186 \times 291 \cdot 5$cm.)
Wells' Diploma work, exhibited at the R.A. in 1866. The picture contains a number of portraits, and was highly praised by the *Art Journal*: 'a finer portrait-picture has not been seen within our recollection in London, or any capital of Europe.' The remarkable resemblance between the central figure of the soldier loading his gun and the soldiers in Degas' *Execution of the Emperor Maximilian* (painted a year later in 1867) is one of the more curious coincidences of art history

The Navy

Considering the size and importance of the British Navy, it is surprising that there are not more pictures relating to it. W. L. Wyllie and Edoardo de Martino painted imperialistic naval reviews, with rows of ironclads proudly puffing smoke. Sailors were favourite subjects for flirtation pictures; they also often feature in many homely scenes showing 'The Return of the Sailor' to the cottage, usually as a bronzed Jack Tar with a parrot, surrounded by an adoring family. G. B. O'Neill's *Manning the Navy* (**254**) deals in a

255 JOHN J. LEE (fl. 1850–1860) *Sweethearts and Wives* Mr. and Mrs. Norman Parkinson, signed with monogram and dated 1860, $33\frac{1}{4} \times 28$in. (84·5 × 71·2cm.)
Sailors coming ashore at Liverpool Docks to meet their sweethearts and wives. The ship in the background is H.M.S. Majestic, which had done service in the Baltic during the Crimean War, but was by that time on Coastguard service

jolly, humorous way with the Navy's methods of recruiting, but makes no allusion to the notorious press-gangs, still prevalent at the time. J. J. Lee's *Sweethearts and Wives* (**255**) shows sailors coming ashore at Liverpool docks. The painters only seemed interested in the popular image of the sailor – plucky, boisterous, hopelessly amorous.

30

THE QUEEN, GOD BLESS HER!

'Take up the White Man's Burden,
Send forth the best ye breed,
Go bind your sons to exile
To serve your captives need.'
Rudyard Kipling, *The White Man's Burden*

The imperialist spirit is detectable in many pictures of the 1880s and 1890s. Even the neo-classical pictures of Leighton and Alma-Tadema perhaps derived some of their popularity from associations with the Greek and Roman Empires. But there were many other pictures which reflect in a more positive way the influence of that popular, patriotic imperialism that was the signature tune of the late Victorian period. Of course, Britain already had a large empire by 1850. 'We seem, as it were, to have conquered and peopled half the world in a fit of absence of mind,' wrote Sir John Seeley in *The Expansion of England* (1883). At first the Empire was a commercial and trading affair, as the Dutch empire had been, but in the late nineteenth century a new competitive spirit entered. In the resulting race for territory, Britain added, between 1871 and 1900, 66 million people and $4\frac{1}{4}$ million square miles to her already large Empire. There were always plenty of Little Englanders who protested, but the idea of Empire had caught the popular imagination. It was personified in the soldiers, explorers and adventurers – men like General Gordon, Livingstone and Rhodes – whose exploits gave the Victorians ample outlet for their need to hero-worship.

It was the innumerable colonial wars which proved the most fertile ground for artists. Lady Butler was in the front line as usual, and *Remnants of an Army* (**256**) is typical of her dramatic approach to military subjects. Most of her pictures deal with the campaigns and battles of the early nineteenth century, but they are no less imperialist in spirit for that. Imperialism glorified the past as well as the present. Every schoolboy read Fitchett's *Deeds that won the Empire*; its pictorial counterparts were paintings like *The Boyhood of Raleigh* by Millais and Collier's *Last Voyage of Henry Hudson*, recalling the heroes and the deeds that had made England great. Although the Victorian age produced many great explorers, their exploits do not seem to have appealed to artists. There are no pictures of Livingstone, Speke or Burton, and it was left to contemporary illustrators to reconstruct graphic accounts of their expeditions. Only Millais' *North-West Passage*

256 LADY BUTLER (1846–1933) *The Remnants of an Army* (detail) Tate Gallery, London, signed and dated 1879, 52 × 92in. (132·1 × 233.7cm.)

Lady Butler became the doyenne of Victorian military artists. This picture records an incident in the terrible retreat from Kabul, during the first Afghan War of 1842. Dr. Brydon was the only man to survive out of an army of 16,000 men, and is shown here arriving in the frontier town of Jellalabad, on 13th January, 1842

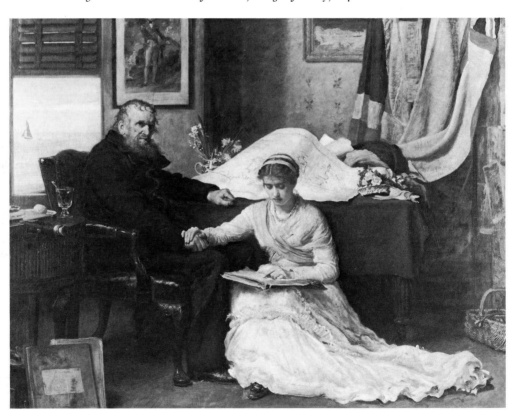

257 SIR JOHN EVERETT MILLAIS, Bt. P.R.A. (1829–1896) *The North-West Passage* Tate Gallery, London, signed with monogram and dated 1874, 69½ × 87½in. (176·5 × 222·3cm.)

In the 1870s, arctic exploration was much under discussion, and in December 1872 a deputation approached the Chancellor of the Exchequer for assistance in sponsoring arctic research. The model for the old sailor was Captain Edward Trelawny, the friend of Byron and Shelley

(**257**) is on the subject of exploration, with its bulldoggy sub-title 'It might be done, and England should do it.'

Many of the deeds which won the Empire seem to have been disasters and defeats, which the Victorians cherished almost more than victories. As we remember Dunkirk, they remembered the Retreat from Kabul, the Charge of the Light Brigade, and Majuba Hill. They perhaps also remembered Isandhlwana (**258**), a particularly disastrous episode. Fripp's picture of the last heroic defenders gives substance to both the lines and spirit of Sir Henry Newbolt's poem *Vitae Lampada*:

> 'The sand of the desert is sodden red,
>   Red with the wreck of a square that broke;
> The Gatling's jammed and the Colonel dead,
>   And the regiment blind with dust and smoke.'

Bravery and devotion in the face of official bungling has always been a quality particularly admired in England, and it is this spirit which runs through many imperialist pictures.

258 CHARLES EDWIN FRIPP (1854–1906) *The Battle of Isandhlwana, January 22nd, 1879* National Army Museum, signed, 55 × 88in. (139·7 × 223·6cm.)
The thin red line of the British square. An incident in the Zulu War of 1879, when a small detachment of 1,200 British troops was wiped out by a force of 20,000 Zulus

259 RICHARD CATON WOODVILLE (1856–1926) *The Charge of the 21st Lancers at Omdurman, 1898*
Walker Art Gallery, Liverpool, signed and dated 1898, $60\frac{3}{8} \times 96\frac{3}{4}$in. (153·4 × 245·8cm.)
Imperialism triumphant. The charge of the 21st Lancers (in which Lieutenant Winston Churchill took part)
was mainly prompted by the desire of its commander, Lt. Colonel Rowland Hill, to gain battle honours for his
Regiment. He ordered a charge, against vastly superior forces, on his own initiative. Although heroic (three V.C.s
were awarded) it made very little difference to the outcome of the battle

260 ROBERT TALBOT KELLY (1861–1935) *The Flight of the Khalifa, Omdurman, 1898* Walker Art Gallery, Liverpool,
signed and dated 1899, 51 × 78in. (129·5 × 198·1cm.)
The rascally Khalifa and his followers flee in disarray before the might of the British Army. The Egyptian campaign
of 1896–9 was the high point of British imperialism and military strength; both were soon to be irreparably shattered
by the Boer War

It is certainly present in Caton Woodville's *Charge of the 21st Lancers at Omdurman* (**259**). The charge is now the most celebrated episode of the battle, but it was in fact unnecessary, foolhardy, and contrary to orders, giving it just that 'Light Brigade' flavour the public delighted in. The imperialist spirit not only demanded pictures of the British army, but also of the enemy retreating in disarray, as in Kelly's *Flight of the Khalifa* (**260**). There is perhaps no better expression of the spirit of British imperialism than J. E. Hodgson's picture *The Queen, God Bless Her!* (**261**). With these two Kipling-esque soldiers, drinking the loyal toast out of their water bottles, this book ends, as it began, with the Queen.

261 JOHN EVAN HODGSON, R.A. (1831–1895) *The Queen, God Bless Her!* Forbes Magazine Collection, signed, 25 × 35in. (63·5 × 88·8cm.)
Imperialism in paint. Hodgson's picture, exhibited at the R.A. in 1885, the year of the death of General Gordon at Khartoum, captures the patriotic spirit of British imperialism – the spirit of Kipling and Rhodes, Jingoism and Jubilees

CONCLUSION

Imperialism in art is really a separate subject, outside the scope of this book. Modern-life painting as a movement was over by the 1870s; late Victorian England produced no 'peintre de la vie moderne', such as Baudelaire searched for in France, although he made the rather surprising choice of Constantin Guys, a charming but lightweight illustrator. But no one in England knew much about Baudelaire, or took any notice of his art criticism. It has often been observed how isolated from the main currents of European art Victorian painting was. Very few painters were aware of, or interested in, what was going on in Europe. Even Rossetti, Holman Hunt and the other Pre-Raphaelites, all patriotic young men, seemed to share the general belief that anything British was best. They admired Italian and Flemish art, but did not include any contemporary painters in their list of 'Immortals'; among the English artists on the list were Hogarth, Flaxman, Hilton and Wilkie, an eccentric choice.

Victorian modern-life painting, itself a small but important tributary of the main-stream of Victorian painting, also shares its insular character. There is very little in European painting to compare it with. One surprising parallel is the work of certain Russian nineteenth-century artists, such as Fedotov and Makowski, whose witty scenes of Russian life strike the English visitor to Russian museums as distinctly 'Victorian' in flavour. For historical ancestors of Victorian painting one has perhaps to look back to Dutch and Flemish painting. The interiors of Ostade, de Hoogh and Terborch tell us much about Dutch life in the seventeenth century; Victorian domestic scenes, particularly those of Wilkie and his followers, are similarly informative, and alike in spirit. To compare Brueghel and Frith is getting into deeper water; obviously Frith is an artist very much of his own place and time, and not of universal significance. Victorian modern-life pictures which make use of symbolism and allegory, such as the work of Madox Brown and Holman Hunt, have undoubted affinities with early German and Flemish art. To speak of Ford Madox Brown's *Work* in the same breath as Van Eyck, Holbein or Durer is probably still considered sacrilegious, but time will no doubt bring a more balanced assessment.

The elements which go to make up modern-life pictures are not in themselves unique in art, but rather the uses to which the Victorians put them. The desire to narrate which is present in all European painting, especially in religious pictures, was carried by the Victorians to much greater lengths. By combining narrative with literary and social themes, they pushed painting over its natural frontiers into the realm of literature. They tried to make pictures into books, but saw nothing contradictory in it. That a picture should aspire to the condition of literature seemed to them admirable; Ruskin praised Hunt's *The Awakening Conscience* for doing so. Many of the themes of modern-life painting were themes already prevalent in literature. Hood's *Song of a Shirt*, for example, continued to inspire pictures of starving seamstresses for over twenty years. Someone with a detailed knowledge of Victorian literature could probably find a literary parallel for all the scenes illustrated in this book. Never before or since have painting and literature been so hand-in-hand. In both, the most emotive image of the age was that of suffering womanhood, the damsel in distress; a reflection, perhaps, of the ambiguous and changing place of women in Victorian society. Pretty women, whether suffering or not, appear in a great many modern-life pictures. For a supposedly puritanical age, the Victorians were surprisingly obsessed with feminine beauty.

Detail and the use of symbolic objects were by no means the prerogative of Victorian artists – as already noted, many parallels can be found in early German and Flemish art. Even the Pre-Raphaelites' use of pure colours on a white ground was nothing new – Waldmuller and other Austrian painters were painting landscapes with 'Pre-Raphaelite' techniques as early as the 1820s. But the Victorian's elevation of everyday clutter into moral symbolism was something quite new, as was their habit of filling their pictures with clues for the spectator to decode. Neither was morality in art a Victorian invention, but the Victorians were alone in trying to make it the prime yardstick by which a work of art should be judged. Art and morality were forced into an uneasy alliance, watched over by the erratic genius of Ruskin. Nor was the combination of sentiment and morality a new one – Greuze and other late eighteenth-century painters had already explored the idea of sentimental domestic scenes with a mildly moralistic flavour. The Victorians carried morality, and sentimentality, much further. Our own age, anti-romantic and anti-emotional, has long distrusted Victorian art for its supposed sentimentality; time and a change of mood has now enabled us to understand and appreciate it better, and to distinguish the genuine sentiment from the deliberate sentimentality. The morality we find harder to comprehend, so far have we moved away from the evangelical and puritanical views of the Victorians. So entrenched was the idea that art should have a serious moral purpose that in 1884 a book was published entitled *Academy Paintings and their Moral Teaching*, in which the author, James Read, discourses at rapturous length about the supposedly profound messages to be culled from a selection of totally trivial works. In the following year Whistler delivered his Ten O'Clock Lecture, and sounded the death-knell of High Victorian art.

But it would be a mistake to take most modern-life paintings too seriously. Except for the outstanding work of Madox Brown, Holman Hunt, Frith and a few others, the remainder should be enjoyed and appreciated for what they are – wonderfully attractive and informative pictures, which conjure up for us, with an immediacy and directness that no other medium can, the mid-Victorian world.

SELECT BIBLIOGRAPHY

It is obviously impossible to list all the books relating to the Victorian social and historical background. I have therefore included only the books I found most useful, arranging them in groups corresponding roughly with the chapter headings of this book. The bibliography relating to art books is more detailed; many of these books themselves have extensive bibliographies.

Reference Books

Algernon Graves *A Dictionary of Artists 1760–1893*, first published 1884, reprinted 1895, enlarged 1901, reprinted 1969 by Kingsmead Reprints
Algernon Graves *Royal Academy Exhibitors 1769–1904*, 8 vols., 1905–6, reprinted in 4 vols. 1970
Algernon Graves *The British Institution 1806–1867*, 1908, reprinted 1969
Christopher Wood *Dictionary of Victorian Painters*, 1971

Periodicals

Art Journal 1849–1912
Art Union 1839–1848
Athenaeum 1828–1912
Magazine of Art 1878–1904
Punch 1841–

General Books on Victorian Painting

J. Ruskin *Academy Notes 1855–9*, 1875
Ernest Chesnau *The English School of Painting*, 1891
R. Ironside and J. A. Gere *Pre-Raphaelite Painters*, 1948
John Steegman *Victorian Taste*, 1950, reprinted 1970
G. Reynolds *Painters of the Victorian Scene*, 1953
F. Davis *Victorian Patrons of the Arts*, 1963

W. E. Fredeman *Pre-Raphaelitism – a Bibliocritical Study*, 1965
R. Lister *Victorian Narrative Paintings*, 1966
G. Reynolds *Victorian Painting*, 1966
J. Maas *Victorian Painters*, 1969
John Nicoll *The Pre-Raphaelites*, 1970
Peter Conrad *A Victorian Treasure-House*, 1973
A. Staley *Pre-Raphaelite Landscape*, 1973
J. Maas *Gambart, Prince of the Victorian Art World*, 1976

Books on Victorian Artists

MADOX-BROWN: F. M. Hueffer *Ford Madox Brown*, 1896
FILDES: L. V. Fildes *Luke Fildes R.A. A Victorian Painter*, 1968
FRITH: W. P. Frith *My Autobiography and Reminiscences*, 3 vols., 1887–8
HERKOMER: J. Saxon Mills *The Life and Letters of Sir H. von Herkomer R.A.*, 1923
HOLL: A. M. Reynolds *The Life and Work of Frank Holl*, 1912
HOLMAN HUNT: W. Holman Hunt *Pre-Raphaelitism and the Pre-Raphaelite Brother-hood*, 2 vols., 1905
HOUGHTON: *Arthur Boyd Houghton*, Catalogue of Exhibition at the Victoria and Albert Museum, 1975
LEIGHTON: Leonée and Richard Ormond *Lord Leighton*, 1975
LESLIE: C. R. Leslie *Autobiographical Recollections*, 2 vols., 1860
MILLAIS: J. G. Millais *The Life and Letters of Sir J. E. Millais, Bt., P.R.A.*, 2 vols., 1899
ORCHARDSON: Hilda Orchardson Gray *The Life of Sir W. Q. Orchardson, R.A.*, 1930
REDGRAVE: F. M. Redgrave *Richard Redgrave, A Memoir*, 1891
TISSOT: J. Laver *Vulgar Society: The Romantic Career of James Tissot*, 1936
TISSOT: *Catalogue of the Tissot Exhibition* Rhode Island School of Design, Providence, U.S.A., 1968
WALKER: J. G. Marks *Life and Letters of Frederick Walker, A.R.A.*, 1896

General Reading

G. M. Young *Victorian England, Portrait of an Age*, 1936
G. M. Trevelyan *English Social History*, 1944
W. E. Houghton *The Victorian Frame of Mind*, 1957
Asa Briggs *The Age of Improvement 1783–1867*, 1959
Joan Evans *The Victorians*, 1966
J. B. Priestley *Victoria's Heyday*, 1972

Gillian Avery   *Victorian People*, 1970
L. C. B. Seaman   *Victorian England*, 1973

Queen Victoria

Elizabeth Longford   *Victoria R.I.*, 1964
Winslow Ames   *Prince Albert and Victorian Taste*, 1967
David Duff   *Albert and Victoria*, 1972
C. Woodham-Smith   *Queen Victoria*, 1972

Society

D. J. Kirwan   *Palace and Hovel*, 1870, reprinted 1963
Charles Greville   *Memoirs*, 1874 etc.
Sir Charles Eastlake   *Hints on Household Taste*, 1878
Adeline Countess of Cardigan   *Memoirs*, 1909
M. E. Perugini   *Victorian Days and Ways*, 1936
Leonore Davidoff   *The Best Circles – Society, Etiquette and the Season*, 1973

The Poor

H. Mayhew   *London Labour and the London Poor*, 1851 and 1861
S. E. Finer   *Life and Times of Sir Edwin Chadwick*, 1952
Kellow Chesney   *The Victorian Underworld*, 1970

Marriage and Family Life

J. C. Jeaffreson   *Brides and Bridals*, 1872
Gwen Raverat   *Period Piece*, 1952
Katherine Moore   *Victorian Wives*, 1974
Anne Monsarrat   *And the Bride wore . . .*, 1974

Religion

Owen Chadwick   *The Victorian Church*, 1969
John Morley   *Death, Heaven and the Victorians*, 1971

Railways and Engineering

Terry Coleman   *The Railway Navvies*, 1965
F. D. Klingender   *Art and the Industrial Revolution*, revised by Arthur Elton, 1968
Harold Perkin   *The Age of the Railway*, 1970
L. T. C. Rolt   *Victorian Engineering*, 1970

Women at Work

Katherine West   *Chapter of Governesses*, 1949
Patricia Thompson   *The Victorian Heroine*, 1956
Derek Hudson   *Munby, Man of two Worlds*, 1972
Lee Holcombe   *Victorian Ladies at Work*, 1973

Fallen Women

H. G. Jebb   *Out of the Depths*, 1859
S. Marcus   *The Other Victorians*, 1967
'Walter'   *My Secret Life*, 1967
Henry Blyth   *Skittles, The Last Victorian Courtesan*, 1970

The City

G. A. Sala   *Twice round the Clock; or the Hours of Day and Night in London*, 1859
Gustave Doré and Blanchard Jerrold   *London – A Pilgrimage*, 1872
Hippolyte Taine   *Notes on England* (ed. Edward Hyams), 1957
Asa Briggs   *Victorian Cities*, 1964
John Hayes   *Catalogue of Oil Paintings in the London Museum*, H.M.S.O., 1970
Priscilla Metcalf   *Victorian London*, 1972
E. D. H. Johnson   'Victorian Artists and the Urban Milieu' (chapter 19 of *The Victorian City* by Dyos and Wolff, vol. 2, 1973)

The Country

Rev. Francis Kilvert   *Kilvert's Diary 1870–79*
Flora Thompson   *Lark Rise to Candleford*, 1939

Leisure

Stella Margetson   *Leisure and Pleasure in the Nineteenth Century*, 1969
Richard Southern   *The Victorian Theatre*, 1970
Ronald Pearsall   *Victorian Popular Music*, 1973

War

B. Bond   *Victorian Military Campaigns*, 1967

INDEX

The names of artists whose works are illustrated are given in capitals. References to illustrations are in italics